THE TANK MUSEUM

BRITISH MILITARY TRANSPORT
1829-1956

David Fletcher

BRITISH MILITARY TRANSPORT 1829-1956

CONTENTS

INTRODUCTION **4**
LIST OF ABBREVIATIONS **7**
1 GETTING UP STEAM **8**
2 THE FIRST WORLD WAR **46**
3 FIRST FOOTING **70**
4 PEACETIME DEVELOPMENTS **88**
5 OLD LESSONS, NEW VEHICLES **118**
6 RETURN TO THE DESERT **142**
7 SUPPLYING VICTORY **160**
8 TOP GEAR **188**
INDEX **210**

© The Tank Museum 2022

All rights reserved. Except as permitted under current legislation no part of this work may be photocopied, stored in a retrieval system, published, performed in public, adapted, broadcast, transmitted, recorded or reproduced in any form or by any means, without the prior written permission of the copyright owner.

First published in 1998 by The Tank Museum
This new edition published in 2022 by The Tank Museum

David Fletcher has asserted his moral right to be identified as author of this work.

British Library Cataloguing in Publication Data.
A catalogue record for this book is available from the British Library.

Printed book ISBN 978-1-7399027-3-5

Designed and produced for The Tank Museum by JJN Publishing Ltd.
Printed and bound in Malta.

MIX
Paper from responsible sources
FSC® C022612

A mixed selection of British transport enters Arras by the Baudimont Gate on the St Pol road in April 1917. Leading is a chain-drive Commer 3-tonner, next a Talbot tender, a Model-T Ford van and a Sunbeam staff car.

INTRODUCTION

Great Britain was not the first country to test a mechanically propelled road vehicle for military purposes (that honour belongs to France). Neither, come to that, was Britain swift to adopt horseless road vehicles for military or civilian purposes. Yet when war came, when it really mattered, the British Army committed itself wholeheartedly to mechanisation with hardly a backward glance. It is with this development, from hesitant beginnings to thorough accomplishment, that this book is concerned.

In gathering material for this title, I was first struck by a peculiar theme that repeated itself from the Boer War through the First World War to the finish of the Second World War in 1945. And it is this. After each war the military authorities convinced themselves that ordinary commercial vehicles were neither rugged nor versatile enough for active military service and they persuaded industry to produce specialised, high-quality machines on a no-expense-spared basis – which industry did. In each instance, as soon as this expensive programme was underway, the authorities discovered that they could not afford to sustain it and standards were relaxed. In the subsequent war all standards soon vanish when demand outstrips supply, only to reappear at the end.

The result is a transport enthusiast's dream. Hundreds of superbly engineered, top-quality vehicles of highly imaginative design were built by manufacturers all over Britain who could never have afforded to develop them otherwise. This investment enabled the British commercial motor industry to make great strides in terms of general design, which were reflected in its dominance of foreign markets at least up to the outbreak of the Second World War, and it was the desire to examine this story that caused this book to be written.

However, such concepts do not always go to plan and it was only towards the end, when I was gathering the photographs, that a peculiar truth struck home. Selecting photographs is one of the pleasures of producing a book. The pictures may not all be worth quite a thousand words, but each one must be chosen with a view to illustrating as many aspects of the tale as possible and it is quite a juggling act, especially when it comes to the final selection. Dozens of good images have to be rejected because one always feels the need for far too many, and there comes a time when the study floor is literally covered with them. That is when this odd fact emerged. Despite military insistence on the ideal, the majority of vehicles, certainly in the two world wars, that served the British Army were about as ordinary as vehicles could be.

It did not seem to matter where one looked: from desert to jungle, from quagmire to frozen tundra, one found ordinary lorries struggling through and apparently surviving. Nothing fancy, no four-wheel drive nor extra ground clearance. Just the sort of truck one met every day on the public highway, delivering the goods. Yet here it was, in the middle of nowhere, possibly even under fire, trundling along and still delivering the goods. So, is that it – is the whole concept of special purpose military vehicles a myth? Apparently not or we should not continue to produce them, but evidently there is a place for most types in military service.

INTRODUCTION

Which is what, I hope, this book will show. But what is the excuse for writing it? Why should someone whose career is the study of armoured warfare and whose hobby, it seems, is writing about it, bother with something so apparently mundane as transport? Three reasons come to mind; in the first place it rounds off a project, the study of all aspects of British military mechanisation up to 1945 in one series, which the staff at The Stationery Office encouraged me to complete and nursed me through over 12 years. Then, again, transport is a key part of the whole subject. I know there are those who contend that one can pursue a narrow theme in isolation, but I don't believe it. Take just one example. As this book will show, British road transport policy in the years between the wars had a tremendous influence on the type of military vehicle British industry was able to produce. But it went further than that. Government policy favouring railways discouraged the development of powerful lorry engines and, when new tanks were needed, desperately needed, nothing suitable was available. The third reason is simply that all aspects of transport fascinate me.

British military transport is my main theme along with that developed in the Commonwealth – particularly Canada. Yet one cannot entirely separate the Canadian motor industry from that of the United States and in any case American vehicles were equally important to the British Army. Thus, they are dealt with where it is relevant and, naturally, some degree of comparison is inevitable. There is no need to develop this theme in the main text, indeed there is no room, but perhaps it might justify a word or two here.

Throughout the Second World War, and pretty well ever since, American military transport has been held up as the ideal, and justly so. Somehow, their industry managed to create a whole family of standardised military vehicles that functioned extremely well in all conditions and they appear to have done it without serious disruption to

British transport moving along a badly churned, tree-lined road in north-west Europe. Leading the column is a Canadian-built Chevrolet, followed by a British Ford WOT6.

their commercial trade. Even so, right through to the end of the war, huge numbers of regular American commercial trucks with only the most modest concessions to military requirements, served all around the world. Compare this, and indeed British achievements in the field, with that of the Germans.

Even before the Second World War German industry was harnessed to the requirements of the martial state. The motor industry was compelled to develop an ideal range of military vehicles of the highest quality including an enormous range of semi-tracked models, which had no obvious civilian application at all. Yet by the time the war ended the average German transport driver was glad enough to get his hands on anything that could be made to move and soldiers worked through the rigours of a Russian winter, driving lorries with cabs made of compressed cardboard.

The subject is vast. Taking the Second World War alone one could find enough material to make a separate book on the supply and transport aspects of every campaign. By the same token the influences that bear upon transport are endless. Design and availability of vehicles obviously, terrain and climate of course and the very nature of the army they are supplying. Strategic and tactical factors, particularly the latter, are very influential especially when one has two armies, of different nationalities, operating side-by-side, and there is always the human element; the temptation to include personal stories is hard to resist and it matters – vehicles are driven by people. If, in an attempt to give a flavour of every aspect in a readable format, I have failed to give any one adequate emphasis then the apology can only be tempered with the explanation that authors sign contracts for books of a certain size, to match others in the series.

Earlier titles in this series, notably The Great Tank Scandal and The Universal Tank, have not exactly praised Britain's efforts to produce tanks during the Second World War. So, it is with some relief that one may approach this subject in a more confident frame of mind. That things were not perfect the following chapters will show, but invariably, if something did go wrong, it was not due to industry but ministerial interference. The Germans may have built better tanks but, as more than one author has reported, German Army units operating in the Western Desert were advised to use captured British vehicles for vital operations because they were considered more reliable. The fact that for 'British' the Germans probably meant 'Canadian' does not detract from the value of this unsolicited recommendation.

This book opens in the age of the Duke of Wellington and closes with the Suez Crisis of 1956. That is a period of 127 years embracing four major wars and any number of minor conflicts. Its purpose is not only to explain how military transport developed over that period, against the wider background of civilian progress, but why it developed as it did and how it was employed. This last theme, in particular, is probably covered for the first time in a title that is not an exclusive military textbook. That it could be written at all is due in no small part to the efforts of a number of good friends, among whom I particularly wish to thank Bart Vanderveen, Brian Baxter, John Church, Pat Ware and Richard Peskett, whether they realised they were helping or not. However, the opinions expressed, as they say, are entirely my own and the photographs all come from The Tank Museum collection.

David Fletcher
Bovington, 1998 and 2022.

LIST OF ABBREVIATIONS

AA	Automobile Association
AEC	Associated Equipment Company
AMR	Army Motor Reserve
AOP	Auxiliary Omnibus Park
ARP	Air Raid Precautions
ASC	Army Service Corps
ATS	Auxiliary Territorial Service
BEF	British Expeditionary Force
CMP	Canadian Military Pattern
COXE	Combined Operations Experimental Establishment
DND	Department of National Defence
DUKW	D = 1942, U = amphibian, K = all-wheel drive, W = dual rear axles
FWD	four-wheel drive
FVRDE	Fighting Vehicle Research and Development Establishment
GHQ	General headquarters
GM	General Motors
GMC	General Motors Corporation
GS	general service
HQ	headquarters
LCT	tank landing craft
LST	landing ship tank
LVT	landing vehicle tracked
MEE	Mechanisation Experimental Establishment
MT	motor transport
MTC	Mechanical Transport Committee
MWEE	Mechanical Warfare Experimental Establishment
PAIC	Persia and Iraq Command
RAC	Royal Automobile Club
RAF	Royal Air Force
RASC	Royal Army Service Corps
REME	(Corps of) Royal Electrical and Mechanical Engineers
SMM&T	Society of Motor Manufacturers and Traders
WD	War Department
WVEE	Wheeled Vehicles Experimental Establishment

BRITISH MILITARY TRANSPORT 1829-1956

1 GETTING UP STEAM

From the end of the Crimean War in 1855, the Army embarked on a slow road towards almost total mechanisation at a time when the horse was still a significant part of the nation's transport infrastructure. Various patent inventions were pressed upon the War Office, from steam traction engines to chain-track tractors, but the advent of the internal combustion engine changed everything.

1 GETTING UP STEAM

The Aveling & Porter Steam Sapper No 24 *Balloon* without the crane jib or dynamo. Lieutenant-Colonel J.L.B. Templer is the biggest man in uniform.

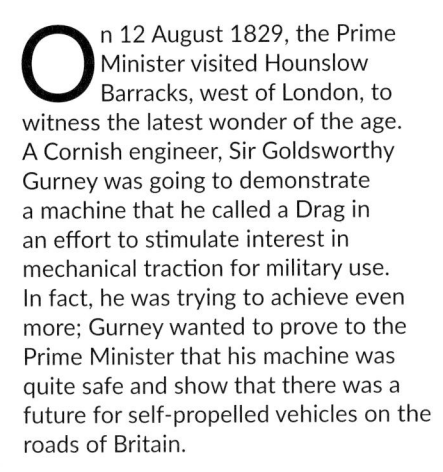

On 12 August 1829, the Prime Minister visited Hounslow Barracks, west of London, to witness the latest wonder of the age. A Cornish engineer, Sir Goldsworthy Gurney was going to demonstrate a machine that he called a Drag in an effort to stimulate interest in mechanical traction for military use. In fact, he was trying to achieve even more; Gurney wanted to prove to the Prime Minister that his machine was quite safe and show that there was a future for self-propelled vehicles on the roads of Britain.

The Drag wasn't much to look at. What the Prime Minister saw was a small, four-wheeled cart with two rows of seats and a kind of boot, or trunk at the back. There were no horses at the front, obviously, but if he looked closely the Premier would notice a small chimney on top of the boot and perhaps be aware that above it the air was simmering. When he got closer, he might be able to sense that the air was quite warm for the cart was powered by steam.

Gurney's Drag was not the first machine of its kind. Many other inventors had already built similar machines and in 1826 Sir Goldsworthy himself had produced a large steam vehicle, with a body like a stage coach, which ran in London for a while. The trouble was that the public did not like steam carriages on the roads; they had visions of the things going off bang and scalding everyone in their immediate vicinity. Indeed, the Drag had been designed to eliminate this fear because it was intended to tow, or drag, a passenger-carrying vehicle rather than form an integral part of it – the reasoning being that if the Drag went up the passengers should not go with it.

The boot at the back of the Drag housed a furnace and boiler, feeding a pair of cylinders in the chassis, which drove cranks on the rear axle. It was driven by Gurney himself on this occasion and his illustrious passenger, the British Prime Minister, was none other than the great Duke of Wellington, hero of India and the Peninsula – the victor of Waterloo. Standing on the side lines, the journalist John Herepath watched as his friend Gurney ran the Drag around the barrack square towing the Iron Duke and his entourage in a carriage hitched on behind. Later in the day the Drag was linked up to a wagon containing 27 guardsmen, which Herepath estimated weighed about 4 tons and he further calculated that it got up to 17mph as it circled the parade ground, all under perfect control. Wellington declared himself suitably impressed. It was, he said 'of great national importance' adding 'it is scarcely possible to calculate the benefit we shall derive from such an invention'. Then he got into his horse-drawn carriage and went home.

It was not that steam was any great novelty. The first steam-powered boat had been built in Scotland in 1788 and by 1802 another, the *Charlotte Dundas*, was operating on the Forth and Clyde Canal. Up in the north-east of England steam-powered locomotives had been used on colliery railways since 1805 and the self-taught engineer George Stephenson had been involved in the creation of the steam-operated Stockton and Darlington Railway in 1825. Indeed, on 6 October in the year of Gurney's demonstration (1829) Stephenson, with his son Robert, would astound the world with their locomotive *Rocket* during trials at Rainhill on the newly built Liverpool and Manchester line.

Those early boats in Scotland, and steam railways wherever they sprang up, captured the public imagination. Crowds flocked to watch them, and ride if they could, but when they encountered steam vehicles on the highway, they saw red. Persons of a Luddite mentality placed rocks across the roads to

9

disable them and Turnpike Trusts were encouraged to charge exorbitant rates if a steam vehicle approached their gates. All in aid of driving them off the roads and these tactics succeeded.

In persuading the Duke to witness his trial, Sir Goldsworthy Gurney achieved quite a coup but he had to have a carrot and the location is the clue. If Wellington could be assured of the Drag's military value there was a much better chance that he would back the development of steam road transport generally. In a long letter to the Prime Minister after the event John Herepath made the same point:

'I say nothing of the saving steam-coaches would create to the nation in the military transportation of troops and baggage: nor of the advantage to the public a rapid conveyance of military force might be in times of trouble or war. These are subjects into which your Grace would penetrate farther in a moment, than perhaps it would be in my power to comprehend or describe.' This, remember, was before any network of railways connected the cities of Britain. But all to no avail. Despite his fine sentiments, the Duke of Wellington appears to have done nothing more to help and the pioneers were driven from the streets. 'Steam on Common Roads', as it was called then, suffered a major setback.

The Battle of Waterloo was fought in 1815. Wellington died in 1852 (the same year as Gurney) and in 1854 Britain became involved in the Crimean War – its Army commanded by Lord Raglan who had lost his right arm at Waterloo. Such are the links of history. The British Army that fought in the Crimea was little different from the one Wellington had commanded in terms of uniforms, weapons and tactics, yet by the time the Crimean War ended in 1855 steam-powered ships, bringing reinforcements and supplies were commonplace and a steam railway ran from the port at Balaclava to the uplands near Sebastopol. There were even rumours of a steam-powered road engine.

The fortified port of Sevastopol presented the Allied armies with a considerable challenge and among the weapons developed to reduce it was a huge mortar that weighed something in the region of 42 tons. There were serious problems in getting the great mortar to work properly but even if these had been solved the difficulties of moving the gun onto the battlefield were enormous. As recorded in a previous title,* the military authorities had considered using traction engines to haul the gun but nothing could be supplied in time.

Once the Crimean War ended there was a sudden upsurge of interest in horseless military transport and various patent inventions were pressed upon the War Office. Prominent among these was a traction engine built by the firm Charles Burrell & Sons of Thetford in Norfolk, fitted with a patent device known as an Endless Railway invented by one James Boydell. Burrells was a typical local engineering firm, manufacturing agricultural implements in the wake of the 18th century revolution in farming practice. They built their first steam engine in 1846. Boydell obtained the patent for his Endless Railway in that same year, although it was not his first attempt; in fact, Boydell equipment had been used on horse-drawn military equipment in the Crimea.

The Endless Railway was just one of a number of inventions that anticipated the appearance of caterpillar tracks. In Boydell's case it consisted of a system of flat, wooden feet, attached to a wheel and arranged so that, as the wheel went round, it placed a foot down before it, rode over it and lifted it up afterwards. The object was to spread the pressure

*D. Fletcher and P. Ventham, *Moving the Guns* (The Tank Museum, 2022)

exerted by each wheel on soft ground by giving the wheel a firm surface to work on. The theory was simple enough, but the mechanics of it were not. Each foot, of which there were six around the rim of each wheel, was attached by means of a bracket, passing through the edge of the wheel and hinged in such a way that it would stay flat on the ground as the wheel rolled over it. Strain on the working parts was considerable and it would require great progress in metallurgy before the system was foolproof; unfortunately, by then it would be overtaken by other developments.

In September 1857, Mr W. Lamerton, who is described as the Machinery Superintendent at Woolwich Arsenal, accompanied a Burrell-Boydell engine that was driven by road from the factory at Thetford to London. The distance was near enough 100 miles and the load behind the engine calculated at 28 tons 18cwt. The engine itself weighed 15 tons. Setting off from Burrell's yard on Tuesday 8 September the train first went to Bury St Edmunds to collect part of its load and then, over the next eight days, plodded steadily towards London via Newmarket, Bishop's Stortford and Epping Forest.

Seeking out water often proved difficult and there were many hold ups when the machine had to be stopped to enable horses to pass, but instances of mechanical breakdown were surprisingly few. Indeed, their worst experiences seem to have been on the paved streets of London itself. There was a slope at each end of London Bridge and the surface was slippery, so the driver was obliged to throw the engine into reverse as it came off the southern end because he felt that the load was pushing him forward. This broke some of the gears, but it did not prevent the engine from bringing its train triumphantly into Woolwich just after 5 o'clock on Thursday 17 September.

In February 1858, two officers from the Military College at Addiscombe in Surrey, Colonel Sir Proby Cautley and Colonel Sir Frederick Abbott, witnessed a trial of this Burrell-Boydell engine on behalf of the East India Company. The event was organised by the Ordnance Select Committee at Woolwich and therefore had more to do with hauling artillery, but the two colonels were considering its value as a means of moving troops in India. Their conclusion, contained in a report to East India House, was that the engine, as it stood, was not suitable. Yet they could clearly see its potential and Colonel Cautley stated his view 'that with a perfect engine the Endless Railway apparatus would, at the present time, be most useful in India for the carriage of troops, where there are neither railroads nor steamers in sufficient abundance available'.

In 1859, the government in India ordered a pair of improved Burrell-Boydell engines, which were shown in Hyde Park that August. As in the Duke of Wellington's demonstration 30 years before, a party of guardsmen arrived to act the part of passengers. The two engines went out to Bombay, and two more were subsequently supplied to Calcutta. This implies success but some reports suggested that they were not always popular. Complaints filtered back from India that the Burrell-Boydell engines reared up and waved their front wheels in the air when trying to start a heavy load, drawing the obvious response from Britain that the load was clearly too heavy. Whatever the reason, matters were not improved by a curious trait noted among road-engine drivers, that when faced with a steep hill they always tried to get up it in one go, no matter how heavy their train. A sensible driver would split the train and bring it up half at a time.

With the death of James Boydell in 1859, and the insistent progress of technology, the era of the Endless Railway passed. For the next 10 years military interest in steam traction ebbed. This was due in part to the rapid spread of railways but also to a dearth of interesting or suitable prototypes. Most of the machines purchased during this time were intended either for hauling artillery or for general work around government dockyards and arsenals. The next stage in the story takes us back to India.

In October 1864, a young officer named Rookes Evelyn Bell Crompton arrived in India to join the 3rd Battalion, the Rifle Brigade at Nowshera. Crompton was something of a prodigy, even in that well-educated age, but he exhibited an aptitude for engineering that was unusual among his contemporaries. While waiting for his commission to come through, Crompton had studied engineering practice under Archibald Sturrock on the Great Northern Railway and, in his youth, had even been to the Crimea as a midshipman and was therefore entitled to wear the Crimean Medal.

Crompton was employed as workshop officer with his battalion and in his spare time completed a steam-powered cart for his own use, which he called *Bluebell*. Sometime later, when he was attached to the staff of Lord Mayo, he managed to interest the Viceroy in the prospect of operating steam road engines for government and military purposes. Like the Roman Army in Britain, the authorities in India appreciated the value of good roads for the rapid movement of troops, especially in the frontier regions. In particular, the Grand Trunk Road was a masterpiece of civil engineering, straight and level with good bridges and even tunnels in places. The same could not be said of the transport. The Army in India, and organisations such as the Post Office, employed bullock carts for transport and huge trains of them were required when a regiment was on the move. At an average speed of 2mph, even with frequent replacement of draught animals, progress was limited to about 30 miles a day and, to that extent, the capabilities of transport affected the distance a fighting force could move.

Crompton had heard of developments in Britain and in particular the work of one R.W. Thomson of Edinburgh. Thomson was the original inventor of the pneumatic rubber tyre but he was also one of the first to see that steam engines could be designed for road haulage, as distinct from agriculture, but that more speed would be essential if they were to compete with the railways. Crompton imported a small Thomson road steamer but, finding it a poor design, decided to come home and see if he could not improve things. The Viceroy had him seconded to the Indian Post Office and with the title of Superintendent of the Government Steam Train, Crompton arrived in Britain in 1870.

A Thomson road steamer was so unlike the normal run of traction engines that it deserves some description. To begin with it ran on three wheels, rather than four: a small one at the front for steering and two large driving ones at the rear. Then it had a vertical boiler, instead of a horizontal one, standing on end at the back. This powered two vertical cylinders but the most significant feature was the location of the driver. On most traction engines, before and since, the driver and his mate worked from the back with their view partly obscured by the boiler and its various fittings. On a Thomson engine the driver was situated in a seat at the front, with the novel prospect of actually being able to see where he was going.

Crompton was authorised to order four engines from the firm of Ransomes, Simms & Head of Ipswich but he nearly fell out with Thomson over the type of boiler to be used. Experience in India had convinced Crompton that the boiler favoured by Thomson was useless, especially when wood was used for fuel instead of coal. Crompton preferred the Field-type boiler, used on contemporary fire engines, but Thomson proved so stubborn that it was agreed to complete the first Indian engine with his simpler pot-type boiler. It was delivered from the Orwell Works in May 1871 and soon distinguished itself by burning down the grandstand at Ipswich race course. This was caused by sparks, blown from the engine which was being run on wood fuel since that was what it would have to use in India. Thus, in addition to the expense of four new engines, the Indian Government now found itself saddled with the cost of a new grandstand.

The first engine, named *Chenab*, was due to take part in the Royal Agricultural Show at Wolverhampton. Crompton undertook to drive it there and, afterwards, go on to Edinburgh so that Thomson, an invalid virtually confined to his bed, could inspect it. Crompton found that the pot boiler only generated half of the 100hp, which he deemed essential and it let him down badly at Wolverhampton. Crompton married at this time and his long journey was referred to in the press as Lieutenant Crompton's 'Honeymoon Trip'. *Chenab* towed a double-deck omnibus trailer, capable of seating 130 people, but which ran on just two wheels and had the endearing capability of making most of its passengers seasick.

The onward trip to Edinburgh, and back to Ipswich, was without doubt the longest yet undertaken by a mechanical road vehicle in Britain and, despite the boiler, it was judged a great success. At one point where the road paralleled the Great Northern Railway near Trent, *Chenab* overtook a goods train. On another occasion, in Scotland, a turnpike gate was closed to them. Crompton failed to convince the gatekeeper that he was bound upon government business and ended up using the engine to force the gate open. His commission actually enabled him to exceed the 4mph speed limit and at times he recorded more than 20mph on good stretches.

The four engines, *Chenab*, *Ravee*, *Indus* and *Sutlej* began to arrive in India from March 1872. Crompton supervised their assembly and then took charge of their operation over sections of the Grand Trunk Road between Rawalpindi and Jhelum in the Punjab. With his assistant, Richard Muirhead, Crompton designed special trailers for the engines, including

One of the four Ransomes engines at the head of a road train in India. The engine is fitted with Thomson's segmented rubber-tyred wheels and the first wagon behind the engine is the tender. The rest of the train is marshalled to include two- and four-wheeled wagons with a double-deck omnibus at the back.

a fuel and water tender. Crompton's idea was to mix two- and four-wheeled trailers alternately in each train since this enabled them to track the engine more accurately.

In addition to their daily haulage tasks the engines were used for military exercises and evaluation. Crompton was able to show that an engine in good condition could manage a train of 19 wagons with a total load of 40 tons at an average 5mph over long stretches of the Grand Trunk Road. However, Crompton's work faltered when his period in India ended, in 1875. Muirhead continued the work for a while but the machines were wearing out and the cost of new tyres was a constant drain on revenue. No immediate attempt was made to replace the engines and, in any case, the gradual spread of metre-gauge railways all over the subcontinent reduced their importance.

We shall meet Crompton again but for now return to the Wolverhampton Show of the Royal Agricultural Society of England in July 1871. Among the engines submitted for display and judging was a little machine, of conventional appearance, by the Rochester firm Aveling & Porter Ltd. It had been built to a government order for military purposes and was rated at 6 nominal horsepower (nhp). This curious figure was arrived at by measuring the capacity of the cylinder. It was a rough-and-ready way of comparing the relative power of engines but was nowhere near an indication of what they could really achieve. Thomas Aveling's greatest contribution to the design of engines at this time was the hornplate, an upward extension of the frame, which served to support the various driving shafts. On earlier machines the normal practice was to bolt the driving shafts direct to the boiler barrel, which resulted in a great deal of stress being transmitted to the boiler with the attendant risk of weakening it.

The reason for building such a small engine was to keep the weight down so that it could use existing Army pontoon bridges but, despite this requirement, it performed extremely well, especially when compared with Crompton's big road steamer, which gave a lot of trouble. However, the War Office believed the engine could be lighter still and Aveling & Porter managed to get the weight down from 5.25 to 4.75 tons. In this form it managed to haul a 15-ton load up the 1-in-11 Star Hill at Rochester and was measured at 36.7 actual horsepower. Indeed, it was so successful that the War Office ordered a number of these engines from Avelings and they were known in the service as Steam Sappers.

This title recognised the fact that all such machines were then operated by the Royal Engineers since, in addition to haulage, they could be used to pump water, generate electricity and serve as a mobile crane with a jib mounted at the front. Aveling & Porter built a further dozen Steam Sappers up to 1877, all single-cylinder machines but including two more powerful models rated at 8nhp. Most were delivered to the School of Military Engineering at Chatham. In 1873, Steam Sapper No 8 accompanied Sir Garnet Wolseley's expedition to the Gold Coast, the Ashanti War. It seems to have spent most of its time working a saw bench. This would be done 'on the belt' to use the technical term, with the engine running out of gear, on a governor, and the appliance worked by a belt running around the flywheel.

From 1870 onwards the number of firms engaged in building traction engines was continually expanding. There was hardly a county in England that did not have a manufacturer building such machines within the next 10 years. Many were on a very small scale but some, such as Aveling & Porter, Burrell, or Fowler were large companies by any standards, with an extensive range of products. Not that one should assume from this that traction engines were a common sight on British roads, except around Chatham of course. Rather they were mostly to be found on farms, moving equipment about or driving threshing machines at harvest time. The roads of Britain were generally falling into decay from lack of use.

The years up to 1890 did not see much expansion of military interest in steam although manufacturers tried to tempt the War Office with some interesting designs. The latter included machines with enormous wheels for improved cross-country performance and even four-wheel drive. A further dozen Steam Sappers were added to military stocks between 1878 and 1885, mainly from Aveling & Porter, although by now the term 'Steam Sapper' had become generic for any service traction engine. Among the more unusual acquisitions was Steam Sapper No 24 of 1885, which not only mounted a jib but an electrical generator as well, fixed on a bracket just ahead of the chimney. This machine, at some time named *Balloon*, was attached to the Army Balloon Factory at Aldershot, presided over by the striking figure of Lieutenant-Colonel J.L.B. Templer. No 24 was used mainly to haul gas cylinders from the factory to a nearby launching site. Templer, who was already acknowledged as a pioneer in military aviation circles, soon came to be regarded as an expert on road transport as well.

In 1893, Templer read a paper before the Royal Engineers' Institution entitled 'Steam Transport on Roads' in which he remarked that there were 22,000 miles of turnpike road in Britain and some 8,000 engines operating over them. In fact, the Turnpike Trusts, which had administered Britain's main roads for the last 200 years, were in serious decline and the last true turnpike gate would close down in 1895. In their heyday, early in the 19th century, the roads of Britain were something to be envied; well-engineered and properly maintained, they supported a system of stage and mail coaches, timed to the minute over long routes. But the railway companies had killed all that, just as they were systematically strangling the canal network by taking its freight business away.

That the roads survived at all was due, of all things, to the bicycle. Cycling became a middle-class craze towards the end of the century and the demand for better roads grew until responsibility for them was vested in the county councils. Soon they improved and, despite opposition from the pro-horse lobby, even started to attract mechanical transport again. Another aspect of the leisure industry, the travelling fair, became a familiar sight with huge and beautifully decorated showman's engines pulling long trains of sideshows and rides from place to place. This, in turn, increased the demand for engines that could travel long distances and the trade developed accordingly. Returning interest in roads led to an increased requirement for steam rollers to keep the surfaces in good order. Aveling & Porter, in particular, reduced their output of traction engines in favour of rollers, in which they soon specialised. Traction engines were now regarded, generally, as machines intended for short-range work around the farm while the term 'road engine' was coined for those designed for long-distance haulage. The latter were geared higher, for greater speed, and were often sprung to give a smoother ride but it was still an uphill struggle in the face of railway competition. Even so, as a direct consequence of the spread of steam, there was a noticeable reduction in the number of horses in commercial use on the roads and this affected the Army.

The Berkshire Manoeuvres of 1893 provide a good example of the Army's use of road engines as substitutes for the horse. The manoeuvres were a large-scale operation employing two brigades supported by artillery, engineers, transport and the *Balloon* from Aldershot. Transport of any kind was in short supply so, instead of the camp moving with the troops, it had to be carried and set up in advance. Three locations were used: at Uffington, Idstone and Liddington. In his report to the War Office the officer in charge explained that the brigades had employed eight Steam Sappers which, he calculated, did the work of 38 pairs of horses. Most of the engines were Avelings from Chatham, including No 24 from Aldershot. However, there was also a Fowler, a new Aveling, called *Queen* and hired from the makers, and an ancient, single-cylinder Howard named *Frog*. This last engine's main employment was pumping water at Liddington Camp while the *Balloon*, in addition to its obvious duty of hauling gas cylinders, was used before the exercise to lay out dumps of coal for the engines to burn in their travels.

Both *Balloon* and *Queen* managed some impressive runs with heavy loads but they did not impress the Commander-in-Chief that much. He did not think there was any great advantage in terms of speed and claimed that a steam engine, pulling three or four trucks, was nowhere near as flexible as an equivalent number of horse-drawn wagons. He pointed out that an engine and train was obliged to halt on the road, at the edge of the camp, whereas a horse-drawn wagon could be driven directly to where it was needed. This meant that soldiers who may just have arrived after a long and arduous march had to spend a good deal of time manhandling supplies from the steam train to their camp. Templer, as might be expected, gave a very positive verdict and showed that there was a considerable saving, in terms of men and supplies, when engines were employed in place of horses.

The 1898 manoeuvres, held in the region around Salisbury in August and

Newly arrived engines on the dockside at Durban, waiting to have their chimneys fitted.

September of that year, proved more of a triumph for Templer. A later report on the manoeuvres explains that the engines were retained mainly as a reserve in case anything went wrong with the plan to bring most of the supplies by rail. However, Templer is singled out for praise so the engines must have performed well. In fact, Templer was using the event to try out a variety of engines that he had persuaded various manufacturers to lend him. He concluded, when it was all over, that the best engine for military purposes was definitely the Fowler.

John Fowler and Company of Leeds, was by this time well on the way to becoming the dominant manufacturer of steam road engines in Britain. Following the Salisbury manoeuvres Colonel A.W. Mackworth, Chief Engineer of what was called the Northern Army, said of the engines: 'Of those we used, Messrs Fowler's compressed engines were undoubtedly the best all round.' Everyone knew what he meant, but Colonel Mackworth had got his terminology wrong: for 'compressed' he should have said 'compound'. The term is applied to a system in which steam from an engine's boiler passes first into a high-pressure cylinder and then, while it still has some power left in it, into a larger, low-pressure cylinder. The result was smoother running, a quieter exhaust, less wear and tear on valve gear and boiler tubes and, probably best of all from the user's point of view, a saving of some 30 per cent in fuel and water consumption.

The last decade of the 19th century saw a strong swing towards Fowlers as far as the military was concerned, but it did not result in many orders. Fortunately, at least for the manufacturers, the Boer War broke out in 1899 and in October of that year the War Office announced that some traction engines would accompany the troops to South Africa. Templer was appointed Director of Steam Road Transport but command in the field rested with Captain G.P. Scholfield who was in charge of No 45 Steam Road Transport Company, Royal Engineers, when it was established in the November.

Obtaining engines did not prove to be a great problem. Fowler was able to supply some good reconditioned machines and new ones, but it was difficult to find two that were identical and odd examples of other makes, Aveling & Porter, Burrell, McLaren and Marshall were included. The big problem was finding drivers. Out of 64 men said to be trained in traction-engine driving, Scholfield reckoned that six were adequate so he was obliged to recruit civilians in Britain and South Africa. Having to work in a war zone they were all highly paid, which was resented by the soldiers, but until more trained men could be provided there was no other answer. And, indeed, this problem was never solved while the war lasted.

The engines were delivered to Aldershot and given a limited test over rough ground in Long Valley. The normal trial involved attaching a couple of unladen wagons to each engine and running it about for a while but Scholfield, with the benefit of hindsight, later criticised Templer for not putting them to something more strenuous. The first shipment of engines and wagons sailed from Southampton in the steamship *Bulawayo* in mid-November, but when it arrived at the Cape a month later confusion reigned. Orders and counter-orders were flying about and the poor old Bulawayo found itself shuttled between Cape Town, Durban and Port Elizabeth, dropping engines, wagons and other items of its badly loaded cargo here and there.

To make matters worse, Scholfield discovered that nobody knew where his unit fitted in. He assumed that the Director of Transport would claim the company, but that worthy offered it to the Director of Railways. Scholfield went to see the Engineer-in-Chief who, after considering the matter, decided in favour of the Director of Railways. It was not a bad choice, the post was then held by the lively Canadian officer Percy Girouard, who could be relied upon to let people get on by themselves if he thought they knew what they were doing.

Colonel Templer sailed from Southampton early in December with a further cargo of engines on the SS *Denton Grange* but he did not have such a smooth trip. On arriving at Las Palmas in Gran Canaria to replenish its bunkers, the ship ran aground and could not be shifted. Two of the engines and a number of wagons carried as deck cargo on the *Denton Grange* were transferred to another ship but the rest had to stay where they were for a while. Templer, meanwhile, had gone ahead and found a desperate situation waiting for him. Ships were still shunting about between ports with the first batch of engines while some that had been delivered to Natal in a rush were now not wanted. Taking a grip on the situation, Templer obtained permission to take every engine he could find up-country and selected Kimberley, where they arrived on 3 March 1900, some two weeks after the famous siege was lifted.

A few days later Scholfield received orders to send three supply trains at once to Boshof, some 30 miles east from the railway. The young officer protested that it was foolish to let them go without first doing a reconnaissance of the track but he was overruled and off they went. Late the next day a message, flashed by heliograph, announced that the engines were all out of coal and water, but not yet at Boshof. Setting out with more fuel, Scholfield discovered that they had run into long stretches of very soft sand on the road and used up their fuel trying to get through. Lord Roberts was furious. He was obliged to send mules to Kimberley for supplies and declared that the engines were useless. This was a bit rich coming from Roberts.

When Roberts arrived in South Africa, with Kitchener as his Chief of Staff, the pair had taken it upon themselves to reorganise the transport arrangements. No longer would they accept the tried and tested method of divisional transport; instead they centralised the system and reduced it to chaos. Thomas Pakenham, in his superb book* describes it as one of the great blunders of the war, and that is saying something where the Boer War is concerned. During operations leading up to the relief of Kimberley the Boers had disabled a huge convoy of 200 wagons carrying about one-third of the British rations, and driven off the oxen. Things were so bad that Roberts was ready to give up the entire campaign until General Buller arrived to sort it out. Blaming Scholfield for his misfortune no doubt had its roots in this debacle.

In June, Scholfield's second-in-command, Captain Gardiner, was at Kroonstad with three engines. He was ordered to attach them to an ox-convoy bound for Lindley with 75 tons of stores. Gardiner explained that traction engines and oxen did not work well together but he was ordered to go anyway. He was assured that there was plenty of good water along the route and that he should expect to take four days to get there and three to come back. In fact, it took seven days just to get there. The oxen were in poor shape and every time they came to a river crossing, or drift, the engines had to be used to haul the wagons through. Two days out from Lindley the convoy was attacked by the Boers. They returned next day in greater force and some wagons had to be left behind. Indeed, at one point, the engines with their wagons brought up the rear, with nothing between

*T. Pakenham, *The Boer War* (Weidenfeld & Nicolson, 1979)

them and the Boers, but they made it to Lindley and even went back for the abandoned wagons next day.

Similar tales occur throughout Scholfield's official report of No 45 Company, yet there are also many examples of successful work, but only when the people who understood the engines were allowed to operate them sensibly. By 1901, the demand for engines was increasing. Units throughout the war zone were clamouring for them and orders were cabled back to Britain for more. They arrived, a few at a time, but Scholfield claims that the majority were quite old and in poor condition. Much the same could be said of some of the drivers who, according to the report, were getting high rates of pay but knew nothing of the work and could not even steer. One, who obviously did know his stuff, irritated the officers by getting dreadfully drunk after every trip. As an employer, Scholfield could not spare the man but if he had been a soldier there would at least have been ways of dealing with him.

Summing up at the end of his report Scholfield makes a number of interesting points. He remarks, for instance, that when supplies were carried by steam convoy the Boers rarely bothered them, so escorts could be reduced. He claims, too, that the engines were much more hygienic. It is not something one normally associates with traction engines but the matter is well illustrated. Oxen inevitably pollute the ground and any adjacent water source, whether they are working or not. Worse still they die. In August 1901, a stretch of road between Krugersdorp and Nauwpoort, according to Scholfield, was decorated with, on average, 20 to 25 dead oxen per mile with a stench to match. After the traction engines took over a month later, the route rapidly became perfectly clear and healthy.

Scholfield's report is a model of its kind. Major-General Sir Elliott Wood, the senior Royal Engineer officer in South Africa, spoke very well of it and historians will find in it a mine of information. On the subject of engines, Scholfield explains that there were 21 different types including various models by Fowler, and even then, he was not distinguishing between those with minor differences such as pumps or other fittings. If repairs were difficult the ordering of spares was a nightmare and

A Fowler compound engine of No 77 Company with a water tender and three traction wagons in tow on the high veldt.

there is no doubt about his views for the future.

In addition to No 45 Company there was another military unit operating traction engines in South Africa. This was the Electrical Engineers (Royal Engineers) Volunteers commanded by Lieutenant-Colonel R.E.B. Crompton, now 55 years old. His engines, three Burrells, were principally employed as mobile plant, generating power for electric arc lamps or searchlights, but they were used for other purposes, as told elsewhere.** They are mentioned again here mainly to make the point that Crompton was not, as a reading of his autobiography might suggest (and many writers have subsequently claimed), in charge of all the steam transport in South Africa.*** In any case he returned to Britain within a year whereas the war did not end until 1902.

Experience with the engines under war conditions convinced Scholfield, as it did his fellow officers, that in future it would be wrong for the Army to rely on ordinary commercial engines. It wasn't just the spares situation, although that was bad enough, but the questions that arose regarding quality and suitability. In Britain all this might not matter so much. Excellent workshop facilities existed and spares were readily available, but on a major campaign in foreign parts it was essential to have the best that was available. Broken-down engines, waiting months for new parts, were no use to anyone and in places where water was 30 per cent mud, good coal was unobtainable and abrasive dust got in everywhere, only the best would do. However, before we examine how this problem was resolved, some space must be given to other developments.

In 1896, the firm John I. Thornycroft of Chiswick, London, built a self-propelled steam lorry, effectively the first of its kind to appear in Britain. In passing one should note that one of Thornycroft's sons-in-law, Herbert Niblett, was involved in the project. His name will appear later in this book. The Thornycroft was followed by a

The Foden overtype No 529, which won second prize in the 1901 trial and served with the Army in South Africa.

similar vehicle from the Lancashire Steam Motor Carriage Company of Leyland (later Leyland Motors) and soon many other companies became involved including Foden in 1898. The advantages of such vehicles were easy to see. They were easier to handle than a traction engine with a train of wagons, especially around busy towns. They were faster and, in due course, cheaper.

With the fighting still going on in South Africa, the Secretary of State for War announced in May 1901 that the War Office was interested in lorries and that he proposed to hold a comparative trial, for anyone who wished to enter, at Aldershot in December. The conditions were fairly strict, and included the requirement that each lorry should be able to carry 3 tons and haul a trailer capable of holding 2 tons. Steam was not specified, but whatever type of engine was used the fuel must not have a flashpoint below 75°F.

Four firms had prototypes ready in time for the trials: Edwin Foden & Sons of Cheshire entered an overtype steam wagon; the Straker Steam Vehicle Company of Bristol and Thornycrofts of Chiswick offered undertype steamers; while the Milnes company of London amazed everyone by entering one of the new-fangled lorries with an internal combustion engine. The term overtype described a steam lorry with a horizontal boiler like a traction engine, with the cylinders on top; undertype meant that the cylinders were located beneath the body and such lorries normally had a vertical boiler. Thornycroft actually entered two models. One was their regular commercial product with the boiler at the front, the other was a special military, or colonial model which, in order to give better traction, had the boiler at the back. This placed the greatest weight over the driving axle but it meant that the driver was situated at the back too. When the lorry was loaded he could hardly see where he was going!

The internal combustion-powered Milnes-Daimler lorry at the 1901 trial. Notice that the radiator is slung between the chassis members at the front and how the guard is located ahead of it.

This is not the place to re-tell the history of the internal combustion engine in detail. Suffice it to say that cars, powered by such engines, had been produced, mainly in Germany and France, from about 1885 and by 1901 were relatively commonplace although still regarded mainly as a novelty for the idle rich.

The application to commercial vehicles followed quickly and the German Mercedes-Daimler was regarded as the best in Europe. The British Milnes-Daimler was a licence-built version of this type. Of course, the limitations on fuel prevented Milnes from running their entry on petrol so it was adapted to operate on paraffin. Some sources claim that the original 25hp engine was replaced by a 16hp unit, better suited to running on paraffin, but it may well be that the difference in power represents the result of using an inferior fuel in the same engine.

The trials commenced at Aldershot on 4 December 1901. They began with a road-run of 60 miles, over two days, with each contestant fully laden. The Foden ran on coal, and continued to do so throughout the trial despite a request from the authorities that they

**D. Fletcher and P. Ventham, *Moving the Guns* (The Tank Museum, 2022)
***R.E.B. Crompton, *Reminiscences* (Constable, 1928)

should like to see how it would perform on coke. The Milnes-Daimler used what was described as 'crude Russian petroleum' of a very high flashpoint but regular petrol was used to start it up and achieve the necessary high running temperature. The Straker-Squire used only coke, the conventional Thornycroft started on coke and finished on coal while the special Thornycroft, fitted with a patent oil burner, started on that fuel and later switched to coke when the equipment broke down.

Following a day for examination the vehicles then commenced a continuous six-day road trial, which would take them over some of the toughest hills in the area including two assaults on the notorious Hog's Back between Farnham and Guildford. The roads are described as being very hard on some days, following overnight frost, and soft on others with a good deal of deep mud in places. The final trial was in Long Valley at Aldershot and the route was specially selected to provide variety, but particular attention was paid to getting through boggy ground or crossing streams with steep banks which, presumably, would represent the drifts found in South Africa.

The Foden blotted its copybook on the first day when the makers asked if they might employ a crew of two, which was contrary to the conditions laid down by the testing committee. This was refused at first but on the second day the danger of one-man operation was realised since the driver had to let go of the steering wheel and look away from the road in order to replenish the firebox. The Milnes-Daimler was underpowered and had to drop its trailer after the third day, while the poor oil-fired Thornycroft was off the road for three days of the trial with mechanical problems; mainly, it seems, with the oil burner.

Thus, when it came to the cross-country course it was down to a three-horse race. In fact, most professional observers saw it as between two, the Foden and the standard Thornycroft, after the Straker had to abandon its trailer in a bog. Unfortunately, the Foden suffered an accident at this time. It was being driven through long grass and neither the driver, nor his mate, noticed a deep ditch in front of them. The lorry plunged in, trapping the front wheels and axle, which in turn caused the entire fore-carriage to bend back beneath the boiler. It was a serious blow, although replacement parts were delivered and fitted immediately and the big wagon finished the trial.

Many journalists, anticipating a win for the Foden, or at least a tie with the standard Thornycroft reported as much, and all were shocked to learn that the War Department Mechanical Traction Committee thought otherwise. The £500 first prize was awarded to the Thornycroft while the Foden only came second (£250) and the Straker-Squire third (£100). Foden himself was very annoyed and made sure everyone knew it. He was able to show that his

The Thornycroft colonial steam lorry taking part in the 1901 War Department trial. The long steering shaft from the driver's position at the back is clearly shown.

wagon was fastest over most routes and certainly much more economical on fuel and water. Most commentators have blamed Foden's disappointment on the accident to the front axle, but one wonders if the Committee was not more irritated by the firm's refusal to run on anything but coal, and their addition of an extra man in the crew.

In announcing their decision the Committee added a recommendation that the War Office should purchase both the first- and second-placed entries, which they did. In his report, mentioned earlier, Major Scholfield gives the vehicles' date of arrival in South Africa as the end of February 1902. He used the old term 'lurries' to describe them but, he says, they had little chance to prove what they could do. The best test came in May, while they were based at Kroonstad. There was a sudden requirement to shift 350 tons of supplies for a distance of 21 miles and an opportunity was taken to make it a controlled, comparative trial, between the traction engines and the two lurries. Scholfield, having been in South Africa for so long, measured his loads in the Dutch, short, tons (2,000lb) and noted that a traction engine train could move 17½ tons, while each lurry and trailer could manage 5 tons. It took a traction engine two days to do the return journey whereas a lurry could do it in one day, and a traction engine needed a crew of three while the lurries only required two. Bitter experience had taught Scholfield that in a place like South Africa vehicles often got stuck, and he pointed out how a traction engine could winch itself and its load from such a situation while a lurry could not.

Even so, for this kind of work Scholfield calculated that four traction engines could have done the job in 10 days for £264 compared with seven lurries, which would be required to shift a similar load in the same time at a total cost of £306 16s 8d. He regarded lurries as more suitable for local distribution work but made the interesting comment that they might prove useful to carry infantry if they were needed in a hurry. Apropos his earlier comment, Scholfield also pointed out that, in the event of the lurry getting stuck, the load could at least jump out and push!

In comparing the two lurries, Scholfield came down heavily in favour of the Thornycroft. It had given hardly any trouble whereas the Foden had suffered repeatedly from breakages of the final-drive chains and damage to the sprockets. He did suggest that if vehicles like the Thornycroft were to survive in South Africa they could do with bigger boilers, but his men had discovered a weakness in the Foden's frame, which had to be strengthened. In an appendix to his report, summing up the days each lurry spent under repair between March and June 1902 (6 for the Thornycroft, 19 for the Foden), Scholfield includes a footnote that refers to a second Thornycroft lurry and lists the damage discovered when it was delivered. No more is known of this.

In its first interim report, dated 1902, the War Office Mechanical Transport Committee (MTC) announced that, in the way beloved of committees, it had grown. With Major F. Lindsay Lloyd, Royal Engineers, as its secretary the Committee, which included Colonel Crompton and a certain Captain Nugent among its members, had created a number of subcommittees in its image. These included three specific subcommittees representing the interests of the Royal Artillery, Royal Engineers and Army Service Corps (ASC) and one with unspecified responsibilities entitled the 'Experimental and Motor Sub-Committee'.

The three specific subcommittees, as might be expected, used their first reports to establish the ground rules.

They each announced that they should own, operate and repair their own equipment up to a point and had quite firm ideas on what that equipment should be. The Royal Engineers, for instance, came down in favour of a traction engine of about 12 tons, while the ASC wanted traction engine trains for long-distance haulage and motor lorries for local work. The ASC even went as far as drawing up a proposed establishment table for two motor transport (MT) companies. Both, it said, should consist of 8 traction trains and 24 motor lorries, each with a trailer. The traction trains should come complete with 10 traction wagons, twice the number that each engine could pull and, like the sappers, agreed that the engines should not weigh more than 12 tons. Each company would be divided into four sections, and each section, commanded by a lieutenant or second lieutenant, should include three traction-engine drivers and eight lorry drivers; the two obviously being regarded as distinct trades. Logically this would mean that each section within the company would have 2 traction engines, 20 traction wagons and 6 lorry and trailer sets.

The MTC concurred with these findings although it emphasised that general training, both in driving and maintenance, should be the responsibility of some central body and that heavy-duty maintenance work should be similarly concentrated. It was also announced that, by taking the majority view of each subcommittee the parent committee was in a position to announce that the most popular type of traction engine was Fowler's big 10nhp compound type, known as the Lion.

Of some 48 engines ordered by the War Office from Fowler between 1902 and 1909, no less than 23 were of the B5 Lion class and 10 of the larger B6, Big Lion-type. Rated at 10nhp, these excellent machines had a maximum indicated horsepower of 70. They ran on 6ft-diameter hind wheels and weighed around 12 tons. They were about 18ft long and, for military use, normally came with a short awning covering the footplate and working parts.

In 1905, Captain Nugent and a fellow sapper officer Captain R.K. Bagnall-Wild published a set of ideal specifications based on such engines in military service. The specifications run to some 15 pages and make it clear that everything was to be made to the highest possible standard. Axles, for instance, must be of special quality, oil-hardened steel and the wheels of wrought iron with phosphor bronze bushes designed for ease of lubrication and maintenance. The firebox and boiler tubes were to be of copper to give the best conductivity of heat, while springs and differential gear were all to be manufactured of best-quality materials. The precise composition of each item was laid down and a series of devastating tests specified before they could be accepted. Each engine was to be capable of hauling up to 60 tons on ordinary roads for at least 12 miles without refilling with coal or water and of winching the same load up an incline of 1-in-8. The cable was to be 100yds of the best flexible, galvanised steel wire rope. Ideally, the engines should be fitted with 7ft-diameter wheels so that they could wade through water up to 24in deep without extinguishing the fire and, in addition to the standard water lifter, a Worthington steam pump was required, capable of delivering 300 gallons per hour into a tanker trailer, towed by the engine. Having dealt with everything in excruciating detail, even down to the type and amount of paint to be used, the compilers add: 'Before leaving the contractor's premises every portion of the work to be painted on all sides and wherever it is possible for a brush to reach, with another coat of paint.'

1 GETTING UP STEAM

As one modern commentator admits: 'This specification is probably the most extensive that has [ever] been compiled for road locomotive or traction type engines.' It is equally certain that it was never achieved. Cost alone would have rendered it beyond reason yet, even when sensible adjustments had been made, such as the substitution of brass for copper tubes in the boiler, the resulting engines were some of the best ever built. With such good quality material most should still have been running today were it not for the fact that, when no longer required for service use, they were of greater value to the scrap-metal dealer than a commercial operator.

Throughout 1902 and 1903, Fowler B5- and B6-class engines were tested by the military authorities on some prodigious haulage trials. In many cases, trains of 60 tons were moved between the maker's factory in Leeds and the military depot at Aldershot and detailed records for many of these runs survive. Fowler often supplied their own staff as drivers and fitters for these trips but they were supervised by the military with great care. Railway companies were contracted to have dumps of coal waiting at suitable locations and it was considered good practice to have a man riding ahead on a bicycle to check the route and watch for obstructions. Water supply was a perennial problem and there are accounts of surreptitious extractions from horse troughs or even wells in people's gardens. As an example of how things could go wrong, the following concerns a run in August 1902, which got off to a bad start.

Leaving the Balloon Factory at Aldershot on Monday morning the engines picked up their trains at the ASC depot and set off in the direction of Reading. Unfortunately, someone got the directions wrong and, instead of heading direct for Frimley, the party took the alternative route via Frimley Green where a bridge, carrying the London & South Western Railway over the road was under repair. Temporary supports beneath the bridge reduced headroom to the extent that the engine had to have its chimney removed to get through. Not that this helped much because the living van that formed part

Two Fowler compound engines on a long cross-country run, drawing water from a duck pond. Each train includes one of the Fowler armoured wagons built for the Boer War. The wagon at the rear of the first train was used as an office and accommodation for the officers.

A Wellington steam tractor by Fosters of Lincoln in service with the Army Service Corps. Notice the large water tanks on each side of the boiler.

of the train was 4in too high. Nothing could be done to reduce the height so the party resorted to digging deep ruts in the road for the wheels of the van, only to find a water main running so close to the surface that this idea had to be abandoned. The second engine therefore took the living van on a long detour through Farnborough where it crossed the railway and rejoined the rest at Frimley Green just before 10.00pm that night, and there the party elected to stay until morning. Not that any of this availed them much. Taking a detour in Reading on the Tuesday they found the road so rough that it shook the kitchen range off its mountings in the confounded living van and it was so damaged that they could not use it again!

Although the notorious Locomotives on Highways Act of 1861 – which required a man to walk in front of any self-propelled vehicle carrying a red flag – was repealed in 1896 there were still all sorts of restrictions to make life an economic misery for hauliers. Steam-traction engines over 3 tons in weight, which of course most were, still suffered severe restrictions. And, although some

manufacturers, notably Taskers of Andover, did build small steam tractors within this limit they were not regarded as economically viable by the majority of potential customers. However, the Heavy Motor Car Order of 1903 improved things a little. Now tractors could be built up to 5 tons and, within that weight limit, it was permissible for the machine to be operated by one man. This meant that operators with such small engines could reduce costs and many firms were now induced to cater for the market.

A steam tractor was, essentially, a miniature road locomotive with long-range water tanks and, from 1903 onwards, the War Office began to test them. From this point the matter of range began to dominate. It was not simply a matter of reduced journey times but greater economy in the use of fuel, all of which interested the military authorities as it did everyone else. Indeed, as early as 1902, the Experimental and Motor Sub-Committee had instructed Colonel Crompton to investigate two features with this in mind. One was the provision of an acceptable form of oil burner, the other a system of air-condensing apparatus. Of the former, Crompton established that a burner designed by James Holden, Chief Mechanical Engineer of the Great Eastern Railway, was most effective, and this was later used in a number of military Fowlers. Condensing gear, on the other hand, never did seem to work very well. The idea was quite sound. Exhaust steam was recycled in such a way that it was returned to the fluid state by a blast of cold air and used to top up the tanks. Crompton designed a large machine, described as an 'Experimental Military Hauling Engine', which was ordered from Ransomes, Simms and Jeffries of Ipswich.

It was a revolutionary engine in many respects. First, it was an undertype, with the cylinders under the boiler; second, it was a triple-crank compound with two high-pressure cylinders flanking a large, low-pressure one. It had chain final drive, which almost everyone else had given up on years ago, and a Clarkson oil burner in the firebox. The condenser was incorporated in the canopy, above the footplate where, presumably, it would be cooled by the movement of air as it rushed along. Unfortunately, the engine didn't rush along. Photographs show it posed with a train of wagons, but at least one source suggests that it had more than enough difficulty moving itself, never mind towing anything, and Ransomes are said to have been so embarrassed that they denied any knowledge of it for many years.

In 1903, the Experimental and Motor Sub-Committee proposed holding a trial for tractors designed for long-distance haulage. Specifications were issued and it was planned to hold the trial in the spring. The main requirement was a minimum travelling distance of 40 miles on one fill of fuel; where steam engines were concerned this meant that the water actually left in the boiler at that distance must still be above the minimum level for safety. The winning vehicle stood to earn its builders £1,000, but there was the added incentive of 10 shillings for every mile it went beyond 40 without refuelling. The list of requirements was, in fact, so long and specific that every manufacturer consulted agreed that an entirely new machine would have to be developed

The unfortunate 'Experimental Military Hauling Engine' designed by Colonel Crompton and built by Ransomes. The flywheel is slung low because the engine is beneath the boiler and the canopy also contains the steam condenser.

and, since nobody could have an entry ready for spring, the appointed date was put back to October. Even then only one firm, Richard Hornsby & Sons of Grantham, had a machine ready and since it managed to cover 58 miles it won easily. It was certainly impressive in appearance as well as performance, running on 7ft-diameter hind wheels and weighing 13 tons. Although the layout was conventional, when compared with existing traction engines, the Hornsby tractor was powered by a two-cylinder, Akroyd-type engine designed to run on paraffin. Vaporising of the fuel was initiated by special heating lamps and the machine even had compressed air starting facilities. On a series of runs in the Aldershot area, spread over a four-week period, the big tractor managed a gross load of 38 tons at an average speed of nearly 4mph and covered 374 miles in the process. It was duly purchased for military use.

Throughout 1904 and 1905, trials of various machines dominated the work of the MTC. The majority were still steam-powered but a great deal of attention was paid to the respective advantages of solid and liquid fuels. Small numbers of steam tractors were obtained from different manufacturers including an advanced three-cylinder design from Fowler, which even featured a hydraulic arrangement at the front end enabling the driver to adjust the boiler to keep it level on a hill.

At the same time a number of motor cars were acquired for examination. In 1902, four Wolseleys, along with a Napier, Lanchester and Brooke were obtained and then passed to the various Army depots throughout the United Kingdom. The commanding officer at each depot was expected to submit a report by July 1903. Members of the various subcommittees also made it their business to attend any motor car shows held in Britain and on the Continent to study the latest developments and maintain contact with the trade.

In 1906, for instance, a number of Committee members went along to the Motor Car Exhibition at Olympia, in London, where they noted the number of firms now producing cars with six-cylinder engines and other innovations such as dual ignition (with two sparking plugs per cylinder) and the use of high-tension magnetos. The petrol engine was rapidly coming of age, the crude efforts of the pioneers having by now given way to a scientific approach, coupled with good engineering practice. Four members attended the Paris Automobile Exhibition that same year, paying particular attention to a display of lorries at the Esplanade des Invalides, which included all the vehicles that had taken part in the recent French military trials. They noted, apparently with some surprise, that of the seven vehicles on show only one was steam-powered and one heavy oil, the rest were all petrol. Further, they remarked on the standard of reliability, which was very high, and the average speeds, which were much greater than those considered economical in Britain. They attributed the reliability to the French practice of sticking to conventional designs but paying greater attention

A large Thornycroft undertype steam lorry attended by a bevy of officers at a War Office trial.

Well wrapped in a travelling rug, a sergeant chauffeur at the wheel of an early Wolseley.

to detail; as distinct, presumably, from the British habit of issuing optimistic requirements and expecting manufacturers to build suitable machines from scratch for a price that precluded attention to detail. On the subject of speed, the Committee said 'it must be remembered that rubber tyres were used', as if that, in some way, was simply not playing the game.

For all that, direct interest in foreign products was not so evident in Britain. True, a strange machine known as the Keller tractor had been borrowed from Germany, on the advice of Colonel Crompton, but it was never adopted. The Keller was a four-wheel drive machine but the wheels were flanged and ran around inside larger diameter hoops, which were supposed to give it an improved cross-country performance. The MTC appeared to like the principle, but not the machine itself and in any case there had been similar developments in Britain.

Shortly before the Boer War an eccentric engineer with an equally curious name, one Bramah J. Diplock, had demonstrated a four-wheel drive traction engine at Peckham in Kent. Among those who inspected it was Colonel Crompton who assisted the designer with some suggestions for improvement. But Diplock was of that inventive breed for whom nothing is ever good enough and in 1901 he produced another machine. This also had four-wheel drive but when it was first demonstrated the front wheels were fitted with Diplock's patent device known as the 'Pedrail'. The cost must have been enormous. The engine itself was far more complicated than any type then in production, but the Pedrail wheels were a nightmare of complexity. The rim of each wheel was surrounded by a series of disc-shaped feet, linked by an intricate system of levers, which adjusted themselves to

The undertype, four-wheel drive engine built by Kerr, Stuart of Stoke-on-Trent with Diplock's patent Pedrail wheels on the front axle.

the surface as the engine moved. It was in essence an improved version of Boydell's system but Diplock had even greater ambitions for it. In a book, published in 1902, he proposed a system, not unlike the present method of freight containerisation, by which goods might be distributed from railheads or delivered there as the case may be.* Drawings in the book show special tractors and trailers, all fitted with his Pedrail wheels, which could carry and lift the containers as required. Professor Hele-Shaw of University College, Liverpool, was another eminent engineer who supported Diplock's cause but it was far too ambitious to catch on. Nevertheless, the military authorities took an interest in the system and tested at least one steam tractor at Aldershot.

In 1904 the Grantham company, Richard Hornsby & Sons, demonstrated what they called a chain-track tractor, designed by their managing director, David Roberts. It was a single-cylinder, oil-engined machine, running on a set of complicated crawler tracks and the MTC, having observed its performance, decided to order one on behalf of the War Office. In fact, what Roberts did was to have the big tractor from the 1903 trials converted into a tracklayer

and, in this new form it was delivered in 1907.

This brief excursion into the world of more exotic machines serves to draw attention to another theme which, from the earliest days, runs through the history of military transportation. This is the enduring belief that vehicles designed for military use had much in common with those required for service overseas, and vice versa. Thus, one finds that service personnel were joined on the MTC by representatives of bodies such as the India Office, the Colonial Office and the Crown Agents for the Colonies. The motive behind this alliance was mainly economic but in the majority of instances even the combined budgets of defence and colonial development were insufficient to fund exotic developments, and so it has proved many times since.

From 1907, Bagnall-Wild was the secretary of the MTC and his period in office marked another significant turning point in our story. This was the move away from tractor-drawn supply trains to the use of self-contained lorries, which had begun with the 1901 War Office trials. Not that this move happened at once, as we shall see, but at least it was being considered. In 1907, the Royal Automobile Club (RAC) organised a commercial vehicle trial and the Army Council decided that it would offer a diploma to any entrant whose machine was considered suitable for military purposes. It was noteworthy, however, that in the section devoted to tractors there were only three competitors, all steam, and this was described by the MTC as disappointing. There were some 60 entries in all, but only two diplomas were awarded. One to Thornycroft, for a four-cylinder petrol engine, and one to Maudslays for the way in which the engine in their lorry could easily be reached for maintenance. Both vehicles were purchased for more extensive service trials.

*B. Diplock, *Heavy Goods Transport on Common Roads* (Longmans, Green & Co., 1902)

1 GETTING UP STEAM

The big Hornsby chain-track tractor on a trial run. Despite the large chimney, it is in fact powered by an internal combustion engine.

The majority of vehicles entered were petrol lorries in the 3-ton class, but neither the MTC representatives nor the RAC thought very much of this type. They could see the advantage of the Thornycroft, which was of 30cwt capacity and ran on rubber tyres, but for heavier loads, 3 tons and above, they still believed that the tractor with trailers was the most economical method of moving freight by road, as long as speed was not the main concern. One thing that put them off lorries was the weight factor. A typical steam lorry, capable of carrying 3 tons, weighed 6 tons unladen and this was considered excessive. The reason, of course, was the state of the roads and the fact that all of these vehicles ran on steel-rimmed wheels. The inevitable result was that a great deal of vibration set in, which shook the wagons to pieces so it was essential to build them as strong as possible and, naturally, they were heavy. Two other favourite old complaints were trundled out: self-contained lorries stood idle while they were being unloaded and, if they got stuck in the mire, they could not winch themselves out as a tractor could. Likewise, the MTC preferred the tractor because it could go off and do something else while its trailers were being unloaded.

This opinion was strengthened for a while by the appearance in Britain of a Renard road train from France. This curious system involved a tractor unit which, by means of shafts and universal joints, also provided drive for the centre axle of as many six-wheel trucks as one cared to join on behind it. A three-day trial, commencing with a run from London to Aldershot, was arranged for the benefit of the MTC, but with little success. Although the roads were not ideal, the machine never managed to run in top gear for the entire trip and the MTC inspectors put this down to the tremendous waste of power absorbed by the extended drive shaft. On a cross-country course the tractor, with its train of three wagons, failed to climb every gradient it was put at and the firm's representative refused to allow it to try one test over a small jump. To prove that they were not asking too much, the MTC ran a steam traction engine towing a loaded wagon over the obstacle without ill effect. The MTC report stated that the 'Renard Train as it stands is useless for military purposes'. The report claimed that the loss of power was too great and the time of two hours to uncouple and recouple the train at a weighbridge was ridiculous. On soft ground the driven wheels on each trailer simply dug out the soil beneath them until the suspension reached its limit and they were hanging in space. Despite all this negative reporting the British Daimler company purchased the patent rights and built a few Renard-type machines, one of which was tested by the MTC in 1910 but with no favourable result.

In March 1907, members of the MTC attended the International Commercial Motor Vehicle & Motor Boat Exhibition at Olympia where they observed more interesting trends. One of the first was that steam still dominated, both for tractors and lorries. The Committee members put this down in the first place to the fact that in Britain one could always find water easily, so range was not as important, but they also reckoned that conservative users were not interested in new technology and were too careful to wish to retrain drivers and fitters. This decided the MTC to sponsor the development of internal combustion-engined tractors for military use. The MTC members also observed, with some concern, that the internal combustion-engined lorries on show were all fitted with petrol, rather than heavy oil (paraffin) engines, which the Army favoured. However, as heavy oil engines were fitted to the majority of motor boats on display, the members agreed that something along these lines should be investigated for their own tractor.

Another vehicle at the Exhibition that attracted their attention was a Milnes-Daimler motor omnibus, which they described as a great improvement over earlier models. They ascribed this improvement to the influence of the Metropolitan Police who exercised firm control over the design of buses that were used in the London area. Although this inhibited development in the early stages it meant that, when buses became a common sight on the streets of London, they were of superior quality. In Britain the double-decker had been popular since the early days of horse buses and a typical London motor omnibus of this period could seat up to 34 people, against 26 in a horse bus.

Such vehicles could be useful for military purposes if the need suddenly arose to move a body of troops to places that the railway did not reach; but the first attempt to exploit this possibility was something of a private venture. Thomas Clarkson, a patriotic Lancastrian based at Chelmsford in Essex, was the inventor of a steam-powered bus, a double-decker that was fitted with a flash-type boiler capable of raising steam instantly. Clarkson, the proprietor of the National Bus Company that operated out of Chelmsford, was also a keen supporter of the new Territorial Army, which was created in 1908. Working in conjunction with Colonel R.B. Colvin, Chairman of the Essex County Territorial Association, Clarkson provided transport for the

Territorials, carrying the men and their baggage as far afield as Sudbury in Suffolk, or Folkestone in Kent, in buses emblazoned with slogans such as 'BE PREPARED!' and 'WAKE UP BRITAIN!'

Inspired, no doubt, by Clarkson's enterprise, the War Office decided to try the same thing on a larger scale. It imagined an enemy landing in the Thames Estuary and planned to despatch a force of 500 Territorials to meet it. The day chosen for the exercise was 21 December 1908, the shortest day of the year. The War Office hired 24 buses from three London companies. Each company operated a different make of bus but it came as something of a shock to realise that they were all foreign. General ran French De Dions, Vanguard German-designed Milnes-Daimlers, while the London Road Car Company, who used the fleet name Union Jack, ran Straker-Squires, which were really German Bussings.

The buses picked up the troops at Warley in Essex and then split into two columns, each escorted by motorcycle outriders, which took different routes towards Shoeburyness. The columns met up again at Hadleigh, on the outskirts of Southend, where the troops disembarked and formed up to meet the imaginary attackers. The entire operation was judged a great success and the War Office claimed that many useful lessons had been learnt. Suddenly, it seemed, officialdom was motor mad.

In March 1909, the Automobile Association (AA) sought to prove that whatever buses could achieve, motor cars could do better. They persuaded the War Office to stage a similar exercise with Hastings as the threatened invasion area but with the added premise that enemy spies had already disabled the railway. They offered, through the medium of their members, to carry 1,000 men of the Brigade of Guards from London to the Sussex town in one go. Photographs suggest that each car carried two soldiers, so it seems there must have been 500 of them. It was undoubtedly an amazing sight and strict road discipline, as we understand it today, was clearly ignored. It was a cold day too, for the stout fellows of the Coldstream, Grenadier and Scots Guards all appear to have their legs wrapped in travelling rugs. All of the cars were open to the elements and they appear to have made a mess of the road but the exercise worked. Quite what it did for the War Office is difficult to discover, but the AA obtained a good deal of publicity from it, as did the cause of motoring in general, while Napier & Sons of London, who supplied a fleet of 21 pneumatic-tyred lorries to carry the troops' baggage could not complain either.

Motor cars had become something of a fad with young Army officers. A few years earlier, in 1903, a Motor Volunteer Corps had been formed to foster motoring in the service and provide vehicles for exercises. In 1906 it changed its title to become the Army Motor Reserve (AMR), and turned into something of an exclusive club with premises on Sackville Street in London's West End. Membership was open to anyone under the age of 60 who ran an efficient motor car which, in practice, was limited to some 45 officers. In 1909, the officer in charge of the AMR asked the MTC if it would recommend a particular car that his members could buy, which would be most suitable for military use.

It was explained to him that, as far as the Army was concerned, interchangeability of parts was a vital concern, along with a good stock of spares in the event of war but no particular make was suggested. The result was that each member continued to drive whatever took his fancy and, shortly thereafter, with war imminent, the AMR was disbanded on

A column of steam buses from Thomas Clarkson's National fleet carrying Territorial Army troops on an exercise.

the grounds that the variety of vehicles rendered it more of a nuisance than it was worth.

In 1907, a superb private motor-racing circuit was opened at Brooklands, near Weybridge in Surrey. It was in fact designed by a Colonel Holden of the Royal Engineers and the MTC looked upon it as an ideal place to test new vehicles. They reached an agreement with the Brooklands Automobile Racing Club that permitted them to test vehicles up to 1½ tons weight, as long as the vehicles did not use studded tyres. Tests of speed, hill climbing and fuel consumption could be arranged and were easily monitored so that Brooklands soon became an important venue, not just for the War Office but for many manufacturers who realised its advantages.

At the end of 1909 Captain Bagnall-Wild resigned as secretary of the MTC and was replaced by another sapper, Captain A.E. Davidson. Their report for the year ending March 1910 includes a list of vehicles purchased over the last 12 months and it is interesting to observe that steam was by no means dead:

3   Burrell steam-crane tractors
3   Thornycroft internal-combustion tractors
2   Straker-Squire ambulances
2   Burrell steam tractors
2   Fowler steam tractors
2   Thornycroft 30cwt paraffin lorries
2   Milnes-Daimler 3-ton paraffin lorries
3   Arrol-Johnston 16hp, four-seat motor cars
3   Swift 10-12hp two-seat motor cars.

The point about this list, according to the MTC report, was that only the first eight vehicles, which were built strictly to War Office specifications, had been delivered during the year. The remainder had only been authorised at the very end of the financial year and, in order to get them in time, the authorities had been obliged to take whatever was left on the manufacturers' shelves. It was hardly the wisest way to equip an Army.

Clearly, what was happening had Civil Service accountancy stamped all over it. The finance department counted up what it had left over at the end of the financial year and allowed the Army to buy a few more vehicles. Of course, 1909/10 may have been an expensive year. A number of firms had already supplied special prototype tractors for a War Office trial and, although they might be regarded as private ventures, it may well be that some of the cost was borne by the War Office budget. If so it was an expensive failure and could be described as steam's last fling.

One stipulation imposed by the War Office was a minimum range of 100 miles without refuelling, which indicates a strong bias in favour of the internal combustion engines, as suggested earlier. However, three firms tried to compete with steam. One was Allen and Simmonds of Reading who commissioned a light steam tractor from Taskers of Andover. It was conventional enough in layout but with extra water tanks hanging off everywhere and an air-cooled condenser in the canopy. Another was Stewart and Company of Glasgow who supplied an innovative machine with a rear-mounted boiler generating 200psi with a coil superheater in the firebox and, rather surprisingly, shaft drive. The third was built by the Lowca Engineering Company of Whitehaven, and in many ways it was the most remarkable. It had a vertical flash boiler and enormous condenser at the front with an equally massive water tank at the back but the engine, designed by Mr H. Bentley, the firm's managing director, can best be described as a compound V8 working at 700psi. For some reason not specified, the venerable Colonel Crompton was associated with the design. The makers claimed that it was intended for colonial use and that military interest was incidental but mention of Crompton might give the lie to that. In any event none of the steamers lived up to expectations. Only the Stewart tractor made it to Aldershot and it did not do very well.

Those firms submitting internal combustion designs included Marshalls of Gainsborough, Broom & Wade of High Wycombe, Hornsby, and Thornycroft. The latter two firms took the prizes. Thornycroft came a deserved first but one of the Hornsbys was another tracklayer, powered by a six-cylinder paraffin engine, which was probably the most impressive. Sometime, probably in the financial year 1908/09, the War Office had introduced what it described as an 'Enrolment Scheme'. The idea was that, for the princely sum of £2 per annum a steam-tractor owner would keep his machine in good order and be ready to hand it over when the Army mobilised for war. It wasn't much of an incentive and the MTC knew this. So did the owners, especially when they discovered that in Germany owners received the equivalent of £200 down on each vehicle, plus £50 per annum thereafter. Of course, the German authorities were only prepared to subsidise approved makes and insisted upon very high standards of maintenance, but then it was worth it. Few British owners were tempted by £2 a year and those that were could not be bothered to keep their machines up to scratch. Indeed, the MTC recommended that the number of vehicles enrolled should be maintained at 20 per cent above requirement in the hope that, upon mobilisation, at least a sufficient number would be available in working order to meet immediate needs. They also recommended an increase in the subsidy rate and some form of financial help towards the provision of spare parts.

Two other innovations from 1908/09 deserve a mention. One was the development of petrol-electric lorries in which a conventional engine supplied power, through a dynamo, to an electric driving motor. This gave much better acceleration and made the vehicle a lot easier to drive, since the rugged complexities of a crash-type gearbox were avoided. Two firms were involved, Tillings and Hallford, but the MTC was not impressed. The technology was still in its infancy and they also argued that the mechanic required to service such vehicles should be an electrician too, which they regarded as an unusual combination.

BRITISH MILITARY TRANSPORT 1829-1956

The other machine tested at Aldershot was a monorail vehicle designed by the inventor Louis Brennan. Being essentially rail-borne it does not really fall within the remit of this book but, since the single rail track could be laid almost anywhere it was seen, for a while, as a serious rival to the conventional road vehicle and it put up some remarkable performances on test.

The general interest of the civilian population in cycling, which was mentioned earlier, also had a military counterpart. Like mechanisation itself, cycling was taken up with much more vigour in Continental military formations; in Britain it was largely confined to the Territorial Army. Many local units created cyclist battalions which could be seen, each summer, pedalling off to their summer camps. Of course, their kitbags, tents and other paraphernalia had to be transported separately and the normal practice was to hire private vehicles for the occasion and these invariably seem to have been steam wagons. The reason, no doubt, was carrying capacity. It was cheaper to hire just one 5-ton steamer and trailer than two or three petrol lorries. Matters got slightly more complicated when these battalions were issued with machine-guns and one unit in particular, the 25th County of London Cyclist Battalion, was encouraged by the MTC to conduct an experiment.

It was considered that the ideal vehicle for transporting the machine-gun was the typical London taxi and the type selected was a new four-cylinder (16hp) Panhard then on the point of introduction. In fact the range of purpose-built cabs available at this time was remarkable and it seems likely that they were hired from the firm W. & G. Du Cross of Acton. The Du Cross Cab Company operated Panhards and Napiers and it was three of the former that were supplied for the exercise, although they didn't look much like taxis at this time since they had not yet entered service and simply had rough wooden seats. In addition to the cab driver, each of the two cabs carried a Maxim machine-gun, two men and a supply of ammunition; the third cab transported a fifth man, blankets, tools and more ammunition.

A commercial undertype steam lorry hired by the 25th County of London Cyclist Battalion for their annual camp, posed with a motley crew.

The men of the 25th Battalion, mounted on bicycles and accompanied by the taxis, left Fulham at 4.30pm on 28 May 1910 and arrived at Lewes in Sussex by 9.30pm that same evening. The trip could probably have been done a lot quicker but it was decreed that the taxis must keep pace with the cyclists, which limited the battalion to an average speed of about 10mph. The next day the three cabs accompanied the troops as they fought a mock battle, which involved climbing a steep hill onto the South Downs. The track was deeply rutted and the Panhards grounded part of the way up when the ruts got too deep. They were forced to reverse and proceed by another route in order to meet the soldiers at the firing point. The commanding officer of the battalion had other ideas, however. On his own initiative he had obtained a pair of Autocarrier tri-cars, which he believed would prove more useful than the Panhards. The Autocarriers were local delivery vehicles, which had a platform at the front, supported on two wheels, and a driver sitting over the single rear wheel. However, they were powered by single-cylinder, 5.6hp engines which, as a comment in an MTC report had earlier prophesied, meant that they were not powerful enough for the job.

The logic behind the selection of taxicabs was that there were plenty of them about, all more or less standard, and they could easily be acquired in an emergency; although, as we shall see, they were never used in this way by the British Army.

The Regular Army manoeuvres of September 1910 were used as an opportunity to test, for the first time, a complete divisional transport system at war strength using mechanical vehicles. The MTC report described it as being on a larger scale than anything that had ever been attempted before. Members of the MTC accompanied the various columns over the full seven days of the exercise. Among the innovations was the modification of some petrol lorries to transport fresh meat. Temporary bodies were fitted to the vehicles and the idea was to collect freshly slaughtered carcasses from the depot and deliver them, on a daily basis, to the troops in the field. Unfortunately, it does not sound very appetising. No hooks were provided to hang the meat so it was laid on the lorry floor where it became bruised in transit and covered in what the report daintily describes as 'dust &c'.

Despite the large scale of these manoeuvres, divisional transport was limited. It included 98 steam tractors of which 73 were hired and some subsidised. There were 25 five lorries, of which 15 were hired Foden steamers, four oil-engined tractors and one traction engine. The MTC was not impressed with many of the subsidy vehicles. They did not appear to have been well maintained and would have been rejected if the division was not desperate for transport. The MTC also reported that some of the subsidised vehicles were unsuited to military use and recommended that, in future, subsidy conditions should be tightened up and the subsidy itself increased. This, they argued, would induce owners with suitable vehicles to sign up and, with more frequent and rigorous inspection, encourage them to improve standards

Three Milnes-Daimler lorries in military service. The example nearest the camera is an older model with its distinctive coal scuttle bonnet, the other two are conventional. The same cannot be said of the unusual, high-sided bodies. Could these be the special meat lorries used in the 1910 manoeuvres?

of maintenance. Another lesson of the manoeuvres concerned spare parts; the committee advised that in future units should operate vehicles of the same type to economise on the storage and handling of spares.

However, the real lesson of the manoeuvres was that steam was unsuitable for military purposes and this led to another quandary. To understand it we must first return to 1903, and the campaign in Somaliland. When the War Office decided to send mechanical transport to that theatre they were advised against using steam; the reason was that water was scarce. However, the experts also argued against petrol because in very hot climates they forecast a 50 per cent evaporation rate and that left paraffin. In the event two Stirling lorries were acquired and modified to run on paraffin, but they were not sent to the war. Two other factors influenced the authorities in preferring paraffin: one was the threat that petrol supplies would be difficult to maintain under war conditions and the other was ammunition. There was a horror of the result if a petrol lorry, loaded with live ammunition, should catch fire while moving through a residential area. So real were these fears that such movements were expressly forbidden by the Home Office.

Even so, petrol was now the principal fuel used by the commercial haulage industry, public transport and private cars. Vehicles could be converted to run on paraffin but it was an inefficient fuel and, despite considerable research, the Army had yet to come up with an effective type of paraffin carburettor. Thus the 1910 manoeuvres marked a turning point.

On this occasion ammunition was carried mainly by steam or paraffin tractors but under pressure the Home Office was persuaded that if petrol lorries were modified, mainly by a sheet-metal firewall in front of the load, ammunition could be transported this way in future. Yet, the law forbidding it was not repealed until 1912.

Although it is confirmed by history there seems little reason to doubt that the MTC realised the significance of the steps they took as a result of the 1910 manoeuvres. It was not just the question of making a radical change in the type of mechanical transport to be employed by the entire British Army, it was also a question of massive expansion in the use of such vehicles. The Army was, in effect, committing itself to a programme that would result in almost total mechanisation at a time when the horse was still a very significant element in the nation's transport infrastructure, at least for short-haul work. As late as 1913 the number of horse cabs in London, especially the four-wheeled Growlers, was considerable. Horse buses, although reducing fast, could still be counted in their hundreds in the capital while horse-drawn wagons still accounted for 85 per cent of freight-carrying traffic on the roads of Britain. In altering this balance, commercial operators may have set the mechanisation ball rolling in a small way but the War Office now appeared ready to take the lead in its enthusiasm for a new subsidy scheme.

Even so nothing could be done without considerable cooperation from the motor industry and this, it appears, was immediately forthcoming. The MTC conferred with all the main British manufacturers and, with their advice, matters progressed rapidly. Not that it was all plain sailing. The new subsidy scheme would be a vast improvement on the earlier one but it was not sufficient to obtain the degree of interchangeability of components between makes that the MTC desired. For instance, it was hoped to make engines and gearboxes fully interchangeable. This is not to say identical, but with a standardised pattern of mounting points so that any subsidy engine or gearbox would fit any subsidy chassis. As it was, not even chassis could be standardised without throwing current production methods into chaos. However, the industry was able to achieve a high degree of standardisation – in controls for instance, so that a driver, climbing into a lorry cab in the dark, would not only know where all the controls were, he would tell by their feel exactly what they were and could be confident that they all worked in the same way.

It is indicative of the parsimony which often afflicts government institutions that, having arrived at this momentous agreement, the MTC now found that it could not afford to pay a draughtsman to prepare the essential drawings. One had to be borrowed from the Royal Gun and Carriage Factory while the MTC haggled with the War Office over funds for staff of their own.

No list is available to show which firms the MTC consulted when it shaped the subsidy requirements, but Leyland was undoubtedly one. The Lancashire firm was the first to produce lorries to the new specifications, probably followed by Thornycroft. J.E. Hall of Dartford, makers of the Hallford lorry, were another company involved in the discussions although their products never qualified for the main subsidy because they remained wedded to chain drive.

Of course, it is one thing to decree a subsidy policy and another to make it work. Assuming the commercial vehicle trade agreed to support the proposed scheme, as it did to a surprising extent, acceptable lorries still had to be built and customers induced to buy them, never mind enrol them in an arrangement that could deprive those customers of their own transport in the event of war. Even a cursory study of the conditions, which would be far too long to include here, seems to suggest that they came fairly close to cancelling out the financial advantage unless the firm concerned was already committed to extremely high standards of maintenance, storage and operation of their vehicles. A vehicle operator who did agree to involve himself in the subsidy scheme had, in the first instance, to be prepared for a visit from a War Department inspector every six months. The inspector would check the condition of the vehicle, see where it was being kept and make a report. If he decided that the vehicle was not up to standard the owner would not only lose the subsidy, he would have to pay some

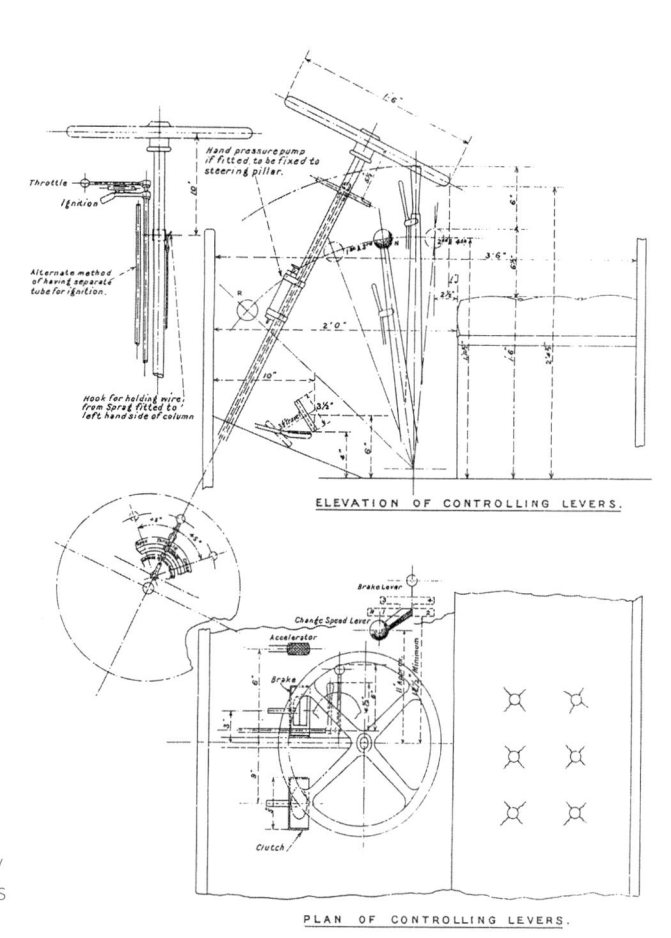

Drawings from the original subsidy specifications showing the standardised controls demanded by the War Office.

of it back. If the vehicle was wrecked while it was in his service the owner had to notify the authorities and either produce a suitable replacement within three months or return any outstanding funds. Under normal circumstances the owner was not allowed to withdraw from the scheme unless he obtained permission and handed back some of the money and, of course, he could not sell the lorry unless the buyer agreed to continue with the scheme.

On the positive side it is true that while the vehicle was operated under the subsidy it could not be hired or impressed for military training. In fact, it took a pronouncement by the Secretary of State for War that a national emergency existed, or, failing that, a proclamation under the Reserve Forces Act of 1882, to require the vehicle to be handed over, but after that the owner had just three days to ensure that it was in full working order and deliver it, by road and fully equipped with spare parts, to a location ordained by the War Department. Such ideals are not always seen as compatible with profitable business practice.

Of course, having persuaded a number of companies to build vehicles to subsidy specifications and various transport firms to join the scheme, some time was bound to elapse before it was fully operational, and the international situation was not getting any better. Faced with what might well prove to be an embarrassing delay the War Office decided to institute a provisional subsidy scheme at once, for approved vehicles already on the road. Had this not been done there was a risk that any sudden outbreak of war would find the Army with an increasing number of mechanised transport companies in the ASC and only a handful of lorries.

The provisional subsidy scheme aimed to register 300 lorries in its first year. It was open to owners of lorries built after 1 January 1910 which, like the main subsidy scheme, came within Class A (those capable of handling a 3-ton payload) or Class B (30cwt). The subsidy would run for a two-year period with an initial payment of £12 if the lorry had a live rear axle, £10 if it had enclosed final drive chains and £8 if the chains were exposed. This was followed by yearly payments of £15, by six-monthly instalments in arrears.

The scheme proved remarkably successful. At the end of the financial year 270 vehicles had been enrolled and it was decided to try and expand it to cover 650 lorries by the next year, including both the main and provisional

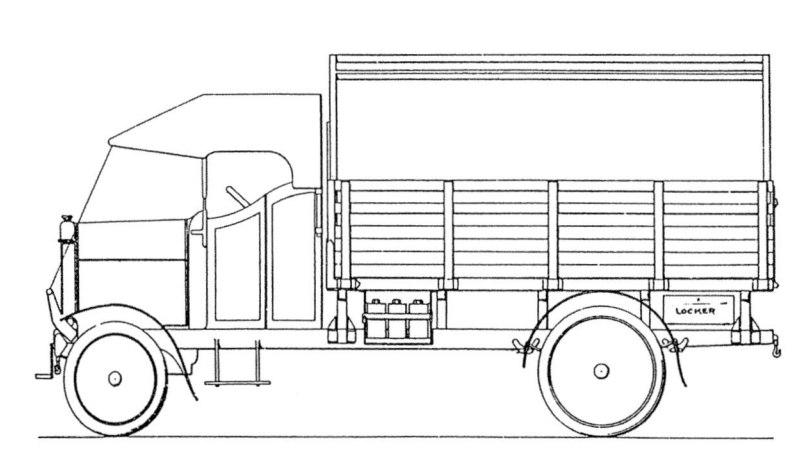

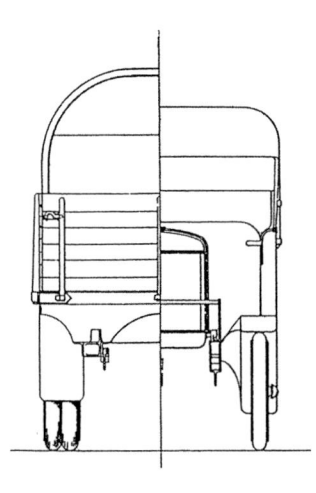

War Office drawings of a typical subsidy-type 3-tonner giving details of body construction.

1 GETTING UP STEAM

'Get out and push.' An embarrassing moment in the 1913 subsidy trials with the inspectors in attendance. The lorry appears to be a chain-drive 2½-ton Thornycroft.

schemes. Should war break out the owner would receive the value of his vehicle, calculated on a sliding scale by age, plus 25 per cent.

Meanwhile trials went on, or they should have done. The MTC planned to hold a trial early in 1911 while the roads were still in bad condition due to the winter weather but it proved impossible to meet the cost out of the existing budget. Another opportunity was sought in August when the usual annual manoeuvres were planned but this also failed due to a serious drought that summer. Thus, it was March 1912 before the next trial took place. It included road runs in the Gosport-Winchester-Aldershot-Oxford area and trials on the new motor-racing track at Brooklands in Surrey.

The following financial year, 1912/13, saw the War Office purchasing 23 new lorries including some 30cwt Leylands for the Royal Flying Corps (RFC). There were many small changes to the subsidy specifications as a result of previous experience, following discussions between the War Office and the Society of Motor Manufacturers and Traders. The most obvious were the preference for folding canvas hoods of the 'Cape Cart'-type in place of the wooden canopy originally specified for cabs and the acceptance of what were described as 'Municipal' bodies, meaning tippers.

Trials took place in August 1912 but only attracted a handful of potential subsidy vehicles, two Leylands and a Thornycroft. However, two double-deck buses were also included, a B-Type of London General and a Leyland belonging to the Central Bus Company.

A number of manufacturers took advantage of the War Office trials to run their own vehicles under test conditions, including at least one that was still flogging the old paraffin horse. As a result weaknesses were identified in Leyland back axles, which had to be replaced by a stronger type, and the gearbox on the lighter model was changed for the heavy type used on their 3-tonners.

The continuing difficulty for manufacturers in having their vehicle ready in time for War Office events was highlighted in 1913. Only three were available, Commer, Hallford and Thornycroft, so the trial was brought forward to January and held in the Aldershot-Woolwich area. The manoeuvres that took place in March were specifically geared to transport. Troops were not involved in the normal sense but an ammunition park was established to maintain a fictitious army and involved a lot of convoy work between Hilsea, near Portsmouth, and Aldershot. At the end of that month it was announced that six manufacturers –

The great brewing firm Whitbread operated this subsidy-type Leyland. Notice the two sprags, just behind the rear wheels, which could be dropped to prevent the lorry from rolling backwards on a hill.

Albion, Commer, Dennis, Halley, Hallford and Leyland – were all qualified under the provisional scheme with a total of 475 vehicles enrolled. All of which looked very promising but it did raise the problem of where a sufficient number of drivers might come from. To alleviate this a Special Reserve of drivers was created. Some 1,400 were soon enrolled out of a total requirement for 3,000.

Although it could not be known at the time when the report was written, the financial year 1913/14 was the last full year of peace. Time was running out fast. The number of vehicles enrolled under the provisional scheme rose to 742 by March 1914 and direct purchases also increased. In the main scheme, Leyland, Thornycroft and Wolseley were joined by Clayton & Company (Karrier) and Walker Brothers (Pagefield) in Class A, with Leyland and Wolseley qualified in Class B. The new additions resulted from trials held in October 1913 for which only four contenders were ready plus the usual non-subsidy entrants. The test on the Brooklands racing circuit now included a three-hour continuous run at 22mph for Class A and 24mph for Class B. Finally, in April/May 1914, Commer, Dennis, Leyland, Maudslay and Thornycroft entered vehicles in Class A and the fleet included a Leyland charabanc, which not only went through the trial programme failed, but the Dennis system proved as tough as the examiners could wish and was duly approved. In this, their last report, the MTC took an opportunity to justify themselves. They had been under a lot of pressure from manufacturers of chain-drive lorries to relax their insistence upon live axles in the main subsidy scheme. The lorry builders appealed to an unnamed manufacturer of driving chains, probably Renolds, who sought the opinion of a transport consultant, probably Crompton, who normally advocated chain drive. He, surprisingly, came down in favour of the MTC. At least he qualified this view by saying that all the while the MTC insisted on running vehicles with fairly small wheels, a live axle was the best under war conditions. Lorries operating in deep mud would suffer damage to chain and sprockets where that system was employed but the expert clearly felt that larger-diameter wheels would be more suitable for army lorries in the first place and, in that instance, he regarded chain drive as superior.

Although 'mechanicalisation', to use the contemporary term, was bound to change the supply system it was really the manoeuvres of 1912 that altered things dramatically. The greater range conferred when petrol lorries were employed caused Brigadier General G.R.C. Paul, the Assistant Director of

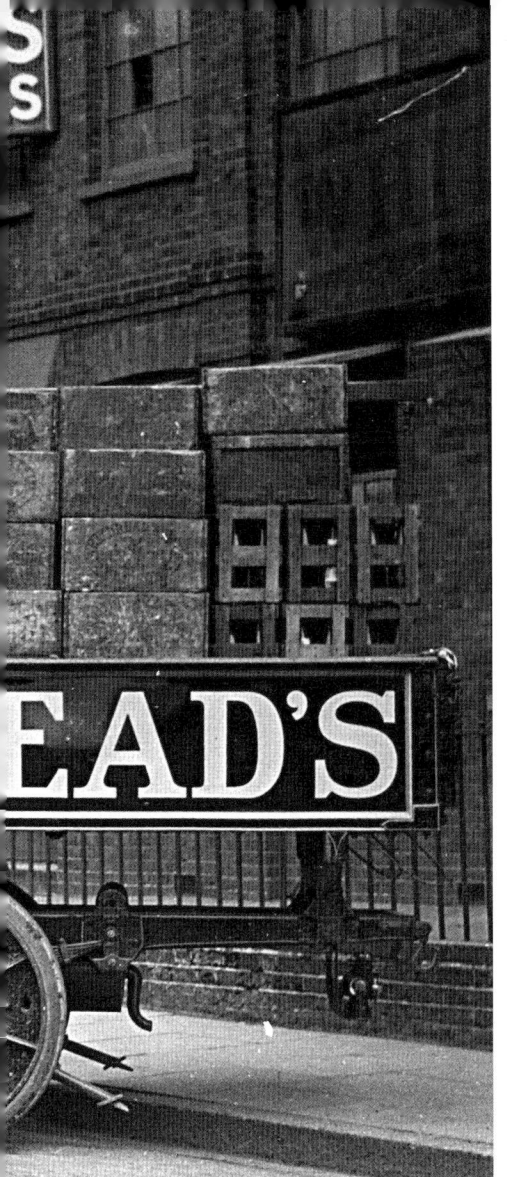

but also served to carry the observers. A final change in the specifications called for reverse gear to be a lower ratio than the lowest forward gear, the object being to provide a final solution to the problem of climbing difficult hills. It was a practice many contemporary motorists were used to. If the vehicle stalled on the hill in the normal way, you drove it up backwards. The evidence, such as it is, suggests that this was not adopted by all manufacturers.

It was during this trial that Dennis proved the efficacy of their worm gear rear-axle design. It was something the MTC had previously expressed doubts about, and a rival Thornycroft design

Another scene from the 1913 subsidy trials with two of the contestants passing a flock of sheep on a misty January day.

BRITISH MILITARY TRANSPORT 1829-1956

Transport, to revise the entire scheme. It must be borne in mind that when this was done the authorities believed that any war in which the Expeditionary Force might become involved would be a mobile one, and the changes reflect this.

Regimental, or first-line, transport would remain horse-drawn since it would need to operate away from the roads and this was considered difficult for motor lorries. The same would apply to second-line transport, which was now to be known as 'Divisional Transport' and, obviously, administered from divisional headquarters. Beyond that, and back to railhead, there would be a single, mechanised third line that replaced two echelons of animal transport. The extra range of motor vehicles meant that the gap between railhead and second-line dumps could be as much as 40 miles. The greatest advantage this bestowed upon troops in the front line concerned rations. Under the old system it might take four days to bring food forwards and that, inevitably, made the provision of fresh bread or meat quite impossible unless, in the case of meat, livestock came forward on the hoof and was slaughtered nearby. Under the new system field bakery and butchery could be carried out on the railway and delivery effected at once. The same supply arrangements applied to ammunition although, for practical reasons, this was controlled by the Royal Artillery rather than the ASC. The mechanised third-line transport would be handled by 3-tonners while 30-cwt lorries were to be used by Army troops and the cavalry.

The provision of motor ambulances came surprisingly high in the War Office list of priorities, the first one being supplied by the Straker-Squire company in 1906. It was based on a 3-ton lorry and bus chassis, itself built to the German Bussing patents, and featured an ornate, wood-framed body with something of the gipsy caravan about it. Reports suggest that it was anything but comfortable, with its chain drive and solid tyres, so an attempt was made to improve things by inserting inflatable tubes between the body and chassis, and by supplying what a report describes as mats and cushions for the seats to cut down vibration – the implication being that cushions for sick or wounded soldiers had not been considered at first. Somewhat belatedly, the Director General of Army Medical Services took advice from the Metropolitan Asylums Board and a gentleman from the London County Council who was experienced in motor-ambulance design. The first result was that two more Straker-Squires on 30cwt chassis were delivered in 1908, followed

A pair of Leyland X-Type 3-tonners. The leading one is marked 'WAR DEPARTMENT SUBSIDISED AVIATION MOTOR LORRY' for obvious reasons; the other was operated by the London furnishing store Warings.

1 GETTING UP STEAM

A pre-delivery line-up of Leyland military vehicles; an ambulance in the foreground and a fire engine third in line.

by some forward-control Wolseleys. The former were described as having more powerful engines but the complaint now was that they were too fast, which seems unusual for ambulances and the next batch, it was announced, would be lower geared.

The report for the financial year 1910/11 states that motor ambulances were stationed in Army depots at Aldershot, Bulford, Portsmouth, Edinburgh, the Curragh at Dublin, Devonport and Malta. The latest models were Leylands equipped, in the words of the report, with 'lever spring suspension', which is later discovered to mean shock absorbers. At the same time it seems there was a marked increase in the number of motor ambulances in civilian service where the trend was towards pneumatic tyres – something the War Office was not quite ready to countenance, although it was suggested that these civilian machines might form a useful reserve in the event of war.

For the remaining years up to the outbreak of war the reports show small additions to the ambulance fleet, all on the Leyland 30cwt chassis, the newest of which featured worm-drive differentials. The report for the financial year 1913/14 states that the original Straker-Squire ambulance, being no longer suitable for the purpose, had been converted into an instructional chassis at Aldershot. Even so, it is clear that none of the vehicles supplied so far were entirely suitable. The reason was that, presumably in the interests of economy, they had been designed to carry either two stretcher patients or 12 seated. The difference in weight between the two loads made it impossible to provide the right sort of springing for both with the result that harder springs for the 12 meant a rough ride for two, while softer springs for stretcher patients would not accept the load if 12 were carried. The report remarks that if ambulances were made to take two stretcher cases only it would be wiser to obtain smaller vehicles which would run on pneumatic tyres. In this the RFC seems to have taken the lead. Among the vehicles they acquired just before the war were three ambulances designed to carry two patients plus a driver and attendant. These were on 20hp Austin, 20/25hp Crossley and 16/20hp Wolseley chassis. In other words, they were basically touring cars adapted to the ambulance role.

While on the subject of emergency vehicles in this period the War Office purchased a few motor fire engines for service at major garrisons; however, these were all of typical civilian pattern.

Commercial vehicles hired for military manoeuvres. A highly decorated Leyland with the Army Service Corps.

45

2 THE FIRST WORLD WAR

For much of the First World War the Class A subsidy 3-ton lorry was the backbone of the British Army's transport fleet. It was built by popular British manufacturers like Albion, Dennis, Leyland and Thornycroft, but at first the increasing demand for transport posed a manpower problem and had to be matched by sufficient numbers of trained drivers.

2 THE FIRST WORLD WAR

Telegraph correspondent, told how trucks were used in relays to smash a route through inhospitable country. A practice likely to wreck more trucks than create equivalent yards of road one might think.

Bearing in mind the harsh usage meted out to transport in the Balkans conflict, it is interesting to record a suggestion offered by Colonel Crompton when he visited the War Office a few days after the First World War was declared. Having secured a suitably high-level interview, Crompton proceeded to explain that the type of vehicle now being used for transport purposes was entirely unsuitable. He pointed out that high ground clearance, wheels of the same size all round and stout bumper bars at each end, equipped with strong towing hooks, would be far better. Crompton was, by now, an old man by any standards but there was nothing wrong with his brain, as his subsequent work on tanks would show.* Yet one wonders where he had been for the last 10 years and whether he seriously believed that, at such a critical time, the War Department (WD) was likely to sanction a complete reconstruction programme for the entire British Army transport fleet.

In his book *Motor Transports in War*, Horace Wyatt, a motoring journalist and secretary to the Imperial Motor Transport Council, observed in 1914 that mechanised transport, still something of a novelty in itself, was about to undergo the first trial of its effectiveness in a major war,** but this was also true of a number of important weapons. The difference, at least as far as the British were concerned, was that their Army depended on mechanised transport for ultimate victory from the very first day. If it failed this test it would not have been possible to substitute horses again on a worthwhile scale. That would have been it.

A short convoy of Maudslay 3-tonners and a Sunbeam ambulance halt while the men examine a wrecked lorry that seems to have been carrying ammunition.

In its final pre-war report, the MTC gave a short account of transport difficulties in the recent war between Greece and Bulgaria. Beyond affirming the obvious fact that motor transport was useful, the Committee's main conclusion seems to have been that the more rugged the country, the tougher the transport needs to be. Roads suitable for anything but oxen hardly existed in the Balkans and one report from Captain A.H. Trapmann, the *Daily*

*D. Fletcher, *Landships and War Cars* (The Tank Museum, 2021)
**H. Wyatt, *Motor Transports in War* (Hodder & Stoughton, 1914)

47

BRITISH MILITARY TRANSPORT 1829-1956

The British Army would come to rely so much on the standard Class A subsidy 3-ton lorry that this might be the best time to describe a typical example – a Pagefield, built by Walker Brothers of Wigan. The chassis was of hefty construction with parallel side members of channel section steel. The suspension consisted of semi-elliptical leaf springs, again far stronger than they might normally need to be, with nine leaves at the front and 12 at the back. The front axle was a rigid beam with heavy-duty steering jaws and the wheels were a cast steel, spoked or lattice pattern with solid rubber tyres, doubled at the rear. The engine, in this case a Dorman, was a four-cylinder unit with cylinders (120mm bore x 140mm stroke) cast in pairs and large inspection panels in the crankcase. These panels were a WD requirement to give easy access to the big-end bearings to enable it to be serviced in situ.

Although rated at 57hp, at 1,500rpm, the engine was fitted with a centrifugal governor, which kept it at 1,000rpm, giving 40hp and a top speed of 16mph; this again being an official WD requirement. The engine was water-cooled of course, the construction of the radiator being one of the more stringent WD specifications. The clutch was of the leather-faced, cone-type, the inner cone being an extension of the flywheel – and with the drive passed from here through a flexible coupling to a four-speed and reverse gearbox. This provided speeds of 3mph, 5¼mph, 9½mph and 15¾mph forwards and 3¼mph in reverse. The footbrake acted on a drum attached to the drive shaft just behind the gearbox and the propellor shaft, with its universal joints, was protected from below by a shield. The magazine *Automobile Journal* was particularly impressed with the Pagefield rear axle. In addition to the normal differential, the banjo housing contained separate geared reductions to the drive shafts that obviated the need for a very large crown wheel which, otherwise, would have reduced ground clearance. The handbrake acted on the back wheels but a sprag was also provided, which the driver could release in a hurry

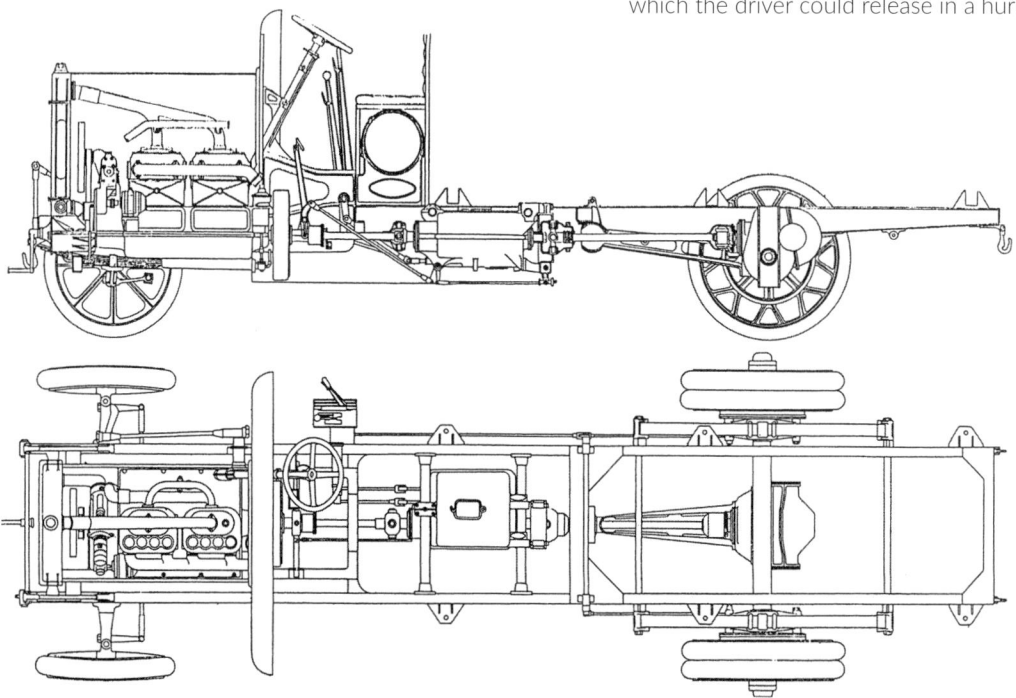

Side elevation and plan drawings of a Pagefield subsidy A-Type chassis.

to prevent the lorry from rolling back on a steep hill.

The driver's cab was spartan to say the least. It could accommodate a crew of three for whom padded seat cushions were provided along with a padded backrest in due course. The 18in-diameter steering wheel was set at a prescribed height and angle from the dashboard and included ignition and throttle controls along with the sprag release. The foot pedal layout was standard, with the brake pedal between the accelerator and clutch. The handbrake and gearchange levers were mounted in a bracket, to the right of the driver on the outside of the chassis. The handbrake had an extended handgrip with a release toggle attached. It was outboard of the gearchange lever, which had a ball-shaped handgrip. The gear shift was a typical H-shaped layout with reverse the foremost position, followed by first and second, then through a gate for third and fourth. Starting was manual, by crank, and lighting normally acetylene headlamps with oil side and rear lights. A number of bodies were acceptable under the subsidy scheme but the standard general service type was inevitably the most common. It formed an open wooden tray with detachable sides, drop-down tailgate and a curved frame for the canvas cover. It had racks for petrol cans and extra kit lockers beneath floor level while the specifications for attachment to the chassis are among the most stringent in the entire subsidy scheme. Although rated at 3 tons for military purposes, the commercial payload for most Class A subsidy vehicles was nearer 4 or 5 tons because the average commercial haulier did not need to make allowance for a crew of three and their kit. Even so, overloading became a serious problem throughout the war and in the case of the Class B, or 30cwt lorries it was almost fatal. In terms of size they were so similar to the 3-tonners that a weight limit was painted in huge letters all

War production gets under way – a view of the Thornycroft factory at Basingstoke in Hampshire.

One make that never went to France, a Belsize, manufactured in Manchester and obviously limited to a payload of 2 tons.

around the body. This in the faint hope that it would discourage soldiers from piling on as much as they could fit into the vehicle.

The MTC ceased to exist on the outbreak of war. Its responsibilities were transferred to the Chief Inspector of Subsidised Transport (CIST) whose department maintained the register of subsidised vehicles. Indeed, the department had gone further: manufacturers of acceptable vehicles had been persuaded to hand over the names of everyone who had purchased a lorry since 1910. The CIST divided the country into areas and appointed inspectors who were either regular ASC officers or newly-recruited personnel with experience of motor transport. These individuals not only checked that firms enrolled for the subsidy were abiding by the conditions, they also investigated what else was available, based on the information obtained from manufacturers. Only lorries engaged on the haulage of foodstuffs or other vital services were exempt; everything else was earmarked for impressment should the need arise.

The first 'MT Mobilisation Depot' was established at Grove Park in south-east London but it was soon in danger of being overwhelmed, with long lines of newly arrived vehicles filling the surrounding streets. Later on in the war it was superseded by an establishment at Bulford Camp on Salisbury Plain. West of London, Kempton Park, otherwise better known for its race course, became a huge MT acceptance depot where new vehicles were prepared for service and stored until they were required.

Mobilisation of the British Expeditionary Force (BEF) was generally smooth and efficient. By September 1914, six divisions were in France complete with their transport. The call-up of subsidy vehicles involved lorries, with their Special Reserve drivers going straight to their concentration points and from there to Avonmouth docks for shipment. In the case of larger fleets, such as those belonging to some of the bigger London stores, they were often sufficient to form complete ASC companies, and it was a colourful array. For the first few weeks soldiers often found their rations coming up in convoys of lorries still adorned in company liveries with such homely names as Harrods, or Waring & Gillow, proudly emblazoned on the sides, with nothing more than a chalk mark or sticker, plus the uniformed crew, to show that they were now military vehicles.

Figures for the period are slightly contradictory but one of the most convincing breakdowns lists 500 lorries in the supply columns, 650 with the cavalry and divisional ammunition

Bromley Road, Catford, lined down both sides with newly mobilised vehicles ready for service.

2 THE FIRST WORLD WAR

Four Karriers and a Dennis, complete with motorcycle escort about to set off for the war.

parks and 50 more either at bases or allocated to special duties. These were split between 19 MT companies. It has to be remembered that at this time the concept of extensive trench warfare had hardly been considered. Base depots were established and the railway system organised to support armies engaged in a mobile form of warfare and as this intensified the system came under considerable strain. During the retreat from Mons, which occupied the latter part of August and early September 1914, the potential for disaster was not confined to frontline troops. Supply columns, setting out from a railhead, often had no more than the sketchiest idea of where their troops were and the distance they travelled was often well beyond anything the planners could have imagined. In addition to this confusion one has to imagine the difficulties of navigating in unfamiliar territory, over roads already jammed with refugees. And, if that were not enough, there was an unforeseen problem with the Allies. At this time the small BEF was sandwiched into line between larger French forces and there were occasions when British and French supply columns met, face-to-face, on roads with a single strip of pavé at the centre, wide enough for just one vehicle. Despite this the actual loss of vehicles during the retreat was surprisingly small.

While the Allies were being pushed back to the River Marne as they struggled to defend Paris, an entirely different war was taking place in the north. The Belgians had been effectively by-passed by the main German advance and made Antwerp the key to their defence. In September, on the initiative of Winston Churchill, then First Lord of the Admiralty, the Royal Navy and Royal Marines were thrown into this void to help but it was a forlorn hope. As the threat to Antwerp increased, attempts were made to get the force out again; many of the men belonging to the Royal Naval Division who left by rail were cornered and forced to escape into neutral Holland and internment, but a successful operation mounted by the Royal Naval Air Service (RNAS) got 70 London buses into the city. The majority of the buses were used to take the wounded and the rearguard out. These buses were Daimler double-deckers of the MET and Gearless fleets but they set an impressive precedent.

In October, the War Office requisitioned 300 B-Type double-deckers from the London General Omnibus Company mainly with volunteer crews who opted to stay with their vehicles. As with the Daimlers these arrived in France still in civilian livery, a striking red and white, and adorned with posters advertising the latest attractions of London's theatreland.

On the outbreak of war, the motoring organisations led by the AA and the RAC mobilised their patriotic members. As we have seen, despite the fact that the AMR had been disbanded in 1912 due to the perceived impossibility of operating such a diverse fleet of vehicles under war conditions, the

BRITISH MILITARY TRANSPORT 1829-1956

2 THE FIRST WORLD WAR

A dockside scene in France. Nearest the camera a 30cwt lorry converted from a B-Type London bus. Next in line stands an overtype steam wagon.

problem of transport shortages was immediately recreated. When cars were needed for the 1913 manoeuvres the War Office had requisitioned taxicabs, partly because they were generally standardised types but also due to the additional skills of their drivers. This was not followed up during the war, except on one famous occasion by the French Army, so it was back to the nightmare of private volunteers again. In fact, it did not result in chaos. Most volunteers were only expected to operate in their locality and, although a number of well-meaning individuals had their cars converted into ambulances, they also remained close to home. However, there was an elite group of 25 motorists from the RAC who took themselves over to France and offered their services to Sir John French. These were not your run-of-the-mill car owners but characters such as the Duke of Westminster and adventurers like Toby Rawlinson, brother of the general, who ran high-powered cars and already knew many senior officers intimately. In the difficult period of the retreat from Mons they acted as couriers, chauffeured officers to and from headquarters and sometimes got caught up in the fighting during reconnaissance missions. It was a period of high adventure, which was only possible in the first weeks of the war; before long things would be getting serious, and no place for amateurs.

A picture of the transport situation in the early part of the war is to be found in an unusual little book *The Motor-Bus in War* by A.M. Beatson.* Beatson was an ASC lieutenant attached to the supply column of an Indian Cavalry Division but his choice of title is misleading. The only connection with motor buses is that many of his lorries were London General Omnibus Company B-Type double-deckers converted into 30cwt lorries. The remainder were Daimlers of the same capacity, including some fitted out as stores and workshop vehicles, along with a few Sunbeam staff cars

and Douglas motorcycles. They arrived in France via Rouen, the Advanced Mechanical Transport Depot for the BEF. Beatson's supply column consisted of 160 lorries divided into two echelons, which operated on alternate days. Thus, one was loading while the other was delivering rations to the troops. Beatson explains that in the early days the cavalry loaded groups of lorries with the range of supplies for a regiment, on the grounds that, in fluid warfare conditions, regiments of horse could be operating independently over a fairly wide area, whereas infantry divisions remained concentrated so that their columns loaded supplies in bulk.

An interesting detail to come out of the book is that, when running in convoy, the driver's mate in each lorry sat in the back, linked to his driver by what Beatson calls a 'communication cord'. This was used to warn the driver if something was coming up from behind to overtake or to tell him to halt if the lorry behind was seen to do so. Beatson also states that his vehicles were painted in a grey-green service colour.

Despite the progress initiated by the subsidy scheme it would be wrong to suggest that steam was eclipsed before the war broke out. Light tractors, including a number of impressed machines, were seen in France in the early days while road locomotives were used for gun haulage behind the lines and steam rollers were employed in large numbers to keep the rapidly deteriorating roads in good repair. Steam lorries, too, rather surprisingly, proved useful throughout the war. Clayton & Shuttleworth was one make employed in France but there is no doubt that Fodens were the most popular. There were disadvantages compared with petrol lorries; it took at least an hour to get the Fodens started from cold and the continual search for water wasted a great deal of time, but

*A.M. Beatson, *The Motor-Bus in War* (T. Fisher-Unwin, 1918)

2 THE FIRST WORLD WAR

when used correctly a Foden steamer could manage twice the load of a subsidy 3-tonner and it was so strongly built that twice that load again was not impossible.

As early as September 1914, the firm G. Scammell & Nephew of Spitalfields, London, obtained a War Office contract to supply 28 steam lorries in four days for service in France. They elected to use Fodens, one of which was to be equipped as a mobile workshop and six trailers were required. This contract being fulfilled to time, further orders followed. There was a serious shortage of experienced drivers and later many of the Fodens came equipped with sprung buffers, like railway locomotives, that were intended to avoid damage when driving in convoy, which was difficult enough with petrol lorries but almost impossible with steamers. In fact, the buffers did more harm than they prevented and were soon removed but the lorries continued to prove invaluable. Some were equipped with Thresh disinfecting equipment and employed in the unsavoury but essential task of delousing clothing when soldiers came out of the line.

Generally speaking, it was not the lot of steamers to operate too close to the frontline. Plumes of steam by day or sparks at night quickly attracted attention from the enemy so they were kept well back and often relegated to road-making work. In this role the Fodens were equipped with special bodies, which had rolling floors, a sort of endless conveyor made of wooden slats, which enabled the crew to empty the load by hand winding the conveyor

A Clayton & Shuttleworth steamer carrying timber. The high-sided body is an open invitation to overloading.

mechanism. Often the road metal jammed in the slats or damaged the mechanism, so a tipper might have been more effective, but the roller system was popular at the time. It takes us well ahead, but rounds off the story of steam, to recount an experience from the great British retreat of March 1918.

The officer commanding a column of Fodens engaged in road work published a stirring account of his part in a post-war issue of the magazine *Motor Traction*. Late one night, unaware of the impending German attack and believing himself to be well behind the lines, this officer bedded his Fodens down for the night, had the fires drawn and prepared to turn in when an officer ordered him to move to Amiens at once. It took an hour to get steam up and by that time the roads were thick with other traffic. His drivers were tired and soon a thick mist came down. Somehow, he not only kept his convoy moving but kept it together. At one time he records taking six hours to cover 4 miles and tells how others around him complained about the sparks his machines threw up when enemy aircraft were overhead. His task was to proceed to a Royal Engineers' dump and take away as much material as possible to prevent it from falling into enemy hands. He was kept on the road for some three weeks, doing one job after another. On one occasion he recalls the wagons being loaded with up to 13 tons of material on each vehicle, which towered so high that no one dared add another thing. Even so, when the time came to move off 50 or 60 men might pile onto each wagon, taking any place they could get including on the GS horse wagons attached to the back of each lorry! Before the retreat ended the majority of his drivers had dropped out with exhaustion, but apart from the need for minor adjustments none of his Fodens showed any signs of the train at all.

In one sense the onset of trench warfare, which really became established in 1915, made the job of the transport services easier. Movement of the battle lines could often be measured only in yards and it became possible to use the existing French rail network, supported by an extensive system of narrow-gauge lines, to keep supplies moving. Indeed, the pressure on transport was relieved to the extent that some manufacturers in Britain were given permission to release a number of vehicles onto the commercial market for a short while. As the transport fleets in France grew, it became possible to create companies of specific makes, which eased the

A classic Foden steam lorry, still carrying the hydraulic buffers, seen here in service with 606 Company, Army Service Corps.

British convoys obeying the 'rule of the road' in France. The long column facing the camera is composed of imported American Peerless trucks.

A Talbot tender with a jolly crew of petty officers of the RNAS during a training run in Wiltshire.

spares and maintenance situation, while experience and careful planning ensured that transport was used efficiently. Road circuits were created in each Corps area in order to keep traffic moving. Special maps were produced, which showed what roads could take two-way traffic and those that could not. Attempts were made to restrict motor traffic to metalled roads and send animal transport over unsurfaced tracks. Speed limits were introduced – and strictly enforced – in villages, towns and on the open road, while columns of vehicles were instructed to run in groups of six with gaps between so that faster vehicles could overtake. Convoys were not allowed to park close to road junctions. Traffic obeyed the French rule of the road, driving on the right, and could only pull over to the side in the direction of travel when parking. It is interesting to compare British practice with the French, especially on the famous Voie Sacrée from Bar le Duc, which kept the suffering garrison of Verdun supplied in 1916. Verdun's very survival relied on a continuous stream of traffic along one battered highway and it was achieved by running the columns as if they were railway trains, using a block signalling system such as railways use to avoid the congestion that would invite concentrated attention from German artillery. It is probably fair to say that few, if any, campaigns in history have relied so entirely upon the efficient use of transport as did the defence of Verdun.

In June 1915, a Ministry of Munitions was created under the redoubtable David Lloyd George, who held this important post until he accepted the Premiership in December 1916. From the summer of 1916 the new ministry assumed all responsibility for the supply

An immaculate AEC 3-tonner with its proud driver.

BRITISH MILITARY TRANSPORT 1829-1956

Girls of the First Aid Nursing Yeomanry strike poses for the camera in front of their Napier ambulance.

of transport to the Army, including the RFC, and subsequently added the Royal Navy and various government organisations at home. For a time, there was some division of responsibilities with the Army's own Quartermaster General's department, which only appears to have created confusion, but as experience within the ministry grew it settled down.

A chapter in the History of the Ministry of Munitions lists most of the British vehicle types used during the war and indicates those which, for one reason or another, were restricted to home use only and those which were only supplied in limited numbers. Oddly, the Wolseley 3-tonner, a fully-fledged subsidy type, is entered in both categories, although there is plenty of photographic evidence to prove that the type operated in France. Production figures vary but, by taking four popular makes – Albion, Dennis, Leyland and Thornycroft – we learn that the last named built 5,000 vehicles while Dennis produced 7,000 and the other two around 6,000 each. None of this was bad, by the standards of the time, yet there was another company which, in a sense, had been overlooked. This was the Associated Equipment Company (AEC), the bus building offshoot of the London General Omnibus Company. In addition to providing buses for the metropolis, its Walthamstow factory enjoyed a thriving market all over Britain and abroad. It was probably one of the best equipped and organised plants in the country but, although their B-Type bus created a legend for itself at the front it was not really up to much as a load carrier.

Many of the buses taken over to France were soon modified into trucks but the reinforced timber chassis was limited to 30cwt capacity and the chain-driven gearbox regarded as suspect. In 1916, the firm was invited to produce a 3-tonner to subsidy specifications and the result was the impressive Y-Type. With a stronger chassis and conventional four-speed gearbox it maintained the company's reputation while the factory managed to out-produce all its rivals. Although the rival companies had two years' head start, AEC built 8,000 3-tonners, reaching a peak of 20 a day by the spring of 1918 and the chassis was so good it remained in production until 1921.

The increasing demand for transport had to be matched, of course, by sufficient numbers of trained drivers, and they were a rare breed. In pre-war days experienced men were not exactly common and they were soon absorbed on mobilisation. The problem of training new drivers was first solved by the London General Omnibus Company, which had excellent facilities at Hounslow and plenty of experience. Subsequently, the Army opened a driving school at Osterley Park in the western suburbs of London but this later became a centre for training technical staff in vehicle maintenance while the bus company's driving school at Hounslow was taken over for military instruction.

It is easy to imagine what an impressive organisation the London General Omnibus Company was when it is understood that the maintenance system adopted by the British Army for its vehicles was based on that practised by the bus company.

A list of the number and variety of private cars offered for conversion to ambulances when the war broke out would probably read like a catalogue of the world's motor industry and it

BRITISH MILITARY TRANSPORT 1829-1956

Lucky for some. Model-T Ford ambulance No 13 waits while a casualty is lifted from a Mark IV (male) tank *Ernest* of 5th Battalion, Tank Corps.

was nearly matched by the range of bodies designed, either by imaginative individuals or professional motor body builders. An illustration from an early wartime issue of *The Autocar* shows a type reputedly favoured by the French and Belgian authorities, which contained a contraption like a miniature Ferris wheel with four stretchers hanging from it. It might have been easier to load, as each stretcher could be brought round in turn, but the image of it breaking loose and turning while the vehicle was in motion is somewhat daunting. In due course, on the advice of the International Red Cross, a more or less standard body was devised for British ambulances, which could be adapted to fit most larger touring car chassis. The body was wood-framed with a strong outer skin of canvas and inner lining. It was heated and could accommodate four stretchers or eight seated cases with a central aisle for the attendant. Variety was still the order of the day and a series of official photographs taken at the main British depot at Rouen included Argyll, Buick, Crossley, Renault, Vauxhall and Wolseley vehicles, but the most common was the Sunbeam, based on the 12/16hp chassis, which was latterly manufactured by the Rover company when the original firm concentrated on building aircraft engines. This type was known as the

'Heavy Ambulance'. The light ambulance was typified by the Model-T Ford, which was more often seen in other theatres of war where cross-country performance was considered more important than load-carrying ability.

The pivotal year of the First World War was 1916. Huge armies had now been assembled on both sides and soldiers at every level were confronted with the full implications of trench warfare on a vast scale. Indeed, it is probably safe to assume that it was not until 1916 that the British High Command was really prepared to admit that a state of virtually static warfare existed and seemed likely to do so for the foreseeable future. Once this was accepted it followed that there would also be an increased demand for manpower in the firing line. Conscription was introduced as one means of achieving this but other, so-called non-combatant arms were also combed for men. For example, the scale of men attached to a transport unit was reduced and many officers, whose functions were more suited to a mobile state of warfare, were also transferred. Thus began the real war of attrition, which was to decimate a generation. The initial solution to this impasse was a massive escalation in the use of artillery which, inevitably, placed an enormous strain on transport as the demand for ammunition increased beyond any previous conception.

Statistics are grisly things, especially when they are inserted into text, but they do have some value, if only of the 'fancy that' variety. The British Official History volume *Transportation on the Western Front* contains some statistics that should not be overlooked. The history starts by making the undeniable statement that lorries needed for daily use required a hard surface to park on. The normal practice was to line them up on wider roads, but this could not be done where there was a lot of traffic, for obvious reasons. The result was that convoys often ended up parked in places that were some distance from where they worked. Among the examples quoted in the history, and one which can be cited as fairly normal, is that of the ammunition park serving III Corps in July 1916. Its fulltime job was shifting ammunition from a railhead called Edge Hill to a dump just 2 miles away, but it was stabled, to use the old Army term, at Franvillers, which was 7 miles from Edge Hill. Thus the pattern of its day's work was a 7-mile empty run followed by 2 miles loaded and 9 miles back, empty. That is 2 miles of useful work out of 18.

In order to determine what was happening and make future plans, GHQ in France instituted a traffic census. The history quotes the result of one conducted at Fricourt Cemetery on 22 July 1916. In that 24-hour period about 7,300 vehicles, mechanical and horse-drawn, passed the census point. The day was not considered exceptional but during the busiest hours traffic frequency was something approaching eight vehicles per minute. Extrapolating this on a wider scale the statisticians calculated that the Fourth Army alone was consuming 12,000 gallons of petrol per day. On a busy day, during the Somme battle, they estimated that 1,934 tons of material was being brought forward from the railheads for every mile of front, and that included the stone needed to maintain the roads.

Although the range of lorries taken into service had now expanded well beyond even the modest restrictions of the Provisional Subsidy Scheme more were required and one idea, tried at this time, was the design of what might be called an 'off-the-shelf lorry'. The idea was to produce a lorry, which complied with the main subsidy requirements, assembled as far as possible from readily available components. Design and construction was entrusted to the Laycock Engineering Company of Sheffield, whose name appeared on the radiator. They employed the same Tylor JB4 engine as the Pagefield; steering, clutch, gearbox and rear axle were by E.G. Wrigley of Birmingham, and front axle by Kirkstall. The result was a tough 3-tonner, fully up to subsidy standard, which was described as 'excellent' when it was reviewed by *The Automobile*

A long convoy, headed by a Daimler 3-tonner, pauses on the wrong side of a road, which is under repair.

Near miss for a Packard, which almost ended up in a shell hole.

A British-Berna marked as suitable for a payload of 3½ tons.

Engineer in July 1917. Yet it is not at all clear how many were produced or whether they saw any military service.

Since British manufacturers would be incapable of meeting all the services' needs, consideration had always been given to buying vehicles from abroad. Indeed, British MT inspectors had been based in the United States since September 1914 and had already ordered vehicles from Studebaker and a firm called Bain. However, of the range of American trucks in British service, those best remembered would be 'The Three Ps' – Packard, Pierce-Arrow and Peerless. Due in part to the local nature of trade and in particular to the great distances involved, the highway network in the United States was very slow to develop. The first trip, a publicity stunt across the continent by motor truck, was not accomplished until 1911, and even then only in the face of great difficulties. A similar stunt, by a truck carrying a ton of Carnation Milk from Seattle to Washington in 1916, took 30 days to cover the 3,640 miles. Even after the war a pneumatic-tyred truck sponsored by Goodyear claimed a world record with a trip from Los Angeles to New York, which took 14 days. All of which must show that highways outside urban areas were not much to boast about. As a consequence American trucks were generally built to take punishment, a virtue much welcomed by the military.

Before long, most American companies had established agencies in Britain and France and were importing sample vehicles for the authorities to test. MT inspectors also borrowed American vehicles from newly-arrived Canadian units for evaluation and by 1916 it was calculated that 30 per cent of the lorries in service with the British Army were built in the United States. Switzerland was a less likely source of vehicles, but according to the Ministry of Munitions the entire production of the Berna factory at Olten was acquired to prevent the Germans from buying them. If this was so it does not explain why the Saurer range was not snapped up as well. Saurer was Switzerland's largest producer of trucks,

Berna only came second, but despite the fact that a Saurer tested by the British Army before the war was considered very good there is no evidence of any quantity purchases during the war. Berna, on the other hand, had a counterpart in England. British-Berna trucks were assembled in Newcastle-upon-Tyne and they are said to have supplied over 300 vehicles to the services in addition to nearly 600 from Switzerland. Italy also supplied vehicles but their contribution will be considered later.

2 THE FIRST WORLD WAR

In the winter of 1916, the five original Auxiliary Omnibus Companies, which served the five British armies in France, were brought together to form the Auxiliary Omnibus Park (AOP). This was subsequently augmented by another company, which employed single-deck charabancs and a seventh, which was equipped with troop-carrying lorries. A total of 271 lorries, fitted with seats for 20 men, as against 25 men on a double-deck bus, were converted for this purpose, although there were numerous occasions when troops piled into the back of any available lorries when the opportunity presented itself. However, the AOP was created for a particular purpose. At full strength it was capable of lifting all the infantry of a division, in addition to their machine-gun company and pioneer battalion, in one go. Acting under the direct control of GHQ the AOP mustered 650 vehicles, which were kept at a series of locations along the road between Amiens and Ypres. They were held ready for call-out at one hour's notice and, with practice, proved capable of loading the personnel of an entire division in about 30 minutes, transporting it to a given location and unloading it again just as swiftly.

Events in 1917 began with an unexpected withdrawal, by the Germans, along certain parts of the front to their massive defence system known as the Hindenburg Line. This provided a severe test of the flexibility of the British transport services because it was regarded as essential to occupy the abandoned German positions as swiftly as possible. Much of this ground having already been fought over, a great deal of extra work was required to prepare transport routes so that supplies and ammunition could follow the troops. The task of road building fell to the Royal Engineers but transport was required to bring forward the road-making materials and the experience thus gained soon proved extremely valuable.

The long, wet summer of 1917 is associated in British minds with the Salient, that provocative bulge in the front around Ypres. Massive artillery bombardment of a landscape prone to flooding at the best of times produced conditions so unvaryingly grim that one is still amazed to find that the countryside has recovered, even after more than 100 years.

London B-Type double-deck buses of the Auxiliary Omnibus Park carrying troops along a well-drained road in the Ypres Salient.

BRITISH MILITARY TRANSPORT 1829-1956

The line was held, and indeed pushed forwards slowly, over a sea of liquid mud by men whose only cover might be a series of flooded shell holes, but they could not survive without support. The entire Salient was under German surveillance, so any attempt to establish a line of narrow-gauge railway was rapidly punished by enemy artillery and it was only the relative independence of mechanised transport that kept things going. Roads could at least be repaired quickly between bombardments, or diverted if need be, by bringing up lorry loads of rubble to fill in the holes. Even so, convoys could and did get caught and the skeletons that littered the battlefield would be those of lorries, as much as horses or men. The following description, taken from a letter written by a Tank Corps officer in October 1917, gives an immediate and graphic account of transport difficulties during the slow advance towards Passchendaele:

'Nos 16 and 17 Companies (of F [6th] Battalion, Tank Corps) were to go over in front of Weiltje-Frezenberg and thereabouts on 31st July. Summers (OC 6th Bn) asked me if I could undertake to get up all their petrol dumps etc. for them, to where they would fill up for the last time before Zero. This entailed going up from La Lovie every night with Ford box bodies to a point on the right of the road to St Jan.

'The road from Well cross roads north of Ypres through St Jan was a nightmare. Packed with transport of all sorts, unable to get off the road or get ahead or astern and subject to perpetual shelling which started every day at dusk. You sat there in the traffic block and saw the fall of the shells coming towards you down the road, and each good shot taking a lorry or a GS wagon out of the line just as if it was bitten out. It was all very unpleasant and nothing to do about it except to sit with the poor old petrified driver on the Ford front seat waiting for our turn and coughing my guts up (from the gas). The dead horses, smashed wagons, limbers, cookers and what nots were simply bundled into the ditch each side of the road and they formed an almost continuous line both sides from Ypres to St Jan.

'The road we came along was via Poperinghe through Vlamertinghe past Goldfish on to the sleeper road to Salvation Corner, then over the lock by the

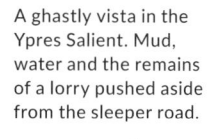

A ghastly vista in the Ypres Salient. Mud, water and the remains of a lorry pushed aside from the sleeper road.

Kaai salient and up to the Dixmude gate, thence Well Cross Roads to St Jan. It got so bad at night and so slow that I asked to be allowed to do it in the daylight and chance it. This was passed and I went in one box body and my Sergeant Major (a very stout hearted fellow) in the other. The drivers were old men of all sorts of trades who had had a 'course' of Ford trucks and were then sent abroad and told they were to be used at the base. From not being able to appreciate what was dangerous and what was not they were of course scared stiff, but with O'Keefe and I to hold their hands they behaved like heroes.

A Glasgow-built Halley with enclosed chain drive, a type used extensively on road construction work.

'We constantly had to stop and time the shells that were bursting on or near the road ahead and then nip through between them. On these occasions the Fords were apt to pop, spit and stop. Our feelings, while a frantic ancient whirled the handle round in an abortive effort to fly the scene, I leave to you. At last, after many days of this we got the whole lot up without a casualty. Just as the very last load was cleared under cover of a wall, a shell fetched the whole gable end over into the lorry and the driver, much alarmed, started off at speed with a load of rubble and without me. All this time we had been very much soaked with gas day and night and I had one very bad dose coming home by Brielen one evening.'

Despite the apparent failure of tanks to achieve a breakthrough, or indeed very much at all, in the appalling conditions of the Ypres Salient throughout that summer it did not destroy everyone's faith in the usefulness of tracked vehicles. A certain Colonel Henry Newton, who had an engineering firm in Derby and was then serving in the Trench Warfare Department, came up with a scheme for a small, tracked load carrier. Prototypes were built by his company, Newton Brothers Ltd, and there is a story that the colonel somehow interested Winston Churchill in the scheme. Whatever the truth, huge orders were placed with Buick, Overland and Studebaker in the United States, which would have resulted in deliveries of some 22,000 Newton Tractors to the Allies in France by late 1918. Production had begun, and some machines had been delivered at the time of the Armistice but none appear to have been employed as intended and the contracts were quickly cancelled.

The Military Tractor Type A, to give the Newton its official title, was about as simple as a vehicle could be. The body was no more than a flat, open tray with the track frames forming the sides, which could handle a payload of 3 tons. The engine, gearbox and final drive were mounted together on a subframe at the back, complete with driver's seat and it looked like nothing more than a small tracked vehicle with the main elements of a farm tractor, less wheels, at the rear. *The Automobile Engineer*, which examined a Buick-built version in August 1919, explained that it was powered by a 27hp, six-cylinder engine and no speed was mentioned, although another source quotes 10mph for the Studebaker version, which seems quite respectable. It was claimed that ground pressure, exerted by the tracks, was less than that of the sole of a man's shoe.

As a supply vehicle, for getting where wheeled vehicles could not go, and able to keep up with tanks, the Newton

A Military Tractor Type A in Tank Corps service, probably after the war.

tractor would probably have been ideal. The driver was perilously exposed but this was never a great consideration in the First World War and in any case the tractor was only a follow-up vehicle, not intended for the first wave of an attack. The Tank Corps employed a few in France and Britain for a while after the war and some are known to have been sold out of service, but the number actually built is not known.

The temporary success of the Battle of Cambrai in November 1917 not only lifted some of the gloom of that dreadful year but also anticipated a return to the Somme. The winter that followed was to witness a change in British transport policy. The change was based on French experience and again seems to have been adopted just in time. In basic terms it meant that the old system of divisional supply columns and ammunition parks was reorganised in favour of transport operated on a pool arrangement. The establishment was based on a section, consisting of 16 lorries, organised in companies of whatever size suited the work in hand. For instance, companies allotted to corps troops comprised two sections, that is 32 vehicles, while divisional companies employed 80 vehicles, or five sections. The object was to obtain the maximum value from each vehicle by releasing it from permanent attachment to any given unit. This new arrangement certainly simplified the workload but it had its drawbacks.

Shortly after the war *The Automobile Engineer* ran a serialised review of the various makes of lorry employed by the British Army, noting in particular how they stood up to the rigorous conditions. One point was common to all reports – that more damage was done by allowing small faults to go unrepaired than by any other single factor. This was undoubtedly due to pressure of work but if it also sounds like a reproach against good workshop practice in the field it is worth noting comments which appeared in the History of the Ministry of Munitions. According to this source, by 1917, when the Ministry's responsibility for mechanical transport was confirmed, the staff was working hard to create some sort of programme for the supply of complete vehicles. At this time no system existed for the supply of spare parts. These were usually ordered in bulk when stocks ran low, causing untold problems for manufacturers. The view in London was that units in the field wasted spare parts by replacing worn items too soon. It was a typical dilemma. On the one hand those concerned with husbanding the Nation's resources; on the other, those upon whom the Nation's very survival depended. Apparent slackness in workshop practice was bound to offend professional journalists in the motor industry but was considered profligate by those who held the purse strings. Unfortunately, they did not have to keep the lorries running. The Ministry was also trying to reduce the demand for American vehicles in order to relieve, where possible, the drain on dollar reserves. Thus, it was deemed essential, as far as the Ministry was concerned, for the military authorities to come up with a planned programme of requirements and at one point the American Board refused to allocate any funds at all until this was done.

The massive increase in the use of mechanical transport was naturally matched by a vast increase in the

A newly repaired Thornycroft J-Type about to go out on a test run from the workshops.

Unloading petrol for the tanks. A pile of 2-gallon cans unloaded from a lorry in the Tank Corps depot at Rollencourt.

Petrol's Part in the Great War—No. X.

SUPPLIES

THIS is a petrol war. Petrol and heavy artillery, according to the consensus of expert military opinion, are to be the deciding factors in the present struggle for supremacy. Speed of transport—of guns and supplies—of men and food—Speed and Weight shall prove the winning weapons.

The transport of supplies at the front is now accomplished by fast motor-lorries, where in the old past the slower method of horse-drawn waggons sufficed. The added efficiency of an army-in-being thus catered for must be almost incalculable.

PRATT'S
Motor Spirit

is used by our own and our Allies' forces—*more than any other spirit*—for operations in the fighting-line, on land and sea, and in the air.

By Appointment.

Anglo-American Oil Co., Ltd.   36, Queen Anne's Gate, London, S.W.

Anglo-American Oil ran a series of newspaper advertisements, which not only informed the public but kept the company's famous brand name to the fore.

demand for fuel. An easy-going attitude in the early days created a situation that was only brought under control by the creation of a Petrol Executive in 1915, which in effect made the huge Asiatic petroleum company Shell the primary distributor of fuel to the Army. From a seriously low position in 1917, matters steadily improved despite the fact that, by 1918, the monthly consumption of fuel by the British Army in France reached eight million gallons, and that did not include the RFC. Petrol was supplied in 2-gallon cans, carried in GS wagons, and petrol tankers were rare. A total of 180 road tankers, of 600-gallon capacity, were impressed

and taken over to France with the object of providing mobile refuelling facilities for MT columns but all they succeeded in doing was to create large road blocks as the lorries lined up to refuel. Anywhere close to the frontline the concentration of vehicles created other dangers so it was discontinued.

Although a system of vehicle registration had existed in Britain since 1903, requiring all motor vehicles to carry number plates, the armed forces were exempt from this rule when the war began. Vehicles were numbered under a War Department system but such numbers were not displayed as were civilian registrations. However, towards the end of the conflict, there were those who began to suspect that service vehicles in Britain were being used for purposes that were not strictly essential or officially sanctioned. It reached a point where the Local Government Board felt it necessary to create a new system of registration for military and service medical vehicles while they were operating in Britain. The system involved painting registration letters on the front and back of each vehicle; the figures to be 5in high and in bright yellow. Separate letter groups were issued to Australian, British, Canadian and US Expeditionary Force vehicles in addition to those of the Red Cross and British Ambulance Committee. Each letter or group to be preceded by a number. The driver was also obliged to carry a card showing that he was authorised to drive the vehicle so that the frivolous use of military transport was curtailed.

In March 1918 the Germans launched their Spring Offensive, which for a while came close to threatening Paris. In the process a number of key Allied railway junctions were deliberately targeted and the network immediately behind the lines was crippled. Road transport was called upon to fill the gap and it was now that the true value of the new pooling system could be appreciated.

The adventures of a steam-lorry company at this time have already been mentioned, but a similar story could probably be told by almost every unit in the ASC. Now that companies could be employed as the need arose, without concern for divisional or corps affiliations, it proved possible to react effectively to any crisis. Even after the German attack had run out of impetus the vital railway system immediately in the rear of the British frontline was seriously disrupted and much of the work devolved upon mechanised transport, including most of the build-up for the crucial Battle of Amiens in August 1918.

After Amiens it was clearly only a matter of time, although most forecasts assumed the war would go on into 1919. Thus, production remained at full stretch and the transport organisation continued to grow. Yet when the crunch came it brought the supply services close to collapse. The Allied advance that got into its stride early in October saw vast numbers of men and weapons moving forwards on a wide front over ground, which was being systematically devastated by a retreating German Army still capable of stubborn resistance.

All this had to be supported by road transport. The main railway system was in a state of total collapse, from enemy demolition, while the speed of the advance precluded the laying of narrow-gauge railways quickly. Lorry columns moved forwards, often in the dark on winter evenings, over damaged roads strewn with enemy dead and abandoned equipment and the question was how long could they go on doing so.

The pace and scale of the advance was outstripping anything that the supply services had been prepared for and, even at the time, there were many who believed that if it went on much longer the pursuit would simply grind to a halt for want of support. The Armistice in November seems to have come in the nick of time although it hardly brought with it the release from labour that many had longed for. An Army of Occupation was moving steadily into Germany while another, less organised army of released prisoners of war, passed in the opposite direction. Both needed feeding and, until engineers managed to get the railway system back into shape, it was the lorries that bore the brunt of the burden.

Coming home. An assortment of military vehicles crowd the deck of a train ferry from Calais as it edges, stern first, into Richborough Military Port in Kent.

BRITISH MILITARY TRANSPORT 1829-1956

3 FIRST FOOTING

Four years of war saw the motor vehicle penetrate into almost every part of the globe where the British Army was fighting – from the deserts of the Middle East, to the jungles of Africa and the mountains of India. It was a war very different in character to the Western Front, with mechanical transport operating at full stretch over huge distances.

3 FIRST FOOTING

That the Great War of 1914–18 was indeed the first world war is undeniable. Some have likened its spread to the ripples on a pond, but the effect was probably more akin to that of a volcanic explosion. Some places were all but overwhelmed while others were lightly touched and others again missed altogether, although in the long run they were few enough.

There can have been few places that knew nothing of war before that time but plenty for whom the arrival of a motor vehicle must have been a traumatic event, not much different to a visit from outer space. Ancient Macedonia, home of Alexander the Great was one such. Siwa Oasis in Egypt – the temple of Jupiter Ammon (visited by Alexander) – another, while the war-torn Bible lands were not spared either. Before long, motor traffic was roaring by the place near Basra, where the Tigris and Euphrates meet, which is reputedly the site of the Garden of Eden. Literally nothing was sacred where transport was concerned.

British-administered Egypt became the base first for operations against the Senussi and later the starting point for a move north into Palestine against the Turks. The Senussi was a religious sect rather than a tribe, with extreme Islamic convictions. In 1914, the sect was engaged in a desultory struggle against the Italians in Tripolitania, fighting from bases at Sollum and Mersah Matruh on the Egyptian coast. In addition, the Senussi had a secure base at Siwa, deep within the desert some 200 miles south of Mersah Matruh. Attempts by the Central Powers to invoke a jihad against the British probably had more effect on the Senussi than any other Muslim group but even then it did not begin with a thunderbolt. Rather, there was a series of what the British Official History dignifies with the term 'affairs' which, even so, had tied up considerable numbers of men and involved the temporary abandonment of Sollum to the Senussi in 1915.

British forces on the coast were supplied by rail up to Mersah Matruh and from there along a route with the rather grand title of the Khedivial Motor Road to Sollum. All this amounted to was a strip of desert, which had been levelled and cleared of stones. It was passable in dry weather but when the rain fell,

Seen here in Bethlehem, this is an earlier pre-1916 example of a Model-T Ford with the angular brass radiator.

BRITISH MILITARY TRANSPORT 1829-1956

A Model-T Ford van in trouble.

Laying a wire netting road over inhospitable ground.

imminent a raid by armoured cars was mounted, which cleared Siwa and the neighbouring oasis of Girba. It failed to trap many of the Islamic warriors or their leader, but it effectively destroyed their base of operations in Egypt and rendered them impotent for the rest of the war. Siwa now became the base for British and Australian Light Car Patrols operating deep within the Libyan desert, but they required an organised supply system. The 200 miles from railhead at Mersah Matruh to Siwa could be reached by two widely spaced tracks and these were used by a Ford Van Supply Column running convoys of 25 vehicles over the route. The round trip, at an average speed of 12mph, took four days although this eased somewhat as the drivers became more experienced in desert driving. It was all a matter of anticipation; of knowing just when to change down as the vehicle encountered soft sand and judicious use of the clutch to keep the car moving.

The Model-T Ford is a legend in its own right, but its contribution to the First World War alone would have justified its fame even if it had never achieved anything else. Built to survive in rural America and to be operated by hands more used to the reins of a horse it was a superb example of simplicity and economic construction. Its narrow tyres, large wheels and in particular the excellent ground clearance enabled it to perform in the worst possible conditions. If it had a fault, it was that of overheating in the arid desert atmosphere. Following various trial solutions, a simple condensing apparatus was developed that retained boiled-off water from the radiator for recycling.

Henry Ford's refusal, early in the war, to allow his vehicles to be used for any warlike purpose except as ambulances is well known. Quite how he expected to enforce it is another matter. Even if he insisted that chassis leaving the Ford plant in Detroit for customers in the war

as it did with a vengeance between December and March each year, the whole thing turned to glue.

Matters took a serious turn in November 1915 when the crews of two British ships, torpedoed by German U-boats, were handed over to the Senussi and marched into the desert. In March 1916, with Sollum reoccupied, the British learnt that the prisoners were located at a place called El Hakkim, some 120 miles from Sollum. They were rescued, in the last stages of starvation, in a raid mounted by the Duke of Westminster with a motorised column of ambulances and armoured cars.*

Suitably cowed, the Senussi withdrew to Siwa and now fermented trouble which, it was believed, aimed at a dual invasion of Egypt from Siwa and the Sudan. When the threat became

*S.C. Rolls, *Steel Chariots in the Desert* (Jonathan Cape, 1937)

zone might only be used as ambulances, it seems unrealistic to expect that the buyers would honour this in an emergency. And how he imagined he could maintain any influence over the Ford factory at Old Trafford, Manchester if the British authorities requisitioned the vehicles for other purposes is even more difficult to understand. Although Ford declared himself a pacifist and made some expensive, if naive, attempts to halt the conflict, he was nothing if not an astute businessman with finely tuned instincts so his declaration may have been no more than a nod in the direction of the non-interventionist Midwest and pro-German customers on the east coast of the United States. Certainly, the British Army was using Fords as carriers and even combat vehicles by 1915 and had purchased nearly 20,000 by the time the war ended.

However, Fords were indeed used as ambulances as well. From 1917 a longer wheelbase version with a capacity of 1 ton was available, which would at least have guaranteed casualties a smoother ride. But, as a load carrier, the original version was, theoretically, limited to an 8cwt payload. In 1925, Lieutenant-Colonel Badcock, who was Assistant Director of Transport to the Egyptian Expeditionary Force, wrote:

'Considering the conditions under which the Ford vans had been running, the results of their work was highly satisfactory. Many of them were on the road for two and a half years, during which time some of them did service in Africa, the Western Desert of Egypt and Palestine.'

Badcock records instances of fitting twin wheels to the rear axles when operating through deep sand, but explains that this resulted in axle failure due to strain. The problem was finally overcome by fitting oversize tyres. If anything was worse than sand it was the rain. A heavy deluge would immobilise virtually all transport except the Fords which, even if they could not be driven were at least light enough to be pushed through.

The first Turkish attacks on the Suez Canal occurred in February 1915. They were beaten off but did serve to expose the vulnerability of this vital lifeline. Even so it was 12 months before any major attempt was made to drive the enemy back, and that was only conceived as a holding action with relatively limited objectives. The initial obstacle was the Sinai Desert which, in places near the coast, was a wilderness of soft dunes. While work progressed on a railway extending northwards from Qantara on the Canal, supplies were moved by camel trains and motor vehicles. Experience soon showed that as far as the latter were concerned the Model-T Ford was the only suitable type. Even then it became necessary to peg miles of wire netting down upon the sand to provide support.

Away from the wire road no wheeled vehicles could operate so the supply services started to use Holt 75hp caterpillar tractors. These were American machines powered by a four-cylinder petrol engine and steered by a pilot wheel at the front or by declutching a track if a tighter turn was required. The tractors had originally been introduced to haul heavy artillery and when they were relegated to supply carrying it was mainly for ammunition. The Holt

A Holt 75hp caterpillar tractor hauling two tracked supply trailers.

BRITISH MILITARY TRANSPORT 1829-1956

A Peerless in the Middle East. These solid American wagons would accept any amount of punishment but they needed a firm surface to operate on.

Company supplied 10-ton capacity tracked trucks, of which each tractor could manage two although they had an unfortunate habit of shedding their tracks during a turn. Various types of wheeled trailer were tried but all proved unsuitable and even the tractors had their problems. Any attempt to steer while tackling a steep slope invariably ended in disaster because the declutched track would start to overrun the driven one, swinging the vehicle the wrong way and causing it to roll over.

North of Sinai, as the advance progressed into Palestine, the nature of the country changed. Good roads existed in places, although they were inclined to turn into mud in the wet season, but where they entered the Judean Hills, on the way to Jerusalem and Jericho, they were very steep, with alarming precipices and hairpin bends, which tested nerves as much as vehicles. The majority of heavy lorries were 32hp Albion 3-tonners and the American 40hp Peerless rated at 5 tons. Colonel Badcock was full of praise for the Albions, saying that they gave very little trouble mechanically and, being lighter, could cross ground that held up the Peerless. However, he favoured the American trucks on hilly routes because of their greater power, although he noted a rapid deterioration in quality in some of the later deliveries. But it required a great deal of skill and not a little courage to handle these big wagons in the hills where a slip, or a temporary loss of nerve, would have them off the road and down the side of the mountain in a moment resulting in the loss of lorry, load and at times the driver. Daimler lorries were issued to some of the specialist arms such as signals and anti-aircraft units, but Badcock criticised them on account of their Knight sleeve-valve engines, which required special lubricants, not always easy to obtain at remote desert bases, and they suffered badly from the effects of dust and sand.

Where roads existed, they had to be preserved because the region lacked any heavy type of stone suitable for repairs. As a consequence, a speed limit of 6mph was enforced for lorries and 15mph for lighter vehicles. Roads were generally built with a considerable camber and the normal practice was to operate convoys in the middle of the road wherever possible. Badcock mentions that they also introduced a system of rear lookouts, just as they did

This Crossley tender is towing a Model-T Ford touring car. The badge on the Crossley's door suggests a LAMB, or Light Armoured Motor Battery.

on the Western Front, with the man at the back able to ring a bell in the cab by means of a line if the driver was required to pull over or stop.

When General Allenby took over command in June 1917, the Egyptian Expeditionary Force was already committed to a continued advance. The final year of the war on this front was characterised by a ruthless pursuit, only made possible by the most intensive use of transport that the availability of manpower and vehicles allowed. Yet it was a war so different in character to that of the Western Front that one sees mechanical transport operating at full stretch over huge distances. In the final weeks, up to the local armistice on 31 October 1918, mounted troops and armoured cars covered areas of hundreds of square miles – eastwards into Syria as far as Damascus itself and north to Aleppo, only a short distance from the border with Turkey.

The advance north from Egypt became one half of a huge pincer movement closing in on the Turkish homeland.

The other half came out of the east. Even before war was declared on Turkey in November 1914, the Indian administration had established a force at the head of the Persian Gulf with a view to protecting the oil installations. Once war had been declared this force was enlarged but at this time had no transport whatsoever. Even so, by requisitioning boats, elements of 6th Infantry Brigade were able to move up the Shatt-al-Arab waterway to Kurna, the point where the Tigris and Euphrates meet. The Turks were slow to respond but by the following April they had caused the British Indian forces to move back to Basra, near the mouth of the Shatt-al-Arab, which was now heavily attacked.

The British Army was substantially reinforced from India and the 6th Division, under Major-General Sir Charles Townshend, now began one of the most amazing advances in military history. After retaking Kurna in May 1915 the infantry, supported by shallow-draught gunboats of the Royal Navy, proceeded to follow the retreating Turkish forces up the Tigris. The advance

Norperforce, operating in northern Persia, seems to have acquired some unusual vehicles. This unidentified lorry, probably of American origin, may have come from the Russians. It does not look very well cared for, but the road surface no doubt has a bearing on that.

of the ships, and the precipitate retreat of the Turks soon left the British and Indian troops behind.

At one time Townshend himself, with some 25 soldiers in a small flotilla of craft, was racing ahead, taking the surrender of one settlement after another until he captured Amarah, some 100 miles up the river from Basra. Here he halted to consolidate his force and then continued, taking Kut-al-Amara a good 100 miles further on, by September. Apart from barges on the river, Townshend only had mule transport for his force and precious little of that. However, by November he was almost in sight of Baghdad, at a site called Ctesiphon where he found a substantial Turkish force waiting for him. He was now some 300 miles from his base as the crow flies, and much more as the river winds, but Ctesiphon became his Waterloo.

Townshend's defeat at Ctesiphon, the withdrawal to Kut-al-Amara and the subsequent siege make grim reading. Men were dying of starvation and disease at an alarming rate but Townshend held out until the end of April 1916. By then all food reserves had gone and hope of relief was dwindling so the entire force of over 8,000 men was obliged to surrender. Things did not improve for many of them after that.

In July 1916, command of the army in Mesopotamia was given to General F.S. Maude. He immediately decided to expand the mechanical transport services and, by September, Lieutenant-Colonel F.W. Leland, ASC, had come out from Britain to take charge. On arrival in Basra, Leland found that the British were, as usual, extending railways all over the place but that mechanical transport was limited to one company equipped with Star ambulances, built in Wolverhampton and another with Peerless, Napier and Fiat lorries. The Peerless 3-tonners were restricted to the base area but early experience convinced the Army that they were too heavy for most roads and limited them to carrying 30cwt loads. The Stars had already been condemned as unreliable, due to weak front axles, but Leland pointed out that he still had all 50 of them running at the end of the war, so they could not have been that bad. But it was the Fiats that were outstanding.

Rated at 1-ton capacity, but running on pneumatic tyres, which was unusual for British or American commercial vehicles, the Fiats were operating right up to

A Model-T Ford in trouble, here being rescued by what appears to be a Talbot tender.

the frontline with considerable success. However, not only was Leland short of transport, his workshop facilities were equally poor and with Maude pressing for a renewed advance on Baghdad there was a lot to be done.

Maude's campaign from November 1916 through to October 1918 not only embraced the capture of Baghdad but extended almost to Mosul by the end. His command was also involved with events in Persia that took British transport as far north as the Caspian Sea. On the Tigris front, Leland had developed a sophisticated floating workshop for his MT, based on barges that could be moved up river as the army advanced. The number of transport companies expanded rapidly. Peerless remained the standard type of heavy truck although other makes were used in small numbers and the Royal Air Force (as it was from April 1918) had 3-ton Leylands. The success of the Fiats caused other makes to be investigated. Britain offered two companies of light Packards fitted with pneumatic tyres. These took so long to arrive that only one MT company was ever up to strength, but the vehicles seem to have survived quite well. As in Palestine, Holt Caterpillar tractors were in use for artillery haulage and they were sometimes called upon to move ammunition and supplies when the going was bad. Leland records that caterpillars pulled British-made Fowler tracked trailers in his theatre, rather than the Holt type used in Palestine.

It was the Fords, however, that excelled themselves once again. They represented by far the largest fleet in that region and drivers were recruited from virtually every nation of the area. Personnel included Indian, Burmese and Mauritian, many of whom had never seen a motor vehicle, let alone travelled in one, before serving with the Army. Leland considered an interesting possibility for recovering broken-down Fords. In Baghdad, when it was captured in 1917, he encountered an amazing breed of Kurdish porters who were able to carry loads of up to half a ton on their backs. Leland reckoned that, with a damaged Model T-Ford lifted onto his back, one of these men could have carried it bodily for 2 or 3 miles! Not surprisingly, the porters were much in demand in Baghdad and the money they could make was more than Leland could afford so the experiment was never tried. In parts of Persia, where better quality roads existed, Leland was able to illustrate the point that when heavier vehicles could be used they were far more economical than masses of small trucks.

Believed to be in Palestine later in the war a Leyland 3-tonner, which has come off the road, provides an indiscreet view of its underside.

The decision to attack the Turks by landing at Gallipoli in 1915 was made in haste, following the failure of the Allies to break through the Dardanelles by sea to launch an attack on Constantinople. That the plan was conceived in ignorance may be deduced from what was known, or rather imagined, about the peninsula in London. Requests for information from the Intelligence Branch at the War Office produced the admission that it was not known if roads in the area were fit for mechanical transport or, indeed, whether there were any roads at all. Higher authority was more positive, but just as ignorant. Colonel R.H. Beadon, in his two-volume

Photographs of motor transport at Gallipoli are few but this appears to be genuine, if of poor quality. A 2-ton Austin, probably a workshop vehicle, is being loaded with great difficulty aboard a Beetle Boat, an early landing craft.

history of the RASC published in 1931, states: 'Now among Lord Kitchener's qualities, and they were both numerous and eminent, knowledge of transport matters was not included.'* For the Secretary of State for War himself had worked out and ordained that, since the troops were to be landed on the beach and only had to walk across the promontory, they would not require any transport at all. What inspired Kitchener to say this is not clear since it was subsequently learned that, early in March 1915, General Maxwell had written to him from Egypt explaining that, from local research, he had discovered that there were no roads so pack animals would be essential. Mechanical transport was used on Gallipoli, but only in support of the landings at Suvla Bay where a wide tract of flat land existed between the fighting line in the hills and the shore. Some 24 30cwt lorries, Model-T Fords of the RNAS and ambulances on the same chassis were employed and the Royal Artillery managed to land a few American four-wheel drive trucks to haul the guns.

According to Beadon, a significant but discounted reason for the lack of initial success on Gallipoli was due to a lack of transport, or at least some adequate means of bringing forward supplies. Admitting that the troops were exhausted following the difficult landing he contends that, with sufficient supplies, they could and would have gone further and probably achieved more effective results. It is a factor not often considered but the presence of transport at Suvla does not appear to have improved matters there so it may be a false conclusion.

Although the First World War may be said to have begun in the Balkans, and fighting continued there for the full four years, it was latterly something of a backwater. Indeed, the war between Serbia and Bulgaria might have been fought out independent of foreign interference, or even interest, without affecting matters too drastically. As it was, both France and Great Britain were bound to support Serbia and so, according to treaty, was Greece although she managed to avoid direct involvement. This placed the Allies in a very awkward position. Serbia was effectively landlocked and the only route that could be used to aid her was through Greece, which was, in its own view, neutral on this front. This seems to have been interpreted freely by both sides. British and French troops effectively occupied the Aegean port of Salonika and used it as a base to support their forces fighting with the Serbs.

The attitude of the Greek Government was not always consistent, but it was in a very difficult position. At one stage, when the British needed fuel, the Greek authorities refused to supply it and placed a sentry at the gates of the Standard Oil Company depot in

*R.H. Beadon, *The Royal Army Service Corps, a History of Transport and Supply in the British Army*, Volume II (Cambridge University Press, 1931)

Salonika. Since the British had their own small depot next door the problem was avoided by simply passing cans over the wall, while the sentry remained oblivious at his post.

On the other hand, when a Bulgarian offensive forced the Allies back across the Greek frontier, no objection was made to the creation of a defensive line on neutral territory.

The task of keeping frontline troops supplied was a difficult one, as it always is in mountainous territory, where extreme weather conditions prevail and railways are few. The range of vehicles available extended from 3-tonners and caterpillar tractors down to the ubiquitous Fords but this was another theatre of war where animal transport was still a vital component. The Fords, as always, earned continual praise although trouble was reported with the bodies, which is not heard from other theatres. It is claimed that, owing to the rough, boulder-strewn roads most had just about shaken themselves to pieces by the time of the Armistice.

As their part of the commitment, British forces ultimately established a front against Bulgaria along the Struma river but it was a good 50 miles from the closest railhead and the two points were linked by a most unsatisfactory road. Since some 40,000 to 50,000 men relied upon this one single supply route a major effort was made to improve it. The Royal Engineers received a substantial shipment of steam rollers, which must have created transport and supply problems of their own, and set about bringing the road up to the best possible standard. It seems hard to credit, in such a country, but one of the biggest problems they are said to have faced was a supply of suitable stone.

Early in 1917, an Allied military mission concluded that Italy would benefit from assistance and decided that six divisions, three British and three French, would suffice. At this time Italy was more than holding its own against the Austro-Hungarian forces on its alpine front but welcomed the help all the same. The British established themselves with a small force at Arquata, some miles inland

A Fiat 15 ter light lorry in British service, on a mountain road in Italy or the Balkans.

A pair of American-built four-wheel drive trucks with the British Army in Italy. The example closest to the camera has a water tank in the back.

from Genoa, and the Italians supplied a fleet of 500 Fiat lorries, with drivers, to service the establishment. Then, in October, came Caporetto, the massive Austrian attack that threw the Italians back and could easily have overwhelmed them. Britain and France immediately rushed six divisions each to the Italian front by rail with their transport following by road. The British column, described as a mixed collection, typical of the wide range of vehicles that a division might acquire after a year or two in France, followed a route which ran from Amiens, via Dijon, Lyons and Nice, and entered Italy at Savona. Averaging about 70 miles a day, with a very high standard of reliability, the column covered some 1,100 miles in two weeks.

With this prompt Allied help the Italians held the attackers and then went back onto the offensive. By the following March many British and French troops were called back to the Western Front in anticipation of the new German offensive but three British divisions remained in Italy. It is interesting to note the scale of transport available to these divisions, including those vehicles donated by Italy: 827 British lorries, 494 Italian lorries, 332 cars, 128 boxcars or vans and 247 ambulances.

Although the Royal Artillery was not generally involved in supply work it ended up playing a part by default. Artillery units were equipped with Holt tractors and American four-wheel drive trucks to haul their guns but the trucks had proved incapable on the steep and twisting mountain roads. The gunners borrowed tractors from the Italians to supplement the Holts; most of the trucks were fitted with drum-shaped tanks inside their wooden bodies and used to supply water to the frontline.

Among the factors that irritated the Germans before the war was their lack of colonies. As a major European power, albeit a relatively new one, Germany felt that it was fully entitled to widespread colonial responsibilities to match those of Britain and France. Unfortunately, it was those colonies that Germany already had, which became involved in the war and is the main reason why it spread its unwelcome influence across Africa. The largest of these colonies was

German East Africa, mainly that area which is now Tanzania.

It is undoubtedly best remembered for the brilliant campaign waged by General von Lettow-Vorbeck and his army of largely local troops. In many respects the fighting in this region had much in common with the Boer War, but with an odd twist. Eschewing all forms of transport except vast numbers of porters recruited locally, and sufficient portable boats to enable his force to cross rivers, von Lettow-Vorbeck operated like a Boer commando. The Allied forces, mainly British, Indian and South African, were commanded by General Jan Christian Smuts who had learned his trade, as a young man, with those very Boer commandos that Lettow-Vorbeck was now emulating.

Since the Germans had the advantage of knowing the country and having local support, along with internal lines of communication when it mattered, Smuts was now obliged to operate more as the British had done in South Africa; a steady advance, consolidating as he went and dependent to an unfortunate extent on ox-drawn transport. Mechanical transport was used but it got off to a bad start. A local expert explained that pneumatic-tyred vehicles would suffer in the bush from punctures, due to the healthy thorns that grew there. As a consequence, the War Office sent out a company of solid-tyred 30cwts, which churned the roads to dust in the dry season and floundered in the mud when it was wet. Ultimately, once again, it was the Fords that saved the day although as Smuts captured more of the East African railway system he was able to improvise trains from Napier and Reo lorries converted to run on rails. The little cab-over-engine Autocar, built in Ardmore, Pennsylvania, was used extensively by British troops in various parts of Africa as well as on the Western Front.

East Africa does, however, provide one of the great transport epics of the First World War, although it has more to do with the Royal Navy than the Army. The aim was to wrest control of Lake Tanganyika from the Germans by sinking the gunboat that ruled there. Two armed motor boats, with the unlikely naval names of *Mimi* and *Toutou* were prepared in Britain and shipped out via South Africa and the Belgian Congo. Most of the journey could be accomplished by rail but there was a gap of about 120 miles over the Mitumba

This Napier lorry has been stripped to the bare essentials and converted to run on rails in East Africa.

BRITISH MILITARY TRANSPORT 1829-1956

A poor but evocative photograph of lorries, probably Napiers, on a bush road somewhere in Africa.

Ensign was a British make, built in north-west London and powered by a Tylor engine. From the name, and the fact that production began in 1914, one might guess that it was produced specifically with war service in mind.

mountain range where the boats would have to go by road. Seen out of the water both craft looked quite big and, for a heavy haulage trip of this magnitude, only steam would do. A pair of big Fowler compound road locomotives was hired, one to haul each boat and a supply wagon. The existing road across the mountains was little more than a track and the team that accompanied the engines had to strengthen over 200 bridges along the route. Water supply for the engines was a nightmare. Much of the time the team had to rely on relays of porters for a regular supply of clean water and it is not surprising that this road section of the trip took six weeks to accomplish. However, it did succeed although the subsequent actions on the lake probably failed to justify the effort.

In German South West Africa, as it was then, General Botha's campaign presented the usual problems of inhospitable terrain, unpleasant climate, tropical diseases and interesting insects. Most of the mechanical transport employed there was operated by the South African Army Service Corps and it was quite a mixed lot. By taking whatever was available, those responsible for supply faced the recurring problem of acquiring spares, which in some cases were obsolete and, in most others, unobtainable. Although the Fords were there, as usual, sandhills could be found along the road that defeated even them. At such places it was common practice to station donkeys, which would assist the motor vehicles over the worst bits.

The campaign in the Cameroons more or less followed on from that in South West Africa but it had this difficulty. There was only one road worthy of the name in the entire 300,000 square miles of the German colony, but the country was a death trap for animals, as the French discovered when they imported hundreds of mules. The British contingent therefore relied on local porters and one Ford van company for their transport needs and the Fords, inevitably, earned unstinting praise. A porter, or carrier, used to the work, could manage a load of about 60lb, meaning that 15 porters equalled the carrying capacity of one Model-T Ford van. The problem was that the carriers bore with them, as it were, the seeds of their own destruction since they were in a region stripped bare of local food supplies. For long trips the journey was divided into so many days' marches with different groups working the various stages. Thus, the column not only had to carry supplies for the troops at the front, it must also bring food for itself, marching in both directions, and for the relays of carriers up ahead. Carried to its inevitable sequel, just as it once was in India, there comes a point where the number of men employed to supply the soldiers is out of all proportion to those actually in the firing line. To make matters worse the rate of sickness among the carriers was such that porters had to be brought in from the British colonies in Africa at the rate of 1,500 a month. No wonder the Fords were admired.

In India the situation was somewhat different in that there was no direct conflict with any of the Central Powers. Their influence was at work, of course, in promoting dissent but there was probably quite enough of that going on in any case. As vast numbers of troops were withdrawn from India to fight elsewhere, any faction with a grievance took advantage of the situation to cause trouble. None more so, of course, than those tribes which inhabited the North West Frontier region, on both sides of the Afghan border.

Naturally, when it came to priorities, India was very low on the scale for more transport. It was inevitable, but ironic, when one considers that at one time India was in the forefront of mechanisation where military transport was concerned. One source claims that early in the war there were no more than a dozen Army lorries in India. Consequently, the authorities were obliged to collect whatever they could from local resources while waiting for new vehicles to arrive from Britain. The result was that within India itself the Army soon found itself with an amazing fleet, which included makes not seen in military colours anywhere else. It would not be the last time that happened. Despite all these handicaps India once again managed to take a progressive step.

The shortage of troops, combined with the increased local threat, encouraged the High Command in India to listen to those who advocated the use of armoured cars. At first these had to be assembled locally but, by their mobility and firepower, they soon proved that

Model-T Ford pick-ups at an African port towing single-axle ambulance trailers.

they could effectively replace large bodies of conventional troops when it came to internal security operations. Where danger threatened, troops were stationed in formidable blockhouses and the armoured cars were used to patrol the areas between. This meant, however, that mechanical transport was needed not only to support the armoured cars but also to escort the transport that kept the forts supplied. Matters did not develop quickly. At many garrisons, local commanders locked the armoured cars up in sheds, rather than use them, while transport, which was still managed by the old Supply and Transport Corps of the Indian Army, was slow to adapt. For one thing in addition to lorries there were separate units for the operation of mules, camels and elephants! In 1915 things started to improve. The Indian agent for Fiat was soon attempting to fill large orders and it is interesting to discover that among those officers involved in organising transport, a Colonel Nugent of the Royal Engineers was prominent. Whether this was the same Nugent who was so involved with the earlier stages of mechanisation in Britain cannot be confirmed, but one rather hopes so. His efforts aside, the most influential character to appear at this time was Lord Montagu of Beaulieu who was retained as Mechanical Transport Adviser to the Government of India. Montagu immediately ordered large numbers of Fords direct from the United States, which got him into trouble, but his other, major contribution will be dealt with shortly.

In May 1916, it was agreed that the ASC should operate in India alongside the Supply and Transport Corps. Soon, four ASC companies were on their way. One was an ambulance company while the

A typical scene on the North West Frontier. The road, beautifully engineered, clings to the side of the mountain, overlooked by strongpoints on both sides and a larger fort at the far end.

other three were equipped with Albion 3-tonners, which were to become the dominant heavy lorry in India. Landing at Karachi in June many of the men from these companies were involved in a terrible incident during a rail journey north. They were packed into a train without adequate ventilation or water and, as it crossed the Sind Desert, they began to collapse from heatstroke and die. Over the three or four days in the train 37 men died and nearly 400 had to be hospitalised.

India has one distinction, in terms of transport, that sets it apart from all other war zones; it was the only place to have lorries designed especially for it. This was due entirely to the efforts of Lord Montagu. Taking his duties very seriously, Montagu toured all areas in which vehicles were operating. He was a man of considerable mechanical aptitude, having been involved in motoring from the earliest days and he already possessed a useful knowledge of transport. He soon realised that, whatever use it might have been on the Western Front, the typical 3-ton subsidy lorry was too heavy for Indian conditions. It was probably not so much a question of ground – the major routes in India were quite well engineered and surfaced – rather it was the topography, especially in the frontier regions. Here, in a stark, unforgiving landscape, roads had to negotiate very rugged country, climbing the sides of high passes, often in a series of hairpin bends and along ledges edged with little more than a fringe of ragged stones. In summer, temperatures often reached 120°F. One problem that had yet to be solved was the preservation of pneumatic tyres. If they were not torn to shreds by the road surface they simply rotted away in store.

On a visit to Britain in 1915, Lord Montagu discussed the problem with two of Britain's leading vehicle manufacturers, Leyland and Thornycroft.

India, old style. An animal-powered supply column extends in both directions as far as the eye can see.

A convoy of Indian Standard Lorries with a locally-built armoured car for escort.

The hazards of a mountain road. A 3-ton Albion is rescued from a very awkward situation.

The result was something that became known as the 'Indian Standard Lorry'. Built to subsidy standards but with a payload of 2 tons, rather than 3 tons, it ran on solid tyres and, but for the cab, looked entirely conventional. The cab had side panels, complete with windows, albeit without doors, and a rigid canvas canopy that stretched forward virtually to the front of the bonnet. Thus, the driver and his mate would be protected against the sun from almost every angle. It could still hardly be described as comfortable but at least it was better than being roasted alive. The lorries were also designed so that they could easily be adapted to run on standard gauge railway tracks.

The design was soon completed and deliveries began late in 1916 from both manufacturers. At first they were supplied to the Supply and Transportation Corps, while the ASC continued to receive Albions. It is not clear just how successful the Standard lorries were in service but relatively few were built. The figure for Leylands is said to be 127 and it may be assumed that Thornycrofts built a similar quantity. It is also worth noting, if one can judge anything accurately from surviving photographs, that after the war 3-ton Albions were far and away the most common make in service, so it may be that the Indian Standard types were not quite up to dealing with the conditions. Considering the subject in retrospect one wonders if the project was ever justified. Surely, the Subsidy B type 30cwt would have suited Montagu's purpose just as well? It was not popular in Europe but it was already in production and even modifying it to take Lord Montagu's tropical cab would have been a much cheaper option than building a new type.

Returning to India late in December 1915, Lord Montagu nearly lost his life when the SS *Persia* was torpedoed in the Mediterranean. As a result, he travelled back to Britain and did not finally arrive in India until December 1916. Much of his time was now spent in dealing with aviation matters but even so he was largely responsible for establishing a driving school near Rawalpindi, which supplied the Army in India and Mesopotamia.

International intervention in Russia after the 1917 Revolution involved British troops in various parts of the country.

Lord Montagu of Beaulieu steps down from a Leyland Indian Standard Lorry, which is being demonstrated on rails.

In the far north, around Murmansk and Archangel, their main task was to maintain and protect supply bases that could be sustained through Murmansk, on the Kola Inlet which was ice-free the whole year round, due to the action of the Gulf Stream. This vestige of tropical warmth did nothing for the land and it proved no place for mechanical transport. Even so, it was tried. Subsidy lorries in the 3-ton and 30cwt classes were delivered along with the ubiquitous Fords, but the season when they could be used was brief. The entire region was snowbound for much of the year, when even the railway suffered, but supply services were maintained with sleighs. But if the snow was bad the thaw was worse. In this season the mud on most roads was so deep that nothing could move, except around the settlements where stretches of corduroy road were created using felled timber. Although the coastline was deeply indented and many rivers ran out from the interior, even they could not be relied upon. In winter, ice breakers were in constant demand while in summer the levels fell so low that nothing with any draught could float. An exercise in ingenuity solved this problem, the Royal Engineers creating large wooden rafts, each of which was fitted with a Model-T Ford ambulance, without its back wheels. These were replaced with paddles, overhanging the back of the raft so that a primitive, shallow-draught stern wheeler was revealed.

War is a dreadful and, ultimately, rather a pointless business but there is no doubt that its influence is profound. Consider how long it might have taken to introduce motor vehicles throughout the world if developments had been left to the normal pace of commercial expansion in peacetime. As it was, within four hectic years the motor vehicle had penetrated into virtually every part of the globe. Whether that was a benefit or not is hardly our concern here but it is remarkable all the same. And it wasn't just a question of primitive natives gaping from the roadside as these strange machines rolled by, drenching them in new and nauseous smells. Thousands of men from these lands had been taught to drive and even learned the rudiments of vehicle maintenance. The 20th century had invaded jungle, desert and mountain range with a vengeance. The whole world had witnessed mechanisation, virtually overnight, and it was not going to go away.

A dockside scene in North Russia. An RAF Leyland is parked alongside the ship while a Model-T Ford van is being unloaded from the aft hold. It can be seen just above the Leyland's hood.

4 PEACETIME DEVELOPMENTS

In 1929, the War Office issued a booklet entitled *Mechanized and Armoured Formations*, known popularly as the 'Purple Primer'. It was compiled by Lieutenant-General Sir Charles Broad and its purpose was to educate serving personnel in the mysteries of mechanical warfare. *Modern Formations* (1931) was the sequel in which the challenges of mechanisation in the British Army as a whole were addressed.

Wars never end in a tidy way. They generate sparks which are easily rekindled. British forces were required for the occupation of Germany and for clearing up in France. At the same time they were involved in Russia, the Middle East and of course India. Close to home the Irish problem, which had flared up in 1916, now came back to life again with a vengeance.

Indeed, the situation in Ireland became so bad that lorries used to transport troops were lightly armoured to protect the men from ambush. In India, the Third Afghan War, which only lasted for most of May 1919, owed much of its rapid success to Lord Montagu's efforts. The road he had authorised through the Khyber Pass was so well engineered that reinforcements and supplies could be hurried forward by lorry in a matter of

4 PEACETIME DEVELOPMENTS

hours. So much so that on one occasion a battalion of infantry was rushed through the Pass in covered lorries, unnoticed by the enemy who thought they were merely supply trucks and let them go by.

Some two weeks after the Armistice in November 1918, the Army Service Corps was granted the Royal accolade by King George V. Its units were scattered across the globe and, with the return to a peacetime economy, it was clear that mechanical transport companies would have to survive on their existing vehicles for some time.

Of the value of mechanical transport there was no doubt whatever and this carried over into civil life. Thousands of men had learned to drive and maintain vehicles during the war and many, as they came out of the forces, saw this as a way of making a living. Many of them who had jobs to return to rejected the idea of subordinate employment and planned to do better for themselves by setting up in business as hauliers. The demand was there, all you needed was a lorry. And this was no problem. The difficulty was getting out of the Army. The demobilisation arrangements were so badly organised, and patently unfair that the men were on the point of revolt. One day in January 1919, the War Office was besieged, Horse Guards Parade and Whitehall being jammed solid with Army lorries, which aggrieved soldiers had brought up to the capital in order to add some point to their protest. These men might be anxious to escape from service life but they did not intend to finish with mechanical transport.

Huge parks of ex-service vehicles already existed at Catford and Kempton Park in London. Hundreds of vehicles were moved to Islington Agricultural Hall for an auction in the spring of 1919. Rarely can such an event have seemed so unpromising. Hardly any of the vehicles looked as if they had a spark of life left in them and many pundits forecast disaster. They could not have been more mistaken. Long before the auction began, the building was thronged by legions of hopeful bidders. A large contingent of police had to be drafted in to maintain order. The end result was that many buyers went home disappointed. Prices went through the roof and bargains appear to have been the exception. Subsequent sales in London and Manchester enjoyed similar patronage and the whole exercise could have ruined the British commercial motor industry. Leyland Motors was one company that saw the danger in time. They re-purchased every one of their old military vehicles that they could get their hands on and initiated a thorough rebuilding programme. This not only kept their staff in work, it ensured that war surplus Leylands, when they did come onto the market, looked good, ran well and sustained their maker's reputation. Meanwhile, the market for new vehicles suffered a serious slump.

One of the themes of this book is the way in which, after each major war, those concerned with transport attempted to specify and build ideal military vehicles. And this regardless of cost, commercial pressure or even common sense to some extent. Now it must be said that this did not happen at once after the First World War. As we shall shortly see, it was not really until 1927 that the War Office sanctioned such a plan with the appearance of the rigid six-wheeler, although the earlier advent of the half-track might be regarded as a false start in this direction. However, there was a scheme, already progressing when the war ended, which for its ambition puts all others into the shade.

The invention of the tank, in 1915, had a profound effect on the whole business of military mechanisation and it inspired some people to believe that

MWEE not only tested new vehicles, it was also empowered to conduct experiments. This was an attempt to improve the cross-country performance of a 6 x 4, carried out in 1931. A standard Morris-Commercial D Type has an extra, driven, steering axle added at the front, making it an 8 x 6.

there was nothing that tracked vehicles could not achieve. Some results of this process have already been noted but in 1918 it was concentrated with the formation of the Department of Tank Design and Experiment at Woolwich. Its original purpose was to create a series of high-speed, amphibious tanks which, it was believed, could revolutionise land warfare. The moving spirit behind this project was Colonel J.F.C. Fuller, the Tank Corps' tactical genius, but the man who turned his ideas into mechanical reality was Lieutenant-Colonel Philip Johnson. An innovative Tank Corps officer, Johnson had visions way beyond his brief and his department embarked upon a whole range of experiments, which aimed at providing the British Army with tracked vehicles to fulfil every purpose. Thus, in addition to tanks, artillery and reconnaissance machines, Johnson's team created prototypes of full- and half-tracked lorries, staff cars and even a despatch rider's motorcycle. These were relatively practical examples, but the Department also indulged in some applied research on the wider aspects of tracked vehicle design, which might, in the fullness of time, have resulted in vast improvements, but it never got the chance.

Johnson was particularly concerned about three factors. First, the matter of rolling resistance; this he attempted to solve with principles not unlike some of Diplock's ideas for his Pedrails. Second, the steering which, with any tracked vehicle, is the principal cause of material stress and waste of power. Johnson introduced a system of curving track, which was intended to overcome this. Thirdly, he investigated suspension, which was a very new field, since none of the wartime British tanks had any springs at all. Springs at every wheel station created a weight problem, which Johnson sought to overcome by a complicated system of wire cables that acted from master springs and, theoretically, carried their effect to all parts of the vehicle. It was the cutting edge of technology at the time. Indeed, it probably went beyond it, and that meant extended development time and considerable expense, which the War Office simply could not justify in peacetime. Johnson's experimental department was closed down in 1923 and a lot of very strange prototypes went to the scrapheap, but the designer had already set himself up for the future by founding Roadless Traction Ltd, which he intended to activate when he retired from the Army.

Johnson's ideas extended beyond the military although he continued to cater for the service market as we shall see. He was steeped in the traditions established by people such as Crompton, Diplock and Kégresse who hoped to extend the benefits of mechanical transport to the very ends of the earth. His vision was encapsulated in a sketch by the motoring artist F. Gordon Crosby, which shows a highway scene in Britain where fully-tracked lorries and buses mingle with tracked motorcycles, touring and sports cars while a tractor, similarly equipped, ploughs a nearby field.

Another problem facing anyone who wished to create a world full of tracked vehicles was that of re-training drivers. Steering tracklayers is an art in itself, quite different from that required for wheeled machines. Johnson's curvable tracks would have solved this to some extent and it was possible, by using a conventional steering wheel linked to the track brakes, instead of the more normal levers, to make it simpler still. This appears to have been the intention behind the design of a 'Caterlorry' that appeared in 1919 and may well be attributable to Johnson. The prototype was a normal Peerless Army lorry mounted on a pair of track frames, instead of wheels, which was designed to be easy enough for the average MT driver to handle with just the most basic instruction. Nothing came of it, but there would be other tracked lorries.

Although it had sold off vast stocks of surplus vehicles, the War Office still maintained a number in service and, under the stringent financial constraints imposed by a peacetime budget, it was clearly not going to be easy to persuade the Treasury to release funds for new types. Indeed, since the pre-war condition of an annual vote for service funding had been reinstated in 1919, the armed forces had been told that they must live off their fat for as long as possible.

Even so, there was a noticeable gap in the military fleet. Although 3-tonners were fine for long-distance convoy work and, at the other end of the scale, the Model-T Ford was still ideal for handling loads up to about half-a-ton, the problem lay somewhere in between. The Army needed a medium payload vehicle with a reasonable cross-country performance suitable for first-line transport duties, so the War Office decided to create a new specification, eligible for a government subsidy, which was intended to come into effect in 1921. It was nowhere near as ambitious as Philip Johnson's schemes, but it was progressive enough to attract criticism.

At first sight it would hardly seem to be an opportune time for persuading the British commercial motor industry to invest in designs for a new subsidy scheme. However, there were some important considerations. One was simply that many manufacturers would welcome something to do. They had the revenue from wartime contracts to invest in research and development and there was bound to come a time when the supply of worn-out Army lorries would come to an end. Equally it was true that not every customer wanted to run a motley collection of tired old military vehicles. They might be acceptable to anyone hoping to start up as a local carrier in his home town, but larger companies wished to project a more modern image that would be enhanced by a fleet of smart new vehicles.

As we have seen, British attempts to produce 30cwt vehicles during the war had not proved successful. Those firms involved in the production of 30cwts had merely developed lighter versions of their subsidy 3-tonners, which were normally overloaded in service and suffered accordingly. Yet experience with Italian types, notably the Lancia IZ and Fiat 15 ter, had revealed that lighter vehicles, fitted with pneumatic tyres,

A side-on view of the Caterlorry, based on a war-surplus Peerless, demonstrating its ability to cross a sunken road.

This 30cwt Crossley has been posed for the camera and is displaying its touring car ancestry.

A Halley 30cwt, built in Glasgow. The firm had been building lorries since 1901 and this is reflected in its construction. The body is a mobile office design which would have only been produced in limited numbers.

Britain was obliged to make a show of strength to restrain Turkish ambitions. Among the units mobilised and sent to Chanak, south of Constantinople, was No 9 MT Company RASC, equipped with the new vehicles. In fact these do not appear to have been subsidy lorries, which were probably not available yet, but most likely Crossleys of a similar type developed during the war for the old Russian Army.

The Chanak affair came to nothing and a similar fate appeared to be in store for the new subsidy scheme. The specifications proved to be so stringent that no potential manufacturer seemed interested in taking it up. The specifications were duly modified in 1923 and four British firms, Albion, Karrier, Clement-Talbot and Crossley offered prototypes. The significance of this was not lost upon the motoring press, which noticed that the second pair of firms was not of the commercial fraternity. They had always been known as builders of good quality private motor

were far better. Specifications were duly drawn up in 1922 and British firms invited to submit designs. At the same time a crisis intervened that appeared to justify the scheme. Greece invaded the Turkish mainland in 1921. The Turkish Army fought back and effectively ended the war in October 1922. Inspired by this success the new government of Kemal Ataturk claimed the right to reoccupy the Gallipoli peninsula and

4 PEACETIME DEVELOPMENTS

cars. This was yet another result of the war. Both companies had watched as the armed forces converted their handsome touring cars into rough utilities, or tenders and they were quick to sense a new market. Even so, the lorries they offered for the subsidy scheme had much more in common with large motor cars than those of their rivals who had adapted commercial vehicle practice to produce lighter vehicles. The secret of this lighter construction, in both cases, was the use of alloys instead of steel for various major components, including wheels, and the fitting of pneumatic tyres, which were stipulated by the subsidy specifications; indeed, they had to be British pneumatic tyres. This move was strongly resisted by the commercial vehicle industry at the time but the War Office was subsequently commended for leading the way in this development, at least in Britain, when the advantages became obvious.

In 1925 Guy, Halley, Thornycroft and Vulcan joined the scheme and it appears to have been successful. The quota of 1,000 was soon filled and the Indian Army adopted similar vehicles. In the same year it was planned to introduce a programme for 15cwt vehicles but this was rendered redundant by a new development in France. In February 1921, the industrialist André Citroën demonstrated a fleet of half-tracked vehicles in the French Alps. The track system had been invented by Adolphe Kégresse while he was in charge of the Czar's motor fleet, but Kégresse fled Russia at the time of the Revolution and ultimately teamed up with Citroën. Interest from Britain resulted in the creation of a London branch trading as Citroën-Kégresse Ltd, which included Sir Ernest Swinton, the tank pioneer, among its directors. The Royal Artillery purchased a few Citroën-Kégresse staff cars but there was clearly a desire for British types and, since the system was adaptable to most vehicles, both

This Burford-Kégresse half-track is at what appears to be an important occasion with one of the Royal Daimlers close by.

Crossleys, in Manchester, and Burfords in London started to produce half-tracked vehicles, with the Kégresse attachment for civil and military use.

The relative success of Citroën's project tempted Philip Johnson to offer his own design. Since the Department of Tank Design and Experiment had been closed down Johnson activated his company, Roadless Traction Ltd, and, from a succession of experimental vehicles, produced a half-track system to rival the French design. Having abandoned cable suspension for a more conventional system and devised a form of track, which employed metal plates and rubber blocks in compression, Johnson came up with a unit that replaced the rear wheels of a standard vehicle, just as Kégresse did, but with a shorter ground contact. Although tested on a whole range of commercial vehicles the Roadless system was only adopted for production by three manufacturers: FWD Motors, Morris-Commercial and Guy Motors. These last two supplied a few Roadless-equipped 30cwt lorries to the War Office.

The half-track was a compromise. It had the advantage over a normal, wheeled vehicle of improved cross-country performance but was simpler for the average driver to control than a fully tracked machine and less of a problem on the road. In addition to its military application many saw it as

A Morris-Roadless civilian demonstrator. Military versions of the half-track had soft-top cabs.

The experimental Renault 6 x 4 vehicle acquired by the RASC Training College.

of the armour in order to sustain the advance. Burford built Kégresse vehicles in the 30cwt and 3-ton class while Crossley concentrated on 15cwt and 30cwt types with just one odd 3-tonner. Morris-Commercial and Guy stuck to the 30cwt size. But the age of the half-track, at least the British built half-track was brief, the pace of invention, liberated by technologies developed during the war, continued to speed up.

By 1925, the permanent military fleet had dwindled, mainly due to wear and tear. Army manoeuvres, held in September of that year over parts of Hampshire and Surrey, could only proceed once a sizeable fleet of commercial lorries had been hired. A Mr G. Streeter, who drove a 3-ton

another step towards freeing the motor vehicle from reliance on well-made roads, which would permit exploitation of resources in under-developed countries where highways and railways were too expensive to justify. It is a recurring theme in commercial vehicle development in those countries with extensive colonial responsibilities and was seen by many as the commercial counterpart of military requirements.

The new tanks employed by the British Army from 1923 onwards had a potential mobility that far exceeded that of the original models from the First World War. Modern ideology now perceived the tank as a sort of land warship, to be operated as part of a fleet ranging far and wide over the countryside with no need to rely upon roads. The half-track helped to support this concept because its mobility was similar. It could transport troops and supplies or tow artillery in the wake

4 PEACETIME DEVELOPMENTS

Commer in the manoeuvres, wrote of his experiences for *Motor Transport*. It was, he said, not quite the holiday he was expecting. He reckoned his Commer as reliable and good as any other make taking part; being relatively high geared it performed well on roads but he noted that mixed convoys were always at the mercy of the slower models. Often, he found, they were grinding up hills in low gear because the vehicle in front could not travel any faster.

At the time Streeter was on manoeuvres the first post-war subsidy scheme was in operation. He personally observed Albion and Halley 30cwts in active service and remarked how much better they were off the road, over wet and rough ground, which the heavier vehicles could not have managed. Yet he did not believe the 30cwts would be as useful for long journeys over good roads because they lacked carrying capacity.

The centre of the universe, as far as the RASC was concerned, was Aldershot in Hampshire. Here they had their main headquarters and training establishments, in particular the RASC Training College presided over by Professor Herbert Niblett, with the honorary rank of colonel, and his staff of enthusiastic officers. Despite its title the Training College was a hotbed of innovation from which a number of

A Guy BAX, 3-ton 6 x 4 chassis on test at MWEE. This one has an experimental suspension system for the front axle.

interesting vehicles had already been developed. In 1925 it made what was arguably one of the most significant contributions to the development of military transport – although the story begins in France.

Since his adoption of the Kégresse half-track system, André Citroën had staged a series of high-profile expeditions, or 'raids' as he styled them, which were intended to prove that his vehicles could go just about anywhere. They crossed the Sahara Desert, the mountains of Central Asia, the Canadian Rockies and parts of Antarctica with a degree of publicity, which only a consummate marketing man like Citroën could engineer. Armies all over the world were examining his vehicles although it has to be said that commercial interest was always limited. As a boy at school in Paris, Citroën had met the young Louis Renault and by 1923 the two men were powerful commercial rivals. Observing Citroën's success in that year Renault set out to prove that the same success could be achieved by a wheeled vehicle.

His designers produced a six-wheeled version of the Renault 10CV car, which made a successful expedition into the Sahara in 1924.

A short time afterwards the RASC Training College obtained a similar vehicle from France and began to test it. In modern terminology the Renault would be described as a 6 x 4 – that is, a six-wheeled vehicle on which the four rear wheels were driven. They were mounted on two axles in a self-contained bogie, articulated to the frame so that the wheels conformed to the surface on uneven ground. Niblett and his team liked the system but discovered some failings in the design, which they set out to remedy. The result was a patent, taken out in Niblett's name, which described a system that gave the maximum possible traction in the worst conditions. It was known as the 'War Department Pattern articulated rear bogie', or WD Pattern bogie, and it soon became the standard by which all others were judged. In order to promote the scheme for both civilian and military

The large and handsome Leyland Bull Terrier mounting a workshop body.

purposes use of the patent was granted free to any British manufacturer who was prepared to design vehicles to British military requirements.

The new WD Pattern bogie was suitable for both 30cwt and 3ton vehicles so new subsidy specifications were prepared for both. There was good reason to be hopeful. The original 1923 scheme was successful to the point that the total of 1,000 registered vehicles was reached by 1926 and this undoubtedly inspired manufacturers to look favourably upon the new schemes. Most of the top names in the British commercial vehicle industry decided to participate. Some, like Guy Motors and later AEC built for the 3-ton class only. Others such as Morris-Commercial and Garner stuck to the 30cwt size, while Crossley Motors and Thornycrofts were among those that built chassis in both sizes. Leyland, who became a major producer, even developed a 5-tonner, the impressive Bull Terrier, which saw limited service.

To what extent did the subsidy scheme succeed in this instance? It is difficult to find accurate figures but circumstantial evidence suggests that the six-wheelers were not popular. Any number of reasons can be proposed but in the main it seems that these new chassis were just a little too closely attuned to military requirements to be entirely suitable for normal trade use.

Few commercial operators needed lorries with the off-road ability of the 6 x 4 and the high loading line of the body, designed to allow free movement of the rear bogie, could be a nuisance when loading and unloading goods. Likewise, the cab was decidedly spartan. By the early 1930s, most British Army lorries were of the forward control type, in order to make best possible use of the chassis, but the cabs were open to the elements, with no windscreen and just a folding canvas hood and side screens

A Crossley 6 x 4 forward control chassis during manufacturer's trials.

and a pin-up apron for the driver if the weather really turned nasty. British transport drivers were a tough bunch, they needed to be, but they preferred an enclosed cab and windscreen if they could get one.

An owner with a subsidy fleet was free to fit the cab and body of his choice but the military style cab and body had to be stored in case the vehicle was required for war service. All of which meant more expense for the user, which was hardly compensated for by the meagre subsidy payments. This divergence between military and civilian requirements is another recurring theme that has never been entirely resolved. Those vehicles supplied direct to the armed forces were mostly operated with wooden general service bodies, but a whole range of specialist applications was created from mobile kitchens and workshops to searchlight vehicles, ambulances and cranes. When the scheme began, petrol engines were universal and invariably quite low-powered. It was War Office policy to use smaller engines coupled to a primary four-speed gearbox and subsidiary two-speed range but subsequent developments included larger engines and a gradual change to diesel by some manufacturers. Whether they were a commercial success or not this range of six-wheelers dominated

British Army transport in the 30cwt and 3-ton classes from 1927 until well into the Second World War despite later developments.

Commercial vehicle taxation was related to unladen weight rather than to size of engine, it effectively stifled the incentive to develop large engines because there was little demand for them. The only exception was in respect of public service vehicles and in many ways the British motor bus industry led the field when it came to developing larger engines and more effective transmissions. But there was another influence at work. In his 1929 budget the Chancellor of the Exchequer reintroduced a tax on petrol, at 4d a gallon. The immediate result was a sudden increase of interest in the compression ignition, or diesel engine. A great deal of work had already been done on the Continent in this direction and a number of British firms, starting with Leyland Motors, began to install imported diesels in their vehicles after paying immense sums for the privilege.

In the meantime, various engine builders in Britain had been developing diesel engines of their own based on experiments carried out by the brilliant research engineer Harry Ricardo. So successful was his work that by 1928 most British vehicle manufacturers had abandoned their foreign interests and swung behind the home industry, which was developing a new, and highly efficient type of direct injection engine.

As a result, the Mechanical Warfare Board was obliged to take notice and its report for 1928/9 dealt with the subject in great detail. In 1933 it stated that diesel engines were the outstanding feature of that year's Commercial Motor Transport Exhibition and concluded that: 'This type of engine is tending to become the standard for all heavy goods and many of the larger passenger vehicles.'

By 1935 diesel engines were well established, despite an increase in duty on oil fuel. One of the Mechanical Warfare Board's members, Mr Shave of the London Passenger Transport Board, estimated that, when every consideration was taken into account, there was a saving of over one penny per mile with diesel-powered vehicles over those using petrol. And so the reports go on, year after year up to the outbreak of the Second World War, reporting technical advances in engine design and remarking on their spread throughout the trade. Yet the Board made no comment on the relevance or application of diesel power to military vehicles. At least, that is to say, the Board describes new military vehicles fitted with such engines and reviews technical matters. What it does not do is attempt to discuss how diesels fit into current military thinking, or how they affect military plans.

The reason is obvious: it doesn't matter. The kind of thinking that resulted in the Crosland Committee report of 1935, to be mentioned later, effectively reduced the War Office to the status of a poodle where the British commercial vehicle industry was concerned. Shorn of whatever influence a subsidy scheme afforded, the military could do little more than watch the direction in which commercial trends led, and follow obediently. Obviously, they still had a say where individual designs and details were concerned but they could no longer lead the way. That was for the trade to decide, but the trade in its turn was being manipulated by government generated taxation and legislation which, to some considerable extent, was reacting to pressure from the railway lobby.

Army Council Instruction 443 of 1927 announced that the responsibility for research, experiment, design, manufacture, issue and repair (among other things) of mechanical transport would be transferred from the department of the Quartermaster General to that of the Master General of Ordnance. The former would remain responsible for provision and repair of RASC vehicles but it was the business of research, experiment and design that was crucial. The change was intended to reflect the great expansion in the use of mechanical transport by the armed forces but it was fiercely resisted by the RASC and regarded with dismay by many civilian engineers, if their influential journal *The Engineer* is to be believed. Major-General S.S. Long, the forthright wartime Director of Supplies and Transport, added his weight to the argument but to no avail.

The problem, from the RASC point of view, was aggravated by concern about loss of prestige but it had a practical aspect. For many years the RASC had taken the lead in design and development of new vehicles and one of its greatest achievements, the WD Pattern bogie, has already been recorded. During this time its officers had not only acquired a great deal of practical experience, they had also formed useful relationships with many manufacturers, which were seen as valuable links between the commercial and military worlds. Now, if an officer wished to continue this work, he was obliged to transfer to the Royal Army Ordnance Corps (RAOC). From this and other causes including premature retirement, the RASC lost many highly qualified men.

Another important manifestation of this change concerned the RASC Training College. Its counterpart at Farnborough was the Tank and Tracked Transport Experimental Establishment, the function of which is self-explanatory. In fact Farnborough also handled some of the more exotic wheeled vehicles and there was already some duplication in the work of the two establishments before they were amalgamated as the

Chosen by 30 Governments

NO less than 30 Governments in all parts of the world have built up big fleets of Albions. Their experts have confirmed, often after severest tests, the Albion's supreme efficiency and absolute reliability even under the most arduous working conditions.

Thirty years' highly developed specialised engineering skill and manufacturing experience are behind every Albion built.

Write to-day for particulars.
Load capacity, 30-cwt. to 5 tons.

The Albion 30/45-h.p. rigid six-wheeler now in use by the British War Office, Government of India, Australian Defence Force, King's African Rifles and the Gold Coast Government.

Albion

ALBION MOTOR CAR CO. LTD
SCOTSTOUN,   GLASGOW.
London: BANK BUILDINGS, 20 KINGSWAY, W.C.2
Also at MANCHESTER,
LEEDS, SHEFFIELD, BIRMINGHAM AND BRISTOL.

Mechanical Warfare Experimental Establishment (MWEE) in 1927. The MWEE was essentially an instrument of the Mechanical Warfare Board, which monitored all aspects of military vehicle production. Its annual reports, including those of the Mechanisation Board, which succeeded it in 1934, are models of balanced, accurate and detailed reporting and they drive home,

Albion Motors made much of their military sales in contemporary advertisements.

better than any other contemporary source, the extent to which military transport developments were linked to the ruling commercial situation. As part of its annual report the Board commented upon trends in commercial vehicle design, having despatched representatives to all the relevant vehicle shows in Britain.

The situation with regard to road haulage in Britain was considered by many as little short of anarchy. It was an inevitable result of the immediate post-war explosion in road transport. Competition was fierce and regulations few. No licence was required to set up in business and the only restriction, beyond the obvious one of staying solvent, was the vehicle taxation law. Tax was calculated on the net weight of a vehicle, not the load it could carry, so manufacturers were encouraged to produce the lightest possible chassis, powered by low-rated engines, to carry the largest possible load. The most unfortunate result of this lack of legislation was felt by the railway companies who lost a lot of their freight business. The government sponsored various Royal Commissions and committees to examine the situation, which resulted in a number of Acts of Parliament in the early 1930s.

The situation in India during this same period was equally active. During a tour of inspection in 1929, Colonel Davidson, representing the Mechanical Warfare Board, noted with approval that active service conditions on the frontier provided the best possible testing facilities for both vehicles and men. In order to pacify the area a circular road was built through the mountainous country of Waziristan, reaching its peak at the isolated Razmak camp, nearly 8,000ft above sea level and said at the time to be the largest armed camp in the world. Being narrow in places and often confined to ledges, the road was normally operated as a one-way route but it was engineered in such a way that steep hills were generally avoided. Instead the road would climb, often for very long stretches, through a series of hairpin bends like the famous Greenwood's Corner, which placed a

A convoy of six 3-tonners negotiating Greenwoods Corner en route for Razmak camp. A damaged section of wall visible behind the fourth lorry suggests that not everyone got round unscathed.

considerable strain on the vehicles and their drivers.

For the men the main problem was an unseen enemy. Even when no state of war existed frontier tribes believed it was their manly duty to attack Anglo-Indian forces wherever they were most vulnerable. Slow resupply convoys, winding their way through the passes, were ideal targets. Snipers, blending into the very boulders of the hillside, only had to disable a couple of lorries by killing their drivers to bring large sections of the convoy to a halt. Although the lorries were escorted by armoured cars it was difficult enough for them to deal with the situation. The ambush at Shahur Tangi, in April 1937, is an excellent example.

The Shahur Tangi is a narrow defile in the mountains of north Waziristan through which the Shahur river runs. The road to the military camp at Wana ran along a ledge for 3 miles in this narrow valley, which has no vegetation in it and looks about as barren as any place on earth. The road, at the time, was unsealed but well maintained with a fringe of stone on the precipitous side. While there was trouble in the area, resupply convoys were being run on alternate days from the railhead at Manzai to Wana or Razmak. The distance was between 60 and 70 miles and, because the amount of transport available was limited, it was essential to complete the trip, there and back, in one day. The shortage of military vehicles meant that hired commercial lorries were being used and the convoy that left Manzai on Friday 9 April 1937 consisted of 31 Thornycroft 3-ton six-wheelers and 16 civilian vehicles. It also included two private cars for the convoy commanders and a Ford van. The escort consisted of 60 men and 4/16 Punjabis, a detachment of Sappers and Miners to clear road blocks and four Crossley armoured cars of No 1 Section, 8th Light Tank Company, Royal Tank Corps. An aircraft was acting as an extra lookout but the fortified posts that covered the pass were not occupied.

The convoy was organised with the lorries in groups of five, with one armoured car leading, another at the rear and the other two interspersed among the lorries, which also carried small parties of the escorting infantry. The whole convoy occupied about 2 miles of road and the leading armoured car *Chitral* with the company despatch rider in attendance, was just approaching the far end of the valley when trouble began.

Transport with a heavy escort of armoured cars on a typical section of the Khyber Pass road.

An ambush in the Pass. A civilian Bedford with a bullet hole through the windscreen stands abandoned on the road. Part of its load has been scattered and two bodies lie at the roadside.

BRITISH MILITARY TRANSPORT 1829-1956

An American Model-A Ford pick-up with a light tank company in India.

Unobserved by the aircraft, tribesmen were hiding all along the hillside overlooking the road and, as if on a signal, they all opened fire. Men leapt from the lorries and quite a few were hit. The first three lorries behind *Chitral* got clear but the driver of the fourth lorry, a hired Bedford, was hit and the remainder of the convoy stopped behind him. The other armoured cars were effectively boxed in. Machine-gun fire from the cars prevented the enemy from rushing the convoy and looting it but snipers on both sides, especially the south, kept everyone pinned down.

The battle raged for two days. Attempts were regularly made to extract more vehicles. Some had been damaged and one caught fire while an escaped horse, rushing up and down in panic, did not help. Even when more armoured cars and infantry reinforcements arrived it was hard work subduing the enemy and by the end of the action seven British officers and 29 other personnel, including civilian drivers, British and Indian infantry had been killed. It was subsequently considered that the escort was inadequate for such a large convoy and that the armoured cars were of limited value since they could not operate off the road. However, in country of this kind that consideration would have applied equally to tanks.

The procurement of military vehicles for India was entirely independent of the War Office in London, but for obvious reasons British vehicles were almost universal and they were invariably similar to their British counterparts. The civilian scene was quite different. A number of American companies had established themselves in India and General Motors products were universally popular. When civilian vehicles were hired for military use they were often Chevrolets and it soon became apparent to the soldiers how much better a six-cylinder engine could cope with the demanding gradients. Some British manufacturers took up the challenge but it is noticeable that by the mid-1930s many of the smaller vehicles in service with the Indian Army were Chevrolets or American Fords. It is probably fair to say that this had as much to do with marketing techniques as quality of product. American firms have, it seems, always known something that it took their British rivals decades to learn. That is, if you endeavour to give the customer what he wants, and make spare parts readily available, you will get the business.

British forces operating in the Middle East came more directly under control from London. There is evidence of some effort to consider conditions outside

4 PEACETIME DEVELOPMENTS

Britain when vehicle specifications were being prepared but the overall impression remains that vehicles were designed primarily for use at home. The result was a spirit of make do, personified by Major Ralph Bagnold, an RASC officer serving in Egypt in 1925. Rather than take a conventional leave each year Bagnold, with a group of like-minded officers, would set off into the desert in a convoy of old Ford cars, adapted for an expedition. They learned a great deal about the skills needed to drive and navigate in the worst possible conditions, often setting out in the face of considerable official opposition. Bagnold himself was one of that select band of eccentric British officers who carve a peculiar niche for themselves. He became obsessed with the desert and was regarded as something of an expert, later putting his experience to good use in the Second World War for the benefit of the Long Range Desert Group.

Colonel Davidson, during his 1929 inspection tour, urged a greater exchange of information between users abroad and manufacturers at home, but the only noticeable results were an increased interest in the design of air filters and the development of good sand tyres. At home most lorries had twin wheels on each rear axle fitted with narrow, high-pressure tyres. In sand these easily became clogged, leading the authorities to demand single, low-pressure tyres all round, a practice that spread back to Britain. Some British military prototypes were completed with enclosed cabs – which in many respects might have been just as welcome at home – but production models invariably appeared with canvas hoods and no windscreen. Drivers had to manage with the pith helmet and goggles.

In 1932, the British Command in Egypt initiated what were known as 'War Office Experimental Convoys' using officers and men from all mechanised branches of the service. The original 1932 event involved a Riley 9hp car, a Morris 12cwt van, a Crossley 3-ton

Rigours of the 1932 Experimental Convoy: the Crossley 3-tonner, with chains around its rear wheels, recovers the Morris van from a swamp.

A Morris-Commercial CDF 30cwt kicking up the dust in the desert. It is fitted with large section desert tyres and appears to be towing a light tank.

A Thornycroft 3-ton, six-wheeler, with tracks on its rear wheels, tackles a heather-clad slope during the 1927 Wool Trials in Dorset.

The impressive Vickers-Armstrong tracked truck on test with a heavy load. Although never tested officially by the Army, it aroused a good deal of interest in military circles.

A Vickers-Carden-Loyd light utility tractor and trailer being tested on a folding boat ferry on the River Stour at Christchurch. The driver sits ahead of the engine, with a cargo pannier on each side.

6 x 4 lorry and a Commer Raider four-wheeled 30cwt, with crews drawn from the Royal Artillery, RAOC, Royal Engineers, Royal Tank Corps and, naturally, the RASC. The route ran for some 5,000 miles out into the desert, back to the Nile, south to the Abyssinian frontier and then east to Port Sudan, with a return run up the Red Sea coast and then inland from Suez to the Nile and back to Cairo. It is probably true to say that it taught the men more about operating British vehicles in a harsh environment than it did about the need to design transport more particularly for such conditions.

Similar vehicle trials in Britain date back to 1925 when the first event was staged at Wool in Dorset, adjacent to the Royal Tank Corps Centre at Bovington Camp. Here, on acres of military heathland, a variety of vehicles including half-tracks and some of the prototype six-wheelers were put through their paces over some unpleasant marshland and challenging slopes. The success of half-tracks at this first trial inspired Adolphe Kégresse to throw his hat into the air and exclaim *'le mort de la roue'* (the death of the wheel) but six-wheelers dominated the 1927 Wool Trials and as far as Britain was concerned it was the half-track that was dead.

From the mid-1930s onwards a location near Llangollen was used for trials since the mountain roads were considered closer to conditions in India, suggesting that the War Office had at least paid some heed to Davidson's advice. These North Wales Trials became an annual event up to the outbreak of the Second World War and manufacturers were encouraged to bring along their own vehicles.

The desert was not so easy to simulate but trials were sometimes conducted in the dunes at Studland Bay in Dorset where much was learned about the performance of tyres, which reinforced the lesson about the advantage of large section, low-pressure covers for use on soft ground.

With the demise of the half-track the subject of first-line transport was reconsidered. The rapid expansion of mechanisation in the British Army had now reached the point when transport for front-line infantry battalions could be studied. This coincided with a time when the British Government had founded a committee to consider the subject of transport in the wilder parts of the Empire. Among the members was Professor Herbert Niblett. Some of the vehicles that took their fancy were tested at Farnborough and at least to that extent came to the attention of the military. However, the majority were clearly both specialised and technically complex, which in turn meant that they were expensive and thus beyond the military budget.

One such vehicle was a large lorry, built by Vickers-Armstrong in 1932, which ran on four sets of tracks. It was marketed for commercial use in under-developed countries but the manufacturer would not have objected to military customers. It was certainly examined by service personnel and even described at some length in the *Royal Tank Corps Journal*, but never adopted, and it appears to have enjoyed no commercial success either. A few all-wheel drive eight-wheelers, complete with road trains, were built by Leyland and AEC for use in Africa and Australia but they also proved too expensive for general adoption. Perhaps it was part of the nature of pioneering colonials that they would make the best of what was available, rather than go to vast expense where transport was concerned. There were few enough places that a Model-T Ford would not go, as Bagnold had discovered, and once the value of a location had been established it was not long before proper roads or railways were extended to reach it.

Even so, Vickers-Armstrong was determined to make a commercial success of tracked vehicles and, in the early 1930s, developed a tiny, tracked tractor for one man, powered by a Ford engine. The firm's publicity department went to great lengths to establish a place for it in the market, showing it doing everything from ploughing and shunting railway wagons to towing canal barges but, as usual, the trade seemed to shy away from such specialised machines. The British Army, however, thought otherwise and purchased them in considerable numbers. The vehicle itself was fitted with load-carrying panniers on each side and supplied with a small, two-wheeled trailer which, altogether, gave a payload of around 15cwt. The vehicles were issued to infantry battalions as a means of transporting soldiers' kit on cross-country operations and appear to have proved quite successful for a while. Yet, inevitably, there were those who believed that a conventional vehicle could be produced to do the same job and the result was another very famous, and typically British product, the 15cwt platoon truck.

Rival designs were submitted by various firms and produced in small numbers but the leader, without a doubt, was Morris-Commercial. Although the little Morris, like its rivals, was constructed mainly from commercial parts it was an exclusively military vehicle; few commercial organisations could have any use for such a thing. It had a very short wheelbase to give a good cross-country performance, but in order to get the best possible use from the body a sort of semi-forward control layout was adopted for the cab, in which the driver and his mate sat with their legs either side of the engine, giving the trucks a distinctive front-end shape. Following trials in Egypt, Morris-Commercial also developed an 8cwt version, which was considered to be more suitable for desert operations, but the 15cwt was

BRITISH MILITARY TRANSPORT 1829-1956

also built by Bedford, Commer, Guy and Ford in considerable numbers. Both Guy and Morris Commercial later produced four-wheel drive variants.

The Road and Rail Traffic Act of 1933 imposed a whole range of restrictions on road haulage, with the intention of retrieving business for the railways. Although heavily criticised at the time, it also protected the efficient road operator from pirates. It did this by a system of licencing, which was graduated in favour of the local haulage contractor while it penalised the long-distance haulier. Linked to the continued system of taxing vehicles by unladen weight it had a detrimental effect on the development of larger lorries and concentrated interest in conventional 4 x 2 types with payloads around 3 tons. Recognising the results of this the War Office decided to investigate the respective merits of 6 x 4 and 4 x 2 vehicles when it ordained the formation of the Crosland Committee in 1935. It was probably no more than a coincidence but, soon after the committee began its deliberations, the government announced a major change in British defence policy. Until 1933, the emphasis had been on the defence of India, which was known as the Eastern Plan. That it lasted so long suggests a failure by the government to appreciate what was happening in Europe.

By 1935, matters could hardly be ignored and a Western Plan, based on a future war in Europe, was deemed to have priority. The Crosland Committee naturally took this into account. It argued that Europe, with its good roads and intensive railway network, reduced the need for six-wheeled vehicles by about 50 per cent and recommended that they should be replaced by conventional four-wheelers. It went on to say that the concept of a subsidy scheme was entirely out of date and suggested that it be replaced entirely by a system of impressment. As far back as 1926, government response to the General Strike had shown that, in an emergency, enough vehicles could be mobilised to keep essential services running. By 1936, it argued, there should be sufficient vehicles available to mechanise a substantial part of an enlarged Army but that, in any case,

A typical result of Crosland Committee thinking. A commercial Bedford WH 2-tonner fitted with oversize Dunlop tyres for military use.

a good deal of tonnage would be handled by the railways.

In 1929, as a result of the earlier Experimental Mechanised Force, the War Office had issued a booklet entitled *Mechanized and Armoured Formations*. Known familiarly as the 'Purple Primer' due to the tint of its covers, the booklet was compiled by Lieutenant-General Sir Charles Broad and its purpose was to educate serving personnel into the mysteries of mechanical warfare. In fact it had a wider readership because it was also published by His Majesty's Stationery Office and sold to the general public despite a panel on the cover that stated it was FOR OFFICIAL USE ONLY and not to be communicated to the press or anyone not holding an official position in His Majesty's Service.

Whether many were sold, except to parties with some professional interest, is another matter. However, to those who did understand its import the booklet was regarded as somewhat revolutionary. Historians tend to concentrate on that part of it which concerns tanks, but in reality it covered all those elements that would go towards creating a comprehensive mobile striking force. In 1931, a revised edition appeared, entitled *Modern Formations*, which took a step backwards by including mounted cavalry divisions but, for our purposes we will concentrate on the transport aspect and, in particular, the return of the bus. The terms 'embus', or 'debus', are employed by the military to describe the process by which troops board transport vehicles or disembark from them, but in this case the meaning was quite literal. Provisional War Establishment tables were included among the appendices in the revised edition. The tables covered various tank formations and what were listed as 'Omnibus Companies, RASC'.

The basic vehicle was deemed to be a 28-seater omnibus, presumably a single-decker in that case, and the total number in such a company was 115, of which 11 were held as spares. The remaining 104 were divided between four sections of 26 buses each, which would be able to lift the four battalions of an infantry brigade, which already had mechanised first-line transport. Individual sections could also be taken from the company to operate as an integral part of a tank brigade. There were minor variations, depending on whether such a brigade was a mixed type, with light and medium tanks or one of the new light tank brigades. Taking the former as an example, one

An early example of the little Morris-Commercial 8cwt. This version was designed specifically for use in the Sudan.

A Morris-Commercial 15cwt of the second series showing the distinctive bonnet shape.

107

An occasion that saw large numbers of Army lorries in London was the 1926 General Strike. Here a long column, mainly composed of wartime vehicles escorted by Peerless armoured cars, waits in the rain.

bus would be allocated to brigade headquarters, six more would work with the light tank battalion while the remaining 15 would be split evenly between the three mixed tank battalions. Within each tank battalion the five or six buses would be allocated to the battalion headquarters and close support section. The odd thing is that, neither in *Modern Formations*, nor in any obvious contemporary document, is there any indication of where these buses were to come from. Very small charabancs on both Crossley and Talbot chassis had been tested by the military authorities and, in the early 1930s the Mechanisation Experimental Establishment (MEE), successor to MWEE, had examined something more modern, a Morris-Commercial Viceroy single-decker. Yet the Viceroy would not have been suitable for the establishment proposed by Broad because it was only a 20-seater. Public service vehicle legislation at this time would not allow a bus with more than 20 seats to be used for one-man operation and this was an important feature for many small operators. On the other hand, larger fleets, who used single-deckers as coaches or buses, were not so worried about the crew aspect and they wanted

to get as many seats as possible onto the chassis. Thus, most manufacturers not catering for the one-man operation market built single-deckers that could carry up to 35 passengers. It seems as if the War Office ideal fell between stools.

Modern Formations devotes a special appendix to the operation of bus columns. Recognising the fact that they could not be expected to operate off the roads it then goes on to discuss how they should be handled when operating in areas where the location of the enemy is uncertain. Surprise attacks were to be avoided at all costs. It would take far too long for 28 men to evacuate their bus and deploy, while encumbered with weapons and equipment (packs would not be worn) and, even if they did, what would the buses do? They needed more room to turn around than the average road provided so the only alternatives must be to remain halted, like sitting ducks, or drive on into unknown territory. The revised 'Purple Primer' laid down that, under such conditions, bus columns would be escorted but they would only proceed in bounds from one suitable turning point to the next when that had been secured from attack. In other words, there would be reconnaissance vehicles operating ahead of the bus column, which would locate a place where the vehicles could turn around and then authorise it to proceed to that place. If this was not possible the infantry would debus, deploy and proceed on foot.

The extent to which this could really be expected to improve the mobility of the brigade is not easy to ascertain. Certainly travelling by bus, even at the regulation military convoy speed of 18mph by day and just 8mph at night, was quicker and less tiring than marching but tanks could go anywhere and buses could not. Even on the roads buses were obliged to travel 100yds apart and dare not get too close to the fighting for the reasons given above. It also becomes clear, when reading *Modern Formations*, that the War Office did not anticipate that they would be able to operate a standard type of bus for the book explains that some will be better on hills than others, some faster on roads. All of which suggests that the War Office intended to hire buses as required. As we shall see this came to pass, under different circumstances, during the Second World War but the closest one can find from this period is an exercise involving 5th Battalion, Royal Tank Corps on Salisbury Plain in 1933. Photographs from the time show the battalion, with its tanks and transport, parked up in a meadow across which, with the greatest difficulty by the look of it, a line of single-deck buses is approaching.

It is, of course, important to keep in mind that *Modern Formations* was placed before its readers as an exercise in the possible. The very title was qualified as *Provisional* on the cover and, as Field Marshal Sir George Milne wrote in the introduction, the instructions were 'based on mechanical equipment already in existence or definitely in view, which would undoubtedly be available upon, or soon after, a declaration of war'. He went on to explain that no attempt had been made to depict the whole future in detail; however, when one can read in the War Establishment tables not

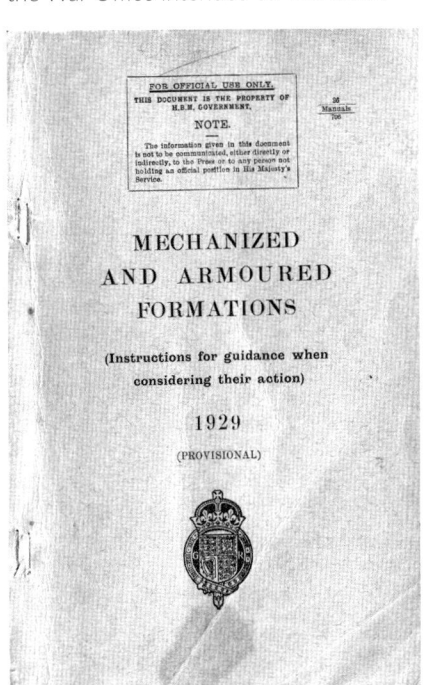

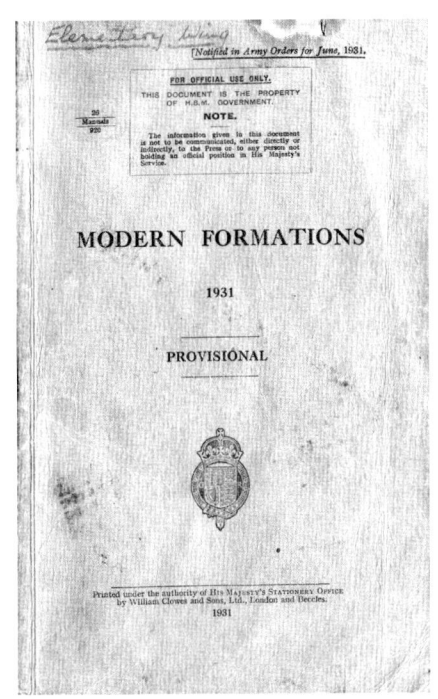

Mechanized and Armoured Formations (1929), known familiarly as the 'Purple Primer', and the revised edition entitled *Modern Formations* (1931).

only the number of buses an Omnibus Company should have, but right down to the number of motorcycles (12), technical clerks (2), coach trimmers (1) and men for sanitary duties (3), it is difficult to imagine how much more detail Milne could possibly want.

The section on supply in *Modern Formations* contains some rather curious observations and opinions which would appear to be Broad's own. They are undoubtedly grounded in the frustration every practitioner of highly mobile warfare feels about the need for a supply train. The author first remarks that mobile formations would 'of course' use railways as much as possible for their supply, which seems very optimistic to say the least. The railway has not yet been invented which could match, in terms of versatility, the flexibility of a mobile force, especially when the railway is not one's own, but the civilian system of a disputed land.

Beyond the railway supplies would be carried in six-wheeled lorries and here Broad starts to reveal his prejudices. Having stated that the bulk of stores required by a mobile, mechanised column would result in 'inordinately long and vulnerable' convoys he goes on to complain that they will require fighting troops for their protection and will, as they advance, require constant resupply in their own right. So much is obvious, but is there an alternative? Broad clearly believes so because his next paragraph shows beyond doubt that he does not like the existing system at all.

'This state of affairs arises, of course, from an organisation in which it requires two men and a powerful engine to move

Morris-Commercial six-wheelers on a cross-country jaunt during the 1927 Mechanised Force exercise on Salisbury Plain.

three tons of goods in a vehicle, which occupies some 20yds of road space, as in the case of the 3-ton lorry.'

Broad's preference appears to be an odd one. He mentions what he describes as a 'Motor Track Train' capable of shifting up to 100 tons of supplies across country at a relatively low speed. It is interesting to note that the inventive ex-Tank Corps officer, Philip Johnson of Roadless Traction Ltd, put forward just such a design at around this time, ostensibly for civil rather than military use but for similar conditions nonetheless. Johnson's drawing showed a conventional caterpillar-type tractor towing a train of tracked trailers, not unlike the Holt system used modestly in the First World War. Nothing came of it but one wonders who was influencing who and just what it was Broad appeared to have against the 3-ton lorry.

The British armed forces had little experience of four-wheel drive. American WD and Jeffery Quad vehicles had been employed during the First World War but very little interest had been shown by British manufacturers since then. The Hathi tractor of 1923 had seen some service but that had been developed by Niblett and his team at Aldershot and then passed on to Thornycroft as a ready-made design for them to manufacture. Hardy Motors of Slough was a specialist firm linked with the British FWD company and AEC Ltd. It produced an impressive four-wheel drive 3-tonner in 1931, using AEC components. It was originally considered as an artillery tractor but the improved performance across country, even when compared with the WD-type six-wheelers, generated enough interest for a number of manufacturers, including Guy and Karrier to develop similar chassis while Commer and Garner concentrated on 30cwt versions.

An early example of the Karrier K3, four-wheel drive 3-tonner during military acceptance trials.

BRITISH MILITARY TRANSPORT 1829-1956

The Army manoeuvres of 1925 have already been mentioned. They were in fact annual events, held in different parts of the country and contrived to test different aspects of warfare. Those of 1927 and 1928 were particularly significant to the cause of mechanisation since they featured tanks and a variety of supporting vehicles organised as an independent striking force. In 1931, the 1st Brigade, Royal Tank Corps, was created to develop this theme further and it was repeated and refined over subsequent years. In 1934, for the first time, the exercise included a Tank Brigade transport element, which was intended to give the armoured force its own integral supply column, capable of maintaining stocks of food, fuel and ammunition. The idea was to create a mobile striking force that could operate entirely on its own for several days, free of any normal supply tail.

The ultimate step was to incorporate this tank brigade into a mobile division. A training pamphlet, issued by the War Office in 1938, gives brief details of the transport serving with a tank brigade in a mobile division. When the brigade is operating with normal lines of communication it is divided into first, second- and third-line echelons. The first line, termed 'Unit Transport' is attached to brigade headquarters, tank battalions and tank brigade signals.

The gigantic 6 x 4 Mercedes-Benz photographed at MWEE in 1929. Its length is emphasised by the fitting of a typical British 3-ton body.

4 PEACETIME DEVELOPMENTS

It carries immediate supplies of food, fuel, lubricants, water and ammunition plus spare parts. Cookers, stores and batteries with charging plant are also included. The second line comprises the tank brigade's own RASC companies with reserve stocks of fuel and ammunition while the third, operating from the railhead, consists of RASC companies organised as a supply section with fuel and ammunition parks. The whole structure to replenish the tank brigade on a daily basis.

When the brigade is operating independently a transport echelon would be created with as few vehicles as possible. These would be loaded on a unit basis with a selection of all necessities. The idea being that when the tanks went into leaguer at night each unit would be replenished at once from its own section of lorries, which should already be carrying everything the tanks and their crews might need. An organisation table included with the pamphlet shows the allotment of 3-ton lorries to a tank battalion. Seven are required for ammunition, seven for fuel, five for unit fitters and one signals vehicle attached to battalion HQ.

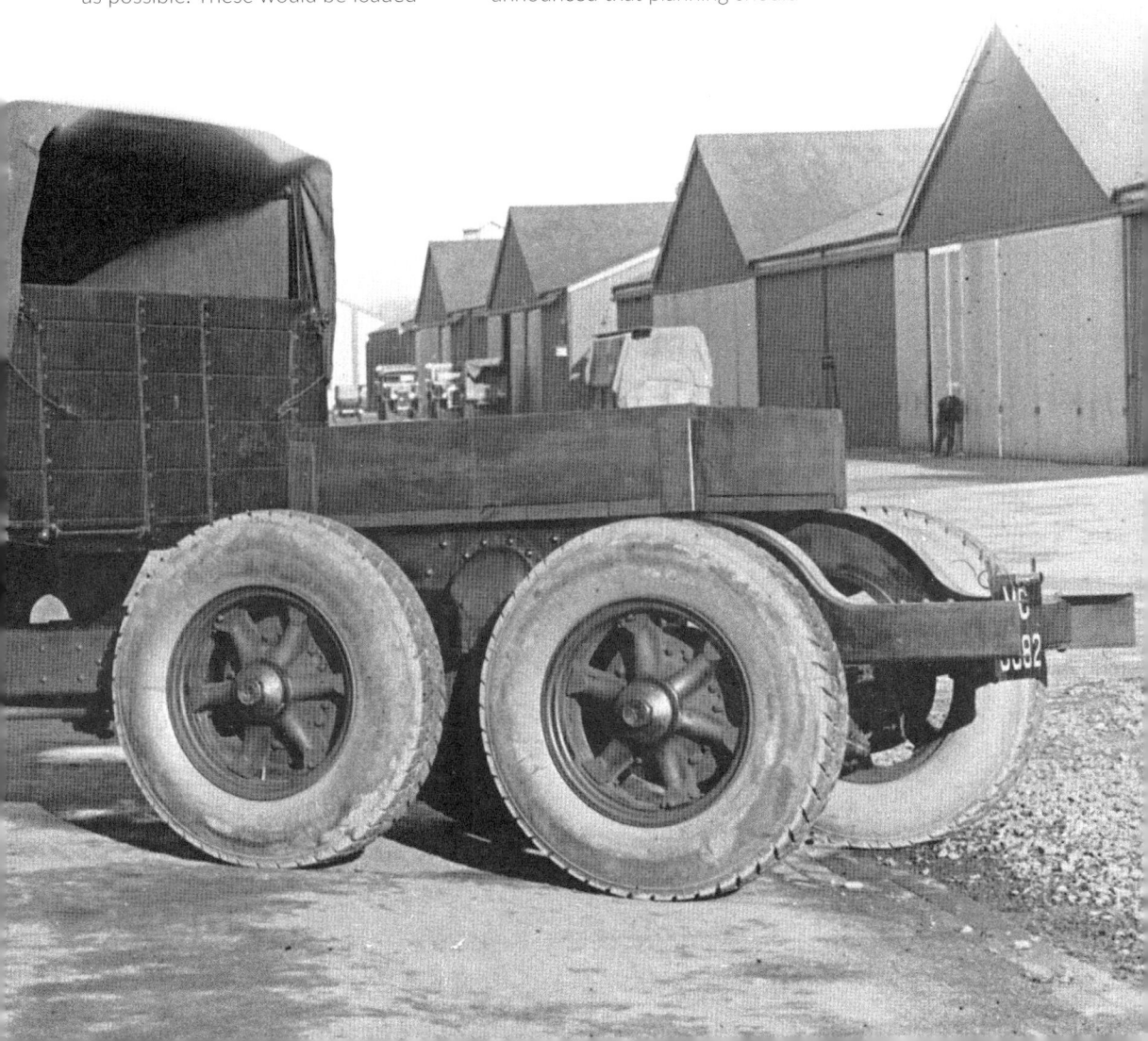

The countdown to war may be taken as starting in 1934. It was in November that the Committee of Imperial Defence announced that planning should proceed 'on the basis of the possibility of war against Germany in five years from 1934', which was not a bad calculation. From a transport point of view, at least in theory, things looked reasonably comfortable. The RASC could be said to be totally mechanised by that time and progress was being made with the infantry. All this, however, related to a peacetime establishment and schemes were now being formulated for a massive expansion of the Army. When the government was obsessed by air defence and the Army was anxious to acquire adequate quantities of good tanks the matter of transport was rather left to look after itself. With the exception of Bedford, who were relatively new to the trade, reliance was placed mainly upon increased production by traditional manufacturers and it is surprising that two of Britain's largest firms, Austin and Ford, were not encouraged to join in. Granted, Austin at this time produced nothing bigger in the commercial line than a taxicab (although they had submitted a prototype 15cwt platoon truck for trials), but Ford already had a 2-ton model in production and some had been tested by the MEE.

Despite the declared intention to concentrate on mass production for rearmament there was no relaxation in the pace of technical development. The 1938 North Wales Trials provide an instance. Held in October that year they were extended in order to make some specific, comparative trials. For some years members of the Mechanisation Board, in their annual reports, had noted the increased use of independent suspension on motor cars, particularly where the front axles were concerned. While it was not common on larger vehicles the value of independent suspension was generally ignored but for the 1938 trials both Crossley and Morris-Commercial supplied four-wheel drive vehicles that employed the system. Indeed, the latter firm offered both independent and conventional suspended vehicles for direct comparison. On certain lightweight scout cars independent suspension immediately proved its value

Part of the diesel revolution: a 5-ton Armstrong-Saurer tested by the Mechanisation Experimental Establishment in 1935.

A Crossley forward control 3-tonner in the markings of 5th Battalion, Royal Tank Corps at Perham Down camp.

but where larger types were concerned it seemed that there was little to choose. As soon as the trial ended the War Office called a conference of manufacturers and experienced service personnel to discuss the matter under the chairmanship of General Davidson and the magazine *Commercial Motor* reported the event. In Britain at this time independent suspension was considered quite a novelty and indeed many of the systems then in use were developed from Continental prototypes. The great advantage claimed was that there was less strain on the chassis over rough ground and, consequently, a reduced risk of body distortion, which was particularly important where vehicles with steel bodies were concerned. Against this there was general agreement that individual wheel movement was restricted, often leaving vehicles with one wheel clear of the ground and it was suggested that more attention needed to be paid to the design of differential locks. It was also true to say that in the main independent systems were more complex than their conventional counterparts.

Traditional systems, with live axles and leaf springs, certainly caused more chassis distortion but from a production point of view they were simpler and made greater use of ordinary commercial parts. This was well illustrated during the trial when a four-wheel drive vehicle entered by Albion Motors managed to wreck its live front axle on one day but was back on the road within 24 hours with a standard, undriven front axle in place. In general, it seems that the discussion proved inconclusive on the subject of suspension but it is interesting to note a call from one manufacturer's representative for more cooperation between firms on technical developments. It was not the sort of thing British industry was used to and there is little evidence to suggest that anyone took much notice. One thing that did make everyone sit up and take note was a claim by a Colonel Crawford, representing the War Office, that there would soon be a call for transport vehicles to be fitted with armoured cabs. Crawford claimed that it was expecting a great deal of an Army driver to give of his best when he felt vulnerable; he complained, too, that most military vehicles were already too heavy.

Under these circumstances it seems fair to suggest that the average British

Hazards of hiring. A civilian Morris-Commercial, registered in Newcastle-upon-Tyne, strains under the weight of a light tank during pre-Second World War manoeuvres.

Army lorry, if required to mount an armoured cab, would be so heavy that the margin left for the payload would hardly be worth bothering about and this is probably why the plan was never adopted.

In the years between the two world wars Britain's armed forces appear to have adopted a very isolationist attitude. At government insistence a policy favouring British industry had been built into the various subsidy schemes, for obvious reasons, but this should not have prevented the services from taking a greater interest in what potential rivals and allies were doing. Some French influence was clearly evident in the adoption of the Kégresse system and its successor, the Renault six-wheeler, but as the MWEE records show the number of foreign vehicles tested over that 20-year period was small.

In 1929, MWEE tested an enormous Mercedes-Benz rigid six-wheeler with a 23ft wheelbase. As already noted, British taxation was set against the development of heavy lorries so it was probably a lack of alternatives that prompted this move. The Swiss Saurer, which had a reputation for quality, was built in Britain by Armstrong-Whitworth, but it was still essentially a foreign design. A four-wheeled Dauntless and six-wheeled Dominant passed through MWEE in 1933, probably on account of their diesel engines, but none were acquired for service. An Austro-Daimler six-wheeler was demonstrated in Britain in the mid-1930s. It was reviewed in various service journals but never appears to have been examined officially. A Czech-built Tatra heavy lorry was tested at Farnborough in 1937, probably at the instigation of Lord Nuffield whose company, Morris Motors, appears to have been acting as agent for the marque in Britain but to no avail as far as the Army was concerned. Indeed, the only foreign firm that seems to have made any serious impression at this time was General Motors from the USA.

In 1938, at the time of the Munich Crisis, General Motors went to considerable lengths to obtain vehicles in a hurry. Their British agent effectively froze all stocks worldwide and placed them at the disposal of the War Office. The immediate threat receded but the authorities were grateful enough for the offer to order from the firm large numbers of Chevrolet 30cwt trucks. These vehicles were purchased through General Motors' Egyptian agents for service in the Middle East. Another result of Munich was the Air Defence of Great Britain Scheme. This was also to have an effect on transport, notably through an increased demand for lorries to transport and supply power for anti-aircraft searchlights. Until that time a typical British searchlight lorry was a 3-on six-wheeler with an auxiliary, engine-driven generator, but a need was shown for something more compact and self-contained.

The outcome was a sudden revival of interest in petrol-electric vehicles in which the internal-combustion engine drove indirectly through an electric motor. It was by no means a new concept, a Dennis-Stevens 3-tonner having been supplied in small numbers at the end of the First World War. Even so the type had declined in popularity since that time and the only British firm to keep the flag flying, albeit in a small way, was Tilling Stevens Motors of Maidstone in Kent. They responded to the new demand with two models shortly before the war and they were joined by Guy Motors, who supplied a petrol-electric version of their 3-ton commercial Otter model and Thornycroft, who came up with a conventionally driven vehicle mounting a generator in front of the main engine.

Munich may have been a premature alarm, but it could hardly be called a false one. War with Germany was not merely on the cards, it was imminent, and no matter what the politicians might be saying in public the Government was well aware of it. Yet there were many other items of defence equipment that were regarded as more important than transport, which now slipped to a very low priority indeed. Some interest was shown in specialist vehicles such as the petrol-electric types mentioned above, but the authorities believed that increased general transport requirements could be met by hiring suitable vehicles and impressment.

Impressment was a War Office responsibility, through the Chief Inspector of Supplementary Transport. It involved RASC officers visiting companies that owned vehicles and earmarking suitable examples of selected makes and models for service. Each vehicle must be well maintained and fit for at least three years' further service. By 1938, a requirement had been established for 10,000 vehicles and visiting officers had built up a register. As soon as the government announced that the country was to mobilise for war the lorry owner was responsible for delivering his vehicles to one of four centres around the country where they would be repainted and prepared for military service. The owner, naturally, being reimbursed in much the same way as he would have been under the old subsidy scheme.

Hiring was done at a local level, based on the Army Command district. The principle of inspection and selection was the same but a wider range of vehicles could be considered since they were intended for local use for a shorter period. Hiring did not necessarily depend upon mobilisation but it had to be set up by prior inspection and agreement in just the same way. Hiring was seen as an emergency measure; to ensure that the mass of transport required during the first weeks of mobilisation could be available and again a figure of 10,000 vehicles was deemed adequate. There were instances of lorries earmarked for hiring also being impressed but the main problem only showed up at the time of Munich. What the War Office had failed to take into account was the need for transport by the Home Office, as part of the Air Raid Precautions (ARP) scheme, and by the Ministry of Transport, for essential civilian services. This was partly solved in 1937 when the Ministry of Transport was granted overall responsibility for the distribution of vehicles and it was further eased by the fact that, in the case of hiring, military requirements were, in theory, only temporary. Thus, was transport prepared for another war.

A Guy Otter petrol-electric searchlight lorry during trials. Cables from the generator run back to a 90m projector emplaced behind the lorry.

5 OLD LESSONS NEW VEHICLES

Heavy vehicle development in Britain had been restricted by legislation created to favour the railways. Those vehicles that existed were hardly suitable for the rigours of Army life so while others were developed, notably by Albion, Foden and Leyland, what Britain could not produce itself was made up with deliveries from abroad, mainly by Mack and White from the United States.

5 OLD LESSONS NEW VEHICLES

Once the impressed vehicles had been repainted and prepared for service most of the surviving six-wheelers were withdrawn from units and returned to their depots for conversion. In the case of 3-tonners this meant removal of the GS body which was replaced by a specialist type, mainly workshop or other technical structures, which were held in store. The majority of 30cwts became ambulances. Even while this was going on, efforts were being made to prepare the British Expeditionary Force (BEF) for its move to France.

Plans for such a force had been made well before the war and they were constantly reviewed but, as always, last minute changes were introduced that upset everything. In April 1939, it was agreed that the number of infantry divisions for immediate despatch should be doubled, from two to four, and the follow-up plan was even more ambitious. The Army Council's intention was to have 15 divisions – both infantry and armoured – in France within a year followed by five more in the next year. Over the same period, they planned to have 12 divisions in the Middle East and four more retained in Britain for home defence. That is 36 divisions in all without counting those already stationed overseas. For the deployment of the BEF alone this meant that some 25,000 vehicles would have to be shipped across the Channel within a few days of the declaration of war.

The immediate result of this change in policy was to lower the standards of the impressment scheme to a dangerous level. While pre-war plans remained in force the Chief Inspector of Supplementary Transport was able to insist upon the most suitable vehicles for impressment.

The plans allowed for concentrating on a limited number of makes and types and making it possible to ensure the best vehicles and an adequate supply of

An interesting mixture of vehicles assembled for shipment to France. The majority, in the foreground, are Humber 8cwt pick-ups but the group includes some 15cwt Bedfords, among them a water tanker in the second line.

On 3 September 1939, Britain was at war. Two days earlier, on 1 September, Germany had invaded Poland. In Britain, mobilisation began that same day, hired lorries were acquired and impressed vehicles started to arrive at collection depots. As in the First World War, many drivers wished to enlist with their vehicles and this caused an unforeseen problem because the depots were only equipped to handle lorries, not people.

spares, but the expansion of the scheme almost reduced these plans to chaos. The demand for vehicles was such that the Chief Inspector was obliged to look at types that should never have been considered. The divergence between commercial and military requirements that had been recognised after the First World War, but largely overlooked by the Crosland Committee, was now well established. The commercial vehicle industry in Britain offered what their customers wanted: these included minimal ground clearance to achieve a low platform level, a low-powered engine to avoid excessive fuel consumption, and above all low cost. The manufacturers met this demand with mass production techniques that resulted in serviceable vehicles, which were not expected to last very long. The trade demanded lorries that could be worked hard for a few years and then discarded; the military wanted durability for their vehicles, which depended on a ready supply of spare parts. The more variety, in terms of makes and models, the greater the range of spares that must be stocked and in this lay the seeds of potential disaster.

The four infantry divisions of the BEF were organised into two corps. For its transport each division required an ammunition, petrol and supply company. Each corps needed an ammunition park, a troop ammunition company, a troop supply column, a corps petrol park and a motor ambulance convoy. Transport was also required for GHQ and line of communication troops. For the latter troops, two transport companies were equipped with heavy vehicles, 6- and 10-tonners, but all other companies employed 3-tonners.

The deployment to France was complicated by the threat to the short sea routes from enemy aircraft and U-boats. No port east of Le Havre was considered safe except Dieppe, which was allocated to hospital ships only. Therefore, personnel entered France via Le Havre and Cherbourg while vehicles came in through Nantes, Brest and St Nazaire. Thus, apart from small parties of drivers who were embarked with vehicles to assist with unloading in France, the majority travelled separately and then went on to their units, returning later by rail to collect their lorries. Convoys then made for the huge British depot established near Le Mans and from there, in due course, to the main concentration area of the BEF between Arras and Amiens. The entire movement of this first wave was completed within five weeks and British troops were soon in line, with the French, along the Belgian frontier.

Better than marching, but not much. Infantry get a lift in an impressed Bedford 3-tonner.

Now began that nine-month period of relative inactivity, which Chamberlain and Churchill describe as the 'Twilight War'. The Allies established themselves but made no effort, either by land or in the air, to interfere with the Germans. Quiet as it seemed this was a testing time for the British due to their extended supply lines. Material coming ashore through Western France was moved up by rail to the immediate vicinity of the front and then distributed by road. But even this arrangement, using good roads and undisturbed by enemy activity, proved that the transport equipment employed was inadequate. Following a visit to the front, Churchill compared the situation behind the French and British lines. 'The emptiness of the roads ...' in the French sector '... was in great contrast to the continual coming and going that extended for miles behind the British sector.' Yet even this could only be achieved during a period of static warfare. A War Office publication of 1951 claims that the main reason why the British Army only planned to have one armoured division and one tank brigade (or at least two-thirds of it) in France before the first year of war ended was on account of the supply situation. A chronic shortage of tanks must have had something to do with it as well, but if such planning was based primarily on logistics it provides an interesting facet of the nature of the Phoney War.

Even as the build-up continued in France another campaign was being considered. Allied plans to assist Finland with a force of three or four divisions were discussed in February 1940 but they foundered on Swedish reluctance to allow belligerent troops to pass through their country. This move, however, directed Hitler's eyes to Scandinavia and he resolved upon a pre-emptive invasion of Norway in order to secure the entrance to the Baltic and maintain supplies of iron ore from Sweden. The Allied reaction was swift enough but resulted in what Churchill dubbed a 'ramshackle' campaign. One British division, the 49th, was allocated but its brigades were to be split and directed to at least four different locations. Since it was not so easy to split up the divisional transport some optimistic souls at the War Office decided that the shortage could be made good by hiring vehicles in Norway. Clearly, they had no idea of the circumstances in that country. A small population, months of ice and snow each year and rugged terrain had not encouraged the development of motor transport on a large scale up to that time and there was little to hire that the Germans had not already snapped up. To make matters worse, much of the country was still in the grip of winter, even in April, and hardly any of the British vehicles which did land were supplied with snow chains.

Morris CD-Type 30cwt lorries at Calais in 1939, still displaying peacetime colours and markings.

After Dunkirk, on 15 June 1940 it was the turn of Le Havre. Here the street is virtually blocked with abandoned vehicles, mostly Bedford 15cwts.

If there was a useful outcome of the campaign it was a small but surprising one. Norwegian forces had managed to capture a German tanker lorry filled with 3,500 litres of fuel, which they passed on to the British forces at Tromsø. It proved invaluable as a means of distributing fuel and the equipment fitted to it was considered so interesting that it was shipped back to Britain for evaluation.

The distribution of fuel was undoubtedly one of the weakest links in the British supply system. That so vital an element to a fully mechanised army should be allowed to reach such a parlous state was undoubtedly due to false economy, but the resulting waste was so great that it verged upon the criminal. Experiments intended to devise the best method of distributing fuel had been carried out continually since about 1930. Bulk fuel tankers had been tested and rejected, on the grounds of vulnerability and slow delivery rate and the authorities finally settled on a 4-gallon, disposable tin can, known as the 'flimsy'. The Government had established two factories, at Avonmouth and in South Wales, so that the cans could be made close to major refineries but, for reasons of economy, neither plant had been tested to capacity before the war began; and neither had the cans.

The original scheme, upon which the entire Army was supposed to depend, involved shipping full cans, packed in pairs within wooden crates. The trouble was that, unless these loads were handled with the greatest care, the crates would break up and the nails securing them penetrated the cans. To make matters worse, cans coming from the new plants were found to be faulty and the scale of leakage was prodigious. Not only that, it was very dangerous. The Board of Trade recognised this and tried to restrict the size of ships that could transport fuel in this way. Yet, under war conditions, such regulations did not always apply. Sometimes, tragic consequences resulted, as when the SS *Pacific Coast* blew up at Brest on 9 November 1939 when her holds were opened and a spark ignited the accumulated vapour. The RASC had developed a system of bulk fuel distribution in the wake of the Board of Trade's censure, which involved the use of road tankers and, when the can delivery arrangements failed, this was just able to maintain adequate supplies to the forces in France.

There was another problem that beset military transport of fuel at this time. It had its roots in a situation first recognised in the behaviour of aircraft engines, a condition known as 'knocking'. As early as 1916, engineers had learned that knocking could be alleviated by the addition of certain aromatics to petrol and in 1921 two engineers in the United States identified tetraethyl lead as the ideal agent to cure the problem. By 1933 the Royal Air Force (RAF) was using a mixture rated at 87 octane, which improved the situation and by the outbreak of war 100 octane fuel was available. Nothing so potent was required for transport and two lower grades were supplied – 72 octane, known as MT72, which was dyed orange or yellow for identification, and MT80, which was coloured red. The former was supplied for B vehicles operating in Britain and the latter for tanks while, in operational theatres MT80 was standardised for both. Pure petroleum spirit, which was undyed, could only be used in small engines, such as generators.

Unfortunately, the new mixture, MT80 with a tetraethyl lead content of 3.6cc per gallon, was found to wreak havoc with many engines, burning the valves out after only a few hundred miles of running and corroding those that were kept in store for any length of time. The problem was never entirely solved. Valves made from better steel helped, as did wider tappet settings, but a document issued in 1945 still warned drivers to carry out daily compression checks and to report any reduction.

New engines were factory tested on unleaded petrol and, if they had to be stored for any length of time, special materials were used.

From fuel to tyres. Apart from the normal commercial type used at home the Army had to fit specialist types to service vehicles. One was the cross-country tyre, with a heavy moulded tread and the other the sand tyre, which was of a smoother pattern. Both were also available in a type that had been developed by Dunlop, the Runflat. This tyre had extra thick side walls that were designed to stay firm even after the tube had been punctured. With a bit of luck a vehicle could keep going for 20 miles or so before the cover collapsed, which was usually enough to get it out of trouble. The main drawback was that such tyres could not be run at lower pressures when crossing soft sand because it did not make any difference. Runflats were generally limited to frontline vehicles since they were expensive to produce and required extra rubber in order to make them strong enough. Once the Japanese had overrun Malaya in 1942 the availability of rubber diminished and resulted in such terrors for the British public as a shortage of golf and tennis balls and, worse still, hot water bottles.

Looking along the sea front towards Dunkirk with a mixture of French and British transport abandoned on the promenade. Further on one can see two sailing barges, lost during the evacuation, and lines of vehicles driven into the sea to create temporary jetties.

BRITISH MILITARY TRANSPORT 1829-1956

Early on 10 May 1940, the Germans launched their offensive against the Allied forces showing a total disregard for Belgian neutrality in the process. According to plan, the Allies entered Belgium from the opposite side to resist the German attack. The armoured cars of 12th Royal Lancers led the British contingent and they were closely followed by troop-carrying lorries of the RASC. The British line was established on the River Dyle but it was pulled back five days later when Holland capitulated and exposed the Allied flank. Only eight days later the Germans were in Boulogne and the British line of communications was cut.

Soon, that part of the BEF which was encircled could only be supplied through Dunkirk, which was also being used by the French, and congestion and chaos ensued, abetted by constant air raids. The system broke down entirely and was only saved by local reorganisation, which involved rounding up abandoned vehicles and sending them off, with whatever was available, to supply such troops as they could find. In this situation a convoy of heavy 10-tonners proved invaluable but, even with drivers working in shifts, the strain began to tell and the stock of vehicles rapidly diminished due to breakdowns and accidents. Before long, all the traffic through Dunkirk was in the opposite direction and, when the port proved too vulnerable, lorries were driven into the sea to create temporary jetties. This also prevented serviceable vehicles from falling into enemy hands.

While the Germans concentrated on the trapped forces huddled in Dunkirk a large portion of the BEF, including newly-arrived reinforcements, was still in being south of the Somme. The supply situation here was aggravated by the almost total collapse of the French railway system, which was under constant air attack. Convoys wasted a great deal of time, and fuel, scouring the countryside looking for abandoned trains, which could be used to keep

British transport captured in St Valery-en-Caux when the British 50th Division surrendered on 12 June 1940.

the fighting forces supplied. In saying that, one cannot ignore the fact that, in addition to their regular duties, RASC personnel were fighting soldiers. There are many instances of these men taking part in actions and it was standard practice to use lorries as road blocks in the event of an attack by tanks. Despite the arrival of British 1st Armoured Division it soon became clear that there would be no holding the Germans once they resumed their offensive. There followed a series of badly coordinated actions as the Allies retreated across France. The order for British troops to evacuate was issued on 15 June.

According to a table published in 1951, compiled from records then held by the Central Ordnance Depot at Chilwell, near Nottingham, over 100,000 vehicles were lost in France, and this does not include combat vehicles. The breakdown is not only by type, but also differentiates between War Department and impressed vehicles. Without trying to list them all it is interesting to examine the relative proportions of some types. As might be expected the WD 15cwts outnumbered impressed types 11,442 to 26. On the other hand, 3-ton 4 x 2 types formed the largest contingent with 11,782 WD against 14,009 impressed. Of the 6-tonners, the figures are 122 WD to 454 impressed and 10-tonners 195 WD to 384 impressed. Despite attempts to disable them large numbers of these vehicles fell into German hands and saw further service with the Wehrmacht. Subsequent studies have cast some doubt upon the original Chilwell figures and a total of around 85,000 is now considered more accurate, but whatever it was it represents a substantial loss. However difficult the situation may have been when the BEF went to France it must now have seemed desperate on its return.

Disasters such as the defeat of the BEF can be turned to advantage.

Young women working in the Guy Motors factory at Wolverhampton, assembling 15cwt general service truck bodies.

The loss of so many vehicles and the need to replace them could be used as an opportunity to encourage the British commercial vehicle industry to standardise. Unfortunately, this was not possible. For one thing more lorries were needed urgently and there was no time to develop new types, but in any case it was not a popular concept. Official records compiled after the war sought to explain this from the commercial point of view. It was claimed that if an entirely new design was prepared that the majority of firms could build there was no guarantee that it would be successful, at least not without a long development period, and this is undeniable. However, what could be wrong with selecting the best existing type and having it built by a consortium?

The answer, which the War Office put forward with uncharacteristic concern for the sensibilities of the trade, was that those firms obliged to abandon their product in favour of another company's design could hardly be expected to give it their best attention. It was argued that a company, which was forced to build one of its rival's models would do so with such bad grace, that the resulting vehicle was bound to be inferior. Even then, with the Germans just across the Channel

American-built White 760 10-ton truck supplied to Britain and used mainly in the Middle East, hence the sand pattern tyres.

and the nation's very survival at stake it seems that company loyalty came first. The War Office even expressed concern about the post-war situation; how, it asked, could a company expect to revive its range and commercial trade if it spent the war building someone else's model? Perhaps the War Office overlooked the fact that, if things got very much worse there would not be a commercial market to worry about. Certainly, it should have been shamed by Canada, the United States and even Germany. In all three countries – and the first two most particularly – a more or less standard design, recognisably an army lorry rather than a commercial type, was built in vast numbers by more than one company, none of which affected their individual identities or business prospects afterwards.

Just how significant this presumed attitude was among British manufacturers is difficult to determine. The loyalty of any firm to its own products is understandable, as is its concern for long-term survival, but if the United States and Canada could make standardisation work one feels that British industry could have swallowed its collective pride and responded for the common good. However, the matter was never put to the test except in a small way, and the British services continued to enjoy an amazing variety of makes and models which, if nothing else, makes the vehicle historian's task more interesting. Another, more valid, objection to standardisation was that it stifled development of new and improved designs, but even this view is not as valid as it sounds. Undoubtedly, where certain specialised vehicles are concerned, new types were designed and produced, but the chances are that this would have happened anyway. Generally speaking, however, when military products of the war years are examined, very little evidence of development can be found. The vast majority of vehicles in production when the war began were still rolling off the production lines when it ended. Most were deemed quite satisfactory and there was no incentive to improve them except in detail.

What Britain could not produce would have to be made up with deliveries from abroad; notably from Canada and the United States. Canadian production will be considered in more detail later but some aspects of American involvement can be mentioned here. British interest, at this time, was concerned mainly with heavy trucks of about 10-ton payload. It has already been noted that heavy vehicle development in Britain had been restricted by legislation formulated to create an advantage in favour of the railways. Such vehicles as did exist were hardly suitable for the rigours of service life anyway so, while others were developed, notably by Albion, Foden and Leyland, quantities of trucks, mainly by Mack and White, were imported from the United States. This, it has to be admitted, was not quite what the Ministry of Supply had in mind but it was the best deal it could get; as customers, the British believed that they could order vehicles to their own specifications but the Americans had two good reasons for resisting this approach. In the first place they firmly believed that they knew more about vehicle production than did the British, and in any case they were convinced that they built better trucks. Further, it made sense to them that before long Britain would vanish beneath the Nazi onslaught just as France had done, and they had already been caught once. The French had ordered large numbers of trucks from the Americans to expand their military transport fleet and, following the German occupation, it looked as if many American suppliers would be left with hundreds of unwanted vehicles on their hands. Much to their relief, no doubt, Britain stepped in and took virtually the whole lot.

These 'Diverted Shipment', or 'French Contract', vehicles as they were variously known, were a considerable blessing at a difficult time, even if they were not

The Mack EH was classed as a 3-ton 4 x 2 in British service.

precisely what the Army would have ordered. It should also be noted that the American companies' reluctance to build vehicles to foreign specifications had the full support of their Government. Unwelcome as the prospect was, there were those in Washington who could see that, in the end, the United States would be fully involved in the war and they saw no sense in permitting their industry to accept contracts for vehicles that the US Army would not use. Rather, it was logical to have these firms build types that were acceptable and encourage foreign armies to use them. The divisional RASC units that managed to get home from France arrived with what they stood up in; they had not been able to bring back a single vehicle with them beyond one staff car, which its temporary owner refused to be parted from. Nonetheless, it proved possible to furnish all units with some transport and in fact it appears that a shortage of drivers posed a bigger problem than did lorries. Continued production and long-term planning would solve these problems but there was a short-term matter that bulked far greater, the defence of the homeland against imminent invasion.

A scheme to requisition civilian transport in anticipation of invasion turned out to be illegal so it was necessary to extend the hiring scheme. However, it was surprising what could be done with goodwill on both sides. At noon on 17 May 1940, a sudden call went out for 2,000 vehicles to collect rifle parties from anti-aircraft searchlight sites around London and carry them to locations where enemy parachutists were deemed to have landed. The result was virtually a re-enactment of the celebrated 'Taxis du Marne' episode that had saved Paris in 1914. With agreement from the Metropolitan Police and Ministry of War Transport, private taxicab owners and members of the cab-drivers' union, the provision was met in its entirety within 48 hours. This was an exercise, it would probably have been too late otherwise, but it was a fine example of what could be done.

Certainly, parachutist scares did arise throughout those tense months but the threat of a concentrated invasion was far more likely. The problem was to decide where it might take place. Rather than stretch the defences too thinly it was deemed wiser to keep the defending troops concentrated where they could be rushed to a threatened area. It was considered unwise to rely on the railways, which could easily be blocked and in any case were required to carry tanks, so it was agreed that motor coaches should be used instead.

There were, it seems, some 50,000 public service vehicles in Britain at that time, presumably not counting trolley-buses and trams. Many were ordinary short-haul buses, mainly double-deckers, which were needed in any case to get people to work. The Army already had about 3,000 single-deckers, and some

Troops return to their coaches after an exercise, which appears to have been staged for publicity purposes. Note how some of the windows have been painted over with just a small rectangle left clear.

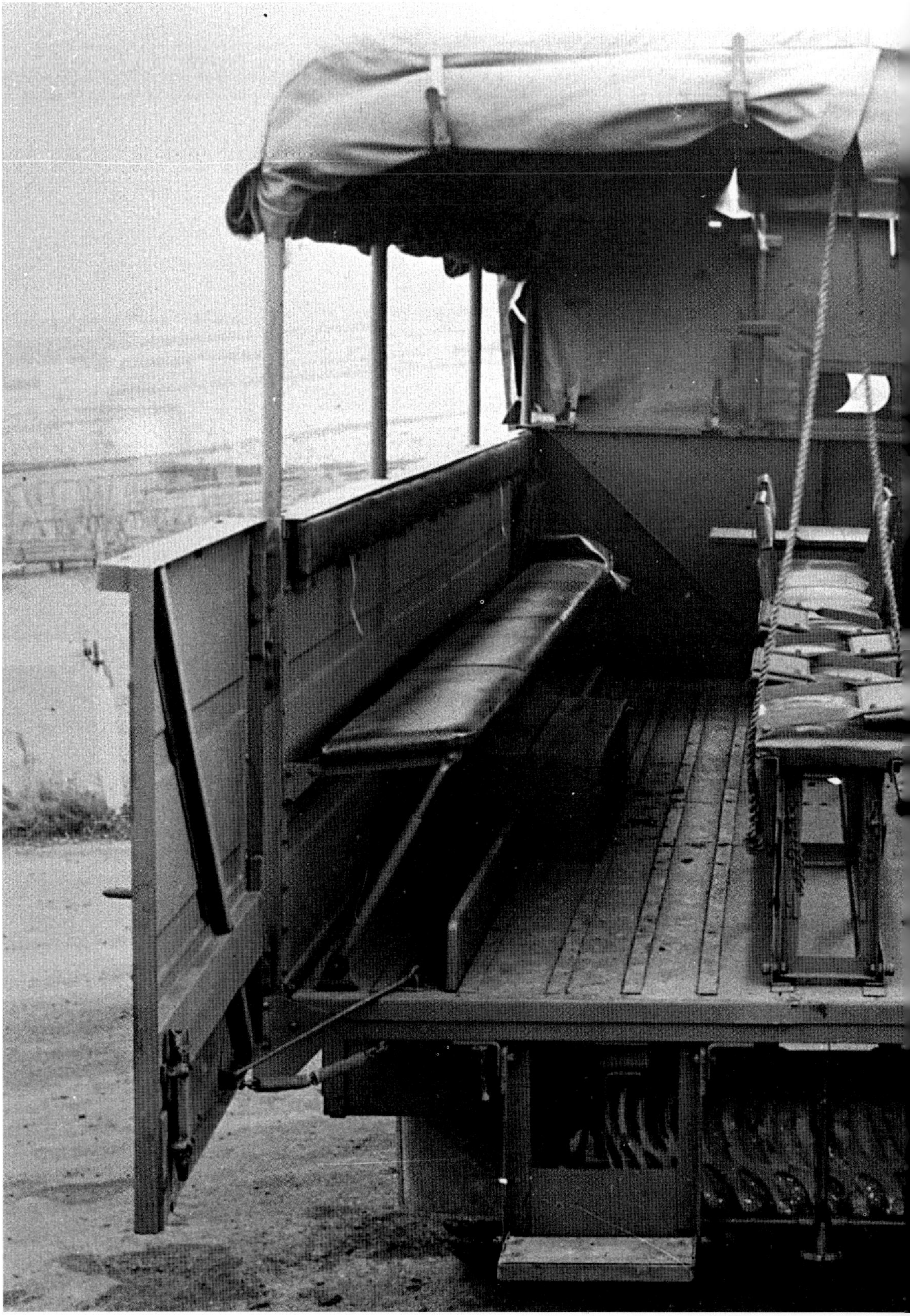

Rear view of a Bedford QLT troop-carrying lorry with the tailgate doors open and seats in place.

had even been lost in France, but the present requirement was estimated at 1,900. The plan was to form 32 Motor Coach Companies RASC, staffed by men returned from France, each company to consist of three sections of 20 coaches. It was stipulated that the coaches must all be of 32-seat capacity because 20 of them, or one section, would then be able to carry an infantry battalion. This requirement immediately limited the choice of vehicles but it was made worse by a further condition that no diesel-powered coaches could be accepted – trained diesel drivers being in short supply.

Subsequently, the force was raised by another 11 companies with an additional 400 coaches in reserve but their new owners were not very happy with them. Many of the coaches supplied to the War Office were not just old, they were positively ancient. And many, too, did not even boast self-starters and breakdowns were frequent. To make matters worse, the Army considered it essential that the coaches should be run off the road when occasion demanded, but being vehicles of very low ground clearance, this was virtually impossible. Not that it stopped soldiers from trying, and this only resulted in more damage. In theory, according to the War Office, the coaches had been acquired for the specific purpose of rushing troops to the scene of an invasion, 'rushing' in this case being a relative term. It was understood that they could also be used for anti-invasion exercises, as indeed they were, but in practice they were being used all the time for conveying troops and the standard of reliability suffered accordingly. Since this could not go on indefinitely a scheme was put forward to develop a suitable troop-carrying lorry.

A prototype, capable of carrying 30 men, was completed by the RASC Motor Transport Depot at Feltham, west of London in May 1941. It was created by extending the chassis of a four-wheel drive Bedford QL 3-tonner and fitting a longer steel body with folding seats. It was found to be perfectly adequate for the job and an order for just over 1,000 followed. As they came into service the motor coaches were released back into the civilian world from which they had come. In addition to the Regular Army requirements there was a demand for transport from the Home Guard. Those battalions that could do so, relied on the loan of vehicles by their members although, one assumes, these would have been subject to civilian restrictions on the use of fuel. London, however, appears to have been regarded as a special case because in July 1941 authority was granted to requisition 1,250 taxicabs whose drivers were enrolled in the Home Guard. Whether this had evolved from the exercise in May 1940 is not clear but, since the cabs could not be requisitioned unless an Action Stations order was issued it was never put to the test. Indeed, it was not until January 1942 that authority was received to create Home Guard MT companies and by then the threat of invasion was considerably reduced. Thus, when these companies were established, by 1943, they tended to be used for general transport duties alongside the RASC, particularly in emergencies created when sections of railway line were seriously damaged by enemy action. This system remained in force until February 1945.

The wartime history of transporting troops by road has some interesting statistics. For example, in the Canadian Army, which claimed to be the most entirely mechanised of any during the war, the proportion of soldiers to vehicles was 3-to-1. In the US Army it was 11-to-1 while Britain was placed somewhere between the two. Not that this implied there was enough transport to excuse soldiers from having to march most of the time. Lorries were needed for too many other tasks so it was essential to introduce some sort of priority arrangement.

As early as 1927, during the original Armoured Force exercise, a mechanised troop-carrying element was introduced in order to provide infantry capable of keeping pace with tanks, and the Mobile Division experiments of the late 1930s emphasised this. By 1939, such a requirement had been built into the structure of armoured brigades with what was known as an infantry (rifle) battalion. In its original form it consisted of an HQ company and four rifle companies. The HQ company included a carrier platoon, equipped with Bren-gun carriers and various support platoons. The rifle companies, each of three platoons divided into three sections, used 15cwt platoon trucks to increase mobility.

By 1943, this arrangement was known as a motor battalion but it operated in a similar way and was intended, according to a War Office pamphlet of the time, to provide the entire fighting portion of a battalion with trucks or carriers so that it could move fast on roads or open desert. In some cases, according to the pamphlet, ordinary 15cwt trucks were being replaced by four-wheel drive armoured vehicles of the same capacity but there is very little evidence that this was ever actually done. The motor battalion was strong on firepower with a preponderance of light machine-guns since its role was seen primarily as defensive, to hold the ground that an armoured brigade had taken. However, at armoured divisional level, infantry was included as part of the attacking force; an infantry brigade of three battalions all of which, by 1944 had transport in the form of 3-tonners.

The defeat of the British Army in France was succeeded by an all-out German assault on Britain from the air as an overture to invasion. This was essentially an aerial fleet action, the tip-and-run raids of later years being then largely unknown. Yet while the threat of such raids existed attempts were made to counter it. The subject being a novel one there was no body of experience to draw upon and, as usual in such

The machine-gun battalion of 5th Corps on exercise in Britain. The vehicles are Bedford 15cwts and in each one the Vickers machine-gun is prepared for anti-aircraft defence.

situations, that beloved British character, the mad inventor, had his day. A number of firms and individuals produced devices that enabled the crew of a lorry to take on low-flying enemy aircraft and the most professional of these, by any standard, was the Motley mount.

In typical form this was a rotating pillar, set into the bed of a truck, attached to which was a small bucket seat for the gunner and one or two Bren guns, mounted on a system of springs not unlike an adjustable desk lamp of the Anglepoise type. Of course, with this mounting in place there was no room for a load of any sort. The Motley mount took up a lot of room and the gunner needed every inch he could get to swing the thing around. Thus, the lorry so equipped was dedicated to shooting down aircraft and added to the convoy for that purpose. The usual carrying vehicle was a 15cwt truck. Without doubt the doyen of these designers was a major in the Royal Tank Regiment, Tom Lakeman. In principle his designs were similar to the Motley but Lakeman was a disciple of the concept of maximum firepower and, instead of a pair of Brens liked to mount four, all directed and fired by one man. He even tried to adapt the arrangement to heavier weapons such as the air-cooled Lewis or Besa, but the one thing he could never do was keep it simple. The majority of Lakeman mounts were masterpieces of complexity with a multitude of springs and cables virtually caging the unfortunate gunner. In fact their value was never adequately tested. Lakeman was one of those fertile, dedicated but awkward people with a knack of rubbing everyone up the wrong way and none of his ideas was ever allowed to settle before he was offering a better one. Ronald Hamilton, designer of the Swiss Roll floating roadway was similar, but that is another story.

Getting back to anti-aircraft lorries, there were at least two examples which, had they been developed, would have been armoured. Based on Bedford MW and Morris-Commercial CS8 prototypes they featured protected mountings for up to four weapons in the truck bed and, in the case of the MW, an armoured cab for the driver. Whether these were attributable to Lakeman as well is not clear, but they went the same way as most of his inventions; nothing was ever heard of them again.

Anyone familiar with Sir Winston Churchill's incomparable, six-volume history of the Second World War will be aware that, besides the onerous duties of Prime Minister, Minister of Defence and self-appointed stimulator of the nation's resolve, he was not above involving himself in anything that attracted his attention, however

RAF personnel, working from a Bedford QL, rigging a small barrage balloon.

A special mount, which enabled the driver's mate to use a Bren gun against attacking aircraft. Here a Royal Tank Regiment soldier demonstrates the system in a Fordson WOT2, 15cwt of 1st Armoured Division.

insignificant. Late in 1940, he suggested to the Minister of Supply that it would make more sense to purchase second-hand cars from civilian owners who had laid them up for the duration, due to petrol rationing, than waste scarce dollars buying new ones from the United States. He was thinking, he explained, of those more powerful types of car, which might be required by senior officers. The War Office was not impressed with the proposal, until officials discovered where it emanated from. Then they realised what an excellent idea it was and placed an initial order for 425 vehicles. This was later increased to include some 1,400 cars of all types, for use at home, which were purchased by the Ministry on behalf of the War Department.

The formation of the Auxiliary Territorial Service (ATS) provided another valuable pool of drivers. Women serving with the First Aid Nursing Yeomanry (FANY) in the First World War had driven ambulances both at home and overseas and they now continued to perform this duty. However, they were mainly employed to drive ambulances belonging to the British Red Cross Society, which imposed strict limitations on the purposes for which their vehicles could be used, in accordance with their international status. The ATS, on the other hand, was primarily raised to provide drivers and operated its own MT companies. In addition to service ambulances they drove staff cars, rode motorcycles under 350cc and handled

The Bedford MW 15cwt complete with armoured cab and multiple machine-gun turret.

relaxed. Women were permitted to drive any vehicle up to 30cwt, including six-wheelers, laden or not and 3-tonners of certain nominated makes, laden or not. This, however, only applied to women over the age of 19 and they were all prohibited from driving any vehicle, which was hauling a trailer.

Although it is not the purpose of this book to discuss particular vehicles in any detail there is some justification for taking a brief look at those significant members of the British commercial motor industry that produced lorries during the war years.

many of the peculiar little vehicles used within RAOC depots to move stores about. When it came to lorries the War Office adopted a rather chauvinistic attitude to its female soldiers. They might drive any four-wheeled vehicle up to 30cwt capacity without restriction, but when it came to 3-tonners, women were not permitted to drive any that were loaded. It has to be said that the women themselves did not expect such concessions and there is no doubt that it caused considerable inconvenience. Later, due partly to pressure from the Air Ministry, these restrictions were

AEC, the firm that built most of London's buses continued to supply six-wheelers in the 3-ton class for some time, in particular those associated with the Royal Engineers' bridging train. However, the firm concentrated mainly on the four-wheel drive Matador, which was primarily employed as an artillery tractor. A six-wheel drive version was developed, particularly for use by the RAF. Armoured vehicles were also built and saw considerable service.

Albion Motors, the only Scottish company that could still be considered

ATS girls parading with their convoy of Guy Ant 15cwt trucks.

as a major producer, continued to produce 6 x 4 3-tonners throughout the war and added a four-wheel drive model to their range. Otherwise they were better known for heavy lorries in the 10-ton class and some equally impressive artillery tractors along with a rather unfortunate tank transporter design, which was ultimately relegated to load carrying.

The Austin Motor Company had virtually abandoned commercial vehicles between the wars but returned early in the war with 30cwts and 3-ton four-wheelers and the classic K2/Y heavy ambulance. When it was realised that the demise of the 3-ton six-wheeler had been somewhat premature, the company was encouraged to produce a version that had a more modern cab than the earlier forward control military types. Austin also built a four-wheel drive 3-tonner, renowned for its noisy transfer box, but did not venture into the production of larger types.

Bedford, the commercial vehicle element of Vauxhall Motors, came very late to the military scene but more than made up for it in the quantity and range of vehicles produced. They had a 15cwt in production before the war and followed it with conventional types in the 30cwt and 3-ton classes – the latter in a bewildering variety. However, their greatest contribution has to be the remarkable four-wheel drive QL of which more than 50,000 were built. Their only venture on the heavy side was a tipper in the 5-ton class.

Commer Cars of Luton made a brief foray into the 15cwt class with their Beetle and the more conventional Q2 and Q15 produced mainly for the RAF. They steered clear of the service 4 x 4 and 6 x 4 types but specialised in short-wheelbase tractor units for semi-trailers, including the impressive Queen Mary aircraft transporters.

An Albion 4 x 4, 3-ton lorry involved in an incident near Lulworth Camp in Dorset. The trailer, carrying a light tank, turned over on the wet road.

Crossley Motors of Gorton had courted quite a lot of military business in the inter-war years but had subsequently decided to concentrate on buses. Their main wartime service product was a four-wheel-drive 3-tonner, which was used principally by the RAF as a load carrier and fire tender.

Dennis Brothers, the long-established Surrey firm, were probably best known to the military for their ubiquitous 3-ton tipper, known as the Pig, and its even less glamorous cousin, which was fitted with a tanker body and pumps to empty drains. However, they also produced a solid, but very civilian looking 6-tonner called the Max.

The staff of life. A Bedford OY 3-tonner fitted with a special body for carrying bread.

137

BRITISH MILITARY TRANSPORT 1829-1956

Foden and Sons, the old-established Cheshire firm, having built steam lorries for the armed forces in the First World War, seemed to ignore the military market thereafter. Moving from steam to diesel power they concentrated on the production of heavy vehicles and supplied the Army with large quantities of six-wheelers in the 10-ton class during the Second World War. They also built a 6-ton four-wheeler, which is worth comparing here with a similar vehicle supplied by ERF, a breakaway company with Foden family connections.

Ford commercial vehicles built in Britain were marketed under the Fordson name originally applied to farm tractors. Like Bedford, they were not strong contenders for military business before the war but they more than made up for it subsequently. Indeed, they had examples in every payload group from 8cwt to 3 tons, including 6 x 4, and they were one of the few firms to produce 4 x 4 military vehicles in 30cwt and 3-ton classes.

Guy Motors of Wolverhampton, although a major military contractor before the war, did not produce anything of outstanding interest after about 1940, having been involved briefly in armoured vehicle construction. However, they were authorised by the Government to build variants of their military range for the limited civilian market and a standard utility type of double-deck bus during the war.

The 3-ton Leyland Lynx, in this enclosed cab version, was a good example of a commercial lorry adapted for military use.

Humber and Karrier were complementary elements of the Rootes Group. Wartime production by the former concentrated mainly on the kind of staff car issued to senior ranks, but they ventured into light trucks and armoured vehicles that included four-wheel drive types. Karrier also built armoured cars (albeit under the Humber marque) and a range of military types that included the unusual four-wheel drive K6 and the inevitable 6 x 4 types.

Leyland Motors ranked as one of the largest commercial vehicle companies in Britain before the war and they produced a range of vehicles that included the 30cwt Lynx, 3-ton 6 x 4 Retriever and 10-ton Hippo as well as a series of fire engines used by the military. They also became involved in the construction of tanks and later took full responsibility for the development and construction of a new model along with much more varied war work. For a period of around two years they virtually abandoned ordinary military vehicles and only resumed production of an improved Hippo in 1944 when it was realised that more vehicles of 10-ton capacity would be needed than other firms were capable of delivering.

The Maudslay Motor Company of Coventry only had one genuine military type in its range, the 6-ton 4 x 2 Militant. But it is included here in order to illustrate another facet of wartime production. Shortly before the war the Government had encouraged firms to develop what were called Shadow Factories as a hedge against the effect of air raids. These were normally constructed on rural sites but not too far away from the main works and managed by members of the parent company staff acting as agents. Primarily these new factories were involved in work for the Air Ministry, hence perhaps the extra awareness of the aerial threat, and in the case of Maudslays it was a lifesaver. The new plant was at Alcester and, following extensive Blitz damage on Coventry in 1942, the entire production line was gradually moved there.

Morris-Commercial Cars will already have registered as a major military vehicle contractor. Wartime production was dominated by the 15cwt platoon truck and its derivatives along with the 6 x 4 CDSW, which appeared mainly as an artillery tractor and breakdown vehicle. However, the firm was also involved in various experimental projects, one of which resulted in the limited production Terrapin Mark I wheeled amphibian.

A Foden DG/6/10 diesel-powered 10-tonner. The horizontal plate ahead of the cab carries a patch of gas sensitive paint that will change colour if gas is detected and warn the crew to put on their masks.

Foden's family rival, ERF supplied their 2C14 6-tonner for military service.

BRITISH MILITARY TRANSPORT 1829-1956

The Scammell company is best known for its range of heavy six-wheelers which, being supplied as gun tractors, breakdown lorries and tank transporters, have no place here. However, they also produced military versions of their famous mechanical horse three-wheelers in both 3- and 6-ton classes. An unlikely military vehicle by any standards, it was actually used extensively in much the same way as its civilian counterpart for short-haul, rapid turnaround delivery work. A licence-built version was even made for the French Army.

Thornycroft of Basingstoke was not only one of the oldest surviving firms in the military vehicle business, it was also a major producer of vehicles that included the four-wheel drive Nubian 3-tonner, 6 x 4 Tartar and the distinctive Amazon crane lorry.

Although this book is concerned with military matters it is only fair to acknowledge the contribution made, especially during the Second World War, by the commercial haulage industry. The pre-war British lorry driver could hardly be described as an individual in search of an easy life, but during the war his task became even more onerous. Fuel rationing certainly cut down congestion on the roads, although it applied to commercial users too, but the strain of night driving under blackout conditions more than cancelled out that advantage. At best an air raid could cause long hold-ups or diversions, which stretched both journey times and fuel consumption while at worst they subjected civilian drivers to the kind of

A Scammell mechanical horse with a tipping semi-trailer as supplied to the Royal Engineers for road maintenance work.

risks that their military counterparts had more reason to expect.

For the first year of the war Government policy was slanted strongly in favour of the railways, and fuel rationing was calculated to enforce this, but that was not all. One source claims that between 1939 and 1945 about 1,400 new statutory rules and orders were issued by the Ministry of War Transport, which affected road transport. Even the appointment of J.T.C Moore-Brabazon, a director of AEC Ltd, and later Lord Brabazon of Tara, as Minister of War Transport in 1940 had no immediate effect but there was a change of policy at the end of that year in favour of road and canal haulage when congestion on the railways reached a chronic state. In 1943, the Government created a Road Haulage Organisation which proved particularly useful during the build-up for D-Day when many oversized loads, often components for the artificial Mulberry Harbours, were carried from where they were built to the coast.

But increased legislation and constant changes of policy throughout the war years brought most haulage firms and their drivers to the last extremes of frustration since they were invariably codified by civil servants without any consultation with the trade. Yet at the same time the work which these men and their vehicles were called upon to do expanded greatly.

This study of the military and civilian transport situation in Britain is an important aspect of the overall story, but in the end a war can only be won by going to the enemy and defeating him on the ground as we shall see in the next two chapters. As the British Army and its Allies dispersed to the various foreign theatres of war, the essential transport went with them. Before long, military vehicles would be found working in every part of the world and on a scale that could never have been imagined, even at the height of the First World War.

The haulage contractor Isaac Barrie of Glasgow engaged in war work carrying newly assembled Churchill tank hulls from Babcock & Wilcox of Renfrew for final assembly at Luton. Various parts of the lorry are outlined in white to improve visibility in the blackout but the load does not appear to be secured in any way.

6 RETURN TO THE DESERT

The launch of any major offensive in the desert campaign depended to a large extent on the accumulation of adequate supplies, and this depended entirely on the availability of transport. Although the 3-tonner was the standard by which all loads were measured by the Army, the quantity of 10-tonners in the Middle East had also increased by the time of El Alamein in October 1942.

The British experience of operating transport in the deserts of the Middle East has already been noted. It was maintained in a small way between the wars but, apart from the development of special, low-pressure tyres little was done to adapt British military vehicles to the conditions. When the Second World War began Britain had garrisons in Egypt, the Sudan, Palestine and Trans-Jordan but the major threat was perceived to be Italian ambitions emanating from their Libyan colony and their recent subjugation of Ethiopia. In 1938, as a response to Munich, the Mobile Division (Egypt) was formed, commanded and trained by the redoubtable Major-General Percy Hobart. The division included two MT Companies RASC, with four companies' worth of lorries, totalling 96 vehicles in all. Although at times of potential trouble the division operated out beyond the railhead at Mersah Matruh its transport remained virtually tied to the coast road so that drivers gained very little experience of driving in the desert itself. Indeed, such desert experience as they did pick up, was of little long-term value because, due to the harsh conditions, the men did not serve in the Middle East long enough to benefit from it or pass it on.

It is stating the obvious to say that conditions in the desert cannot be compared in any way to Europe. It was not simply a matter of sand, heat and wide-open spaces; the sand itself varied in texture and formation, in some places so loose that no wheeled vehicle could cross it; elsewhere it was firm and smooth. Other regions, devoid of sand, offered a surface of rocky lava that had a dreadful effect on tyres and was so hard that it could shake a vehicle to pieces unless it crossed at walking pace. The best surface of all was hard, sun-baked mud, which gave a surface comparable to a British road, though when it rained, as it will do with a vengeance even in Egypt, this was the last surface one would wish to encounter.

Driving in the desert was also terribly boring. Travelling slowly over a featureless landscape on a compass bearing requires a degree of stoicism which, fortunately, is natural to the British character. Even so, when the only event to break the monotony might be the dubious fun of a puncture, a sandstorm or repeatedly digging your vehicle out of deep sand every few yards, the demands on patience were immense.

Navigation was another problem. If vehicles could not follow existing tyre tracks it was necessary to work on a compass bearing, which also requires special skills. The standard Army prismatic compass could only be used effectively at a distance from the vehicle, so the navigator had to stop and dismount to check direction. Even the sun compass developed by Bagnold had its limitations, always assuming one was fitted to the vehicle. Contrary to expectations the sun does not shine all day every day in the desert. In any case navigation is not just a matter of following a bearing. Finding a particular point on a map, in order to arrive at a supply dump or meet up with another convoy, required as much instinct as

The hole in the roof, on this Fordson WOT8 30cwt is square and has a lid, but it illustrates the point. The camel insignia represents General Headquarters and the window in the side of the canopy suggests a command, or office vehicle.

Morris-Commercial 15cwt trucks on a desert excursion at the time of the Mobile Division. Here, on firm ground, the going was easy but it was not to be trusted.

BRITISH MILITARY TRANSPORT 1829-1956

A Bedford 3-tonner goes to the aid of another vehicle which has been caught in a flash flood while its rather numerous crew endeavour to stay dry.

skill, and that cannot be taught of course. Putting up signs did not always work either. Unless the wherewithal existed to create a cairn of stones, a sign on a steel post was favoured, which was fine until it blew over. But wooden posts did not last that long, for wandering Arabs regarded them as an excellent source of firewood.

In order to reduce wear and tear on vehicle springs the RASC decided to lower the payload on the 3-ton lorry by half a ton, which meant that more vehicles were required to move a given amount of material. All personnel agreed that the worst load by far was petrol. Those faults first identified in the 4-gallon flimsy in France were exacerbated by desert conditions. Bumping across the desert in a lorry broke up cases and opened seams in the cans themselves so that petrol trickled away into the sand, and when it wasn't doing that it simply evaporated in the heat. The scale of wastage was such that it could have seriously affected the outcome of the campaign and it is claimed that more lorries, carrying petrol, were lost through fire than from enemy air attack.

The British riposte to the Italian invasion of Egypt in September 1940 was cautious at first. It began as a series of attacks on the fortified camps established by the Italians in the Egyptian desert. The attacks got under way in December and subsequently accelerated at a pace neither side could have imagined, culminating in the amazing British victory at Beda Fomm on 7 February 1941. By the time it was all over and the victors had time to count the spoils, some 1,500 wheeled vehicles, many of them lorries of excellent quality and in full working order, had been captured.

Now arose one of the great imponderables of the Second World War. Moving forward to a position at El Agheila, General Wavell left a small

Desert signpost. Fingers pointing in all directions, on a pole stuck into an oil drum, but notice how the vehicles remain well spread out.

6 RETURN TO THE DESERT

force there to block the road and withdrew the remainder. Not being gifted with second sight he believed that the Italians had been defeated beyond recuperation and saw no need to worry about what they had left in Tripoli. His priority now was to rest and refit his forces in preparation for a move into Greece.

That the British could have pushed on is beyond doubt. Although supplies were at a dangerously low level it is by no means certain, as some histories suggest, that this was Wavell's principal reason for halting the follow-up. Granted, transport was in short supply and the distance from Egypt so great that a further advance could not have been sustained from that source, but the Italians had inadvertently solved both of those problems with what they had surrendered in the way of stores. An advance to Tripoli would probably have succeeded and solved the supply situation – at least until more could be brought in by sea. Wavell may well have suspected that the Germans would do something to assist their Allies but he had good reason to believe that time was on his side. Who could have imagined that within one month General Erwin Rommel would have arrived in Tripoli with a token German force and

A Morris-Commercial 8cwt pick-up halts while the driver distributes cigarettes to the locals. The vehicle sports the combined British/Arabic registration plates seen on vehicles in Egypt before the war. It also has a camouflage net stretched over the front and appears to be loaded with a lot of un-military looking furniture.

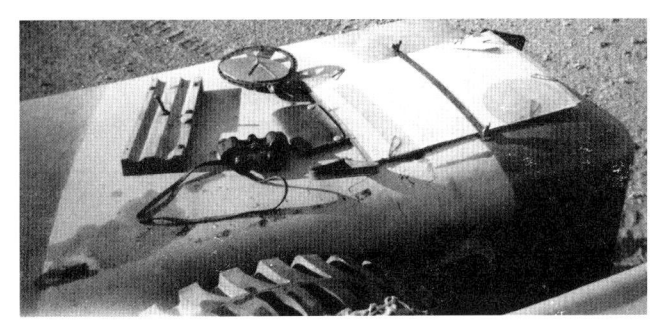

Navigator's tools. Map board, sun compass and binoculars laid out on the cab roof.

Slow going. A pair of Guy 3-tonners progress across a patch of difficult ground on lengths of flexible trackway.

BRITISH MILITARY TRANSPORT 1829-1956

launched a counterattack every bit as amazing as Wavell's, and for a while as successful?

It is beyond the scope of this study to follow the evolutions of the desert war in detail. It was as mobile and fluid as war on land could possibly be and the demands on transport were such that, for all the combatants, resources were stretched to the limit at all times. Both sides poured men and materials into the void, only to see them swallowed up, and not just in a figurative sense. Before any advance could begin vast dumps had to be built up, shielded as far as possible from enemy view yet accessible to one's own side. But all it needed was a modest change of fortune for one army to gain the upper hand, sweep their opponents from the board and capture a hoard that had been transported, at immense risk, for thousands of miles by sea and land.

One gets the impression that, for the British forces, despite their experience of the First World War, supply arrangements for the desert had been worked out to a European standard. Field Service Regulations visualised a maximum distance from railhead to forward delivery point of 80 miles within which second- and third-line echelons operated. Even though the railhead was extended it could never keep pace with the advance especially when, for example, the tanks set off for Beda Fomm. Soon, distances of up to 150 miles had to be covered and it was necessary to adapt the system before it broke down altogether. The third-

Transport spread out across the desert, dispersed to reduce the effect of air attack.

line transport alone was then limited to around 90 or 100 miles, with the second-line covering the next 40 miles. This, however, proved to be unworkable: 40 miles is not just a round trip of 80 miles, allowance has to be made for the time taken to load, refuel and unload a vehicle. Since, in order to prevent damage, convoys were limited to a maximum speed of 10mph, it meant a long day for the driver and his truck with very little time to spare for maintenance. Reducing the round trip to a maximum of 60 miles made some difference but it placed even greater strain upon the brigade and divisional transport. Up to this point in the command structure, some semblance of order was maintained but beyond that it could degenerate into a shambles. The divisional transport echelon then had to spread out across the desert in all directions, carrying supplies to scattered units, and this placed a tremendous strain on what was meant to be a local delivery service, a strain that could only be relieved by increasing the number of drivers and vehicles. The supply of vehicles will be covered shortly but this is probably a good point to record the fact that extra drivers were recruited from Egyptian, Palestinian, Cypriot, Maltese and other local personnel with considerable success.

Although the problem of defending transport from air attack had been appreciated earlier, as we have seen, the Libyan Desert was probably the first battlefield upon which the true meaning of air power was appreciated. There was virtually nowhere to hide and

A forward control Crossley 3-tonner, a searchlight lorry belonging to an anti-aircraft brigade shorn of cab hood and canopy. Notice that it still retains its pre-war registration plates.

even a handful of vehicles, moving with deliberate caution, could stir up a cloud of dust that was visible for miles. Once identified as a warrantable target by roving patrols of the Luftwaffe there was little one could do beyond trusting to luck. With the intention of encouraging resistance most British vehicles were provided with a hole in the cab roof, above the front passenger's seat, through which a Bren gun could be fired at an approaching aircraft. Whether it was used in this way very often is open to doubt, but the idea surely does not deserve the criticism levelled at it by one official publication after the war. This claimed that the dark circle in the roof made vehicles easier to spot from the air and served as a useful aiming point. The odds are that a pilot would see the truck, long before he noticed the hole, and once seen the truck was a small enough target in itself, without worrying about trying to hit the bullseye.

In practice, the general reaction to air attack was to keep one's head down and wait for it to go away. In addition to the unpopular hole in the roof, many lorries operating in the desert had hinged brackets fitted to the sides of the body, which would provide a rest for a Bren gun, and in some cases a sort of raised hook was welded to the front bumper from which the gun could be hung. It was a brave man who took on an enemy fighter single handed with a Bren gun when it was strafing his vehicle. The chances of doing any harm at all were very slim. The South Africans, on the other hand, took a hint from the Royal Navy as one answer to the problem. They created what might be called the highway equivalent of the Q-Ship in the form of a Ford 3-ton lorry, disguised to look like an ordinary truck but which

Camouflage in the desert. Taking advantage of a tiny patch of scrub a lorry attempts to hide beneath a camouflage net, which breaks up its angular shape. But a sign is set up to show who is there.

147

had a quadruple machine-gun mounting hidden inside. The entire upper section of the body was nothing more than a light, canvas-covered frame, which turned with the guns and permitted them to elevate through a flap in the roof. There is no evidence that it went beyond the prototype stage but it would certainly have come as quite a shock to an attacking Messerschmitt.

Picking off a few vehicles here and there was a nuisance but if a major concentration was discovered and attacked the result could be a disaster. The practice adopted to deal with air attack had something of the formal dance about it. Convoys of second- and first-line transport would agree to meet at some barren spot. At the appointed time they would approach from opposite directions and draw up some miles apart. Convoy leaders would then meet to make the final arrangements while the vehicles spread out in line abreast, at least 100yds apart. When everything was ready the second-line transport would move up in this formation to an agreed line, unload and then depart, leaving the supplies on the ground, grouped by type. Now the first-line transport approached, also in line abreast and so marshalled that each vehicle would be aiming directly at its designated load. This would be placed aboard as quickly as possible so that the convoy could depart, hopefully leaving nothing behind to mark its passing.

It is no exaggeration to say that the launch of any major offensive in the desert campaign depended to a large extent on the accumulation of adequate supplies, and this depended entirely on the availability of transport. Operation Brevity, launched on 15 May 1941, owed its very title to expectations of a brief action limited by supply. The shortage of transport was such that 22nd Guards Brigade Group had to borrow vehicles from 4th Indian Division for their attack on Halfaya Pass. Operation Battleaxe, which followed a month later, was on a far larger scale but it was a shortage of tanks and trained crews which delayed it. Again, the operation was supply driven. General Wavell's plan was to employ the largest force that his transport and supply service could maintain but it was not sufficient to dislodge the Axis forces or relieve Tobruk.

Based on a Canadian Ford 098T chassis, this South African anti-aircraft decoy vehicle shows its teeth in the form of four Vickers machine-guns poking through the roof.

6 RETURN TO THE DESERT

A desert supply convoy moving west. Behind it the road stretches straight, as far as the horizon.

Indeed, it was not until the so-called Winter Battle that the siege of Tobruk was lifted. This action, Operation Crusader, was launched in November 1941 and it only pre-empted a German attack on Tobruk by a few days. Thus, both sides had built up considerable forces in preparation and the result was almost certainly the largest armoured battle to be staged up to that time. As part of the long-term planning, the desert railway had been extended to a new railhead at Misheifa, due south of Sidi Barrani, and a supply scheme devised to support a three-pronged attack.

This involved the establishment of three forward bases that supplied a chain of Field Maintenance Centres, which proved to be the ideal solution to administrative problems in the desert. The date of the attack was originally based on the time when a series of supply dumps could be established and the British Official History records that the transport allotted to the creation of these dumps was, at the peak of its involvement, consuming 180,000 gallons of petrol a day.

By the time of Crusader (1941) the British Eighth Army could be considered completely motorised. That is to say, in addition to stores and equipment, which had to be carried or towed by motor vehicles, all personnel, including infantry, could be lifted. However, there was a distinction between those battalions classed as permanently motorised and those that were not. In the latter battalions, sufficient vehicles were allotted to move those elements that employed specialist equipment, such as heavy weapons or radios, but not for the main body of troops. When the battalion had to be moved en masse transport was supplied for the purpose and then returned to the pool.

Crusader was a long battle, but a successful one as far as the Allies were concerned. By early January the Axis forces had been pushed back to El Agheila, via the old Beda Fomm battlefield, but exhaustion had set in on both sides. The port facility at Tobruk was functioning but, even working in conjunction with the railhead at Misheifa, it could not provide enough tonnage to build up resources for a further attack. Yet until Tripoli was taken the supply situation was bound to be difficult. Benghazi would have been suitable if it were not so vulnerable. The most advanced Field Maintenance Centre was at Msus, which was 125 miles behind the most forward British positions. What this meant, in terms of transport, can be illustrated by the fact that, in a convoy of 200 lorries, as many as 40 might be required to carry

BRITISH MILITARY TRANSPORT 1829-1956

fuel and water for the round trip. Yet, on paper, there should have been no shortage of transport. According to figures published in 1952, more than 94,000 wheeled vehicles were on the books in the Middle East at the end of 1941. This was over and above the scale laid down in existing equipment tables by a massive amount. Undoubtedly to those who had need of them there were never enough, but *l'embarras de richesse* has never been a military complaint.

Time was the only answer, in order to build up reserves for the next stage. But again the British underestimated Rommel's impetuosity. He attacked on 21 January 1942 and forced the British back to the Gazala Line, which he himself had tried to hold, facing the other way, in December.

The subsequent actions at Gazala and the long retreat to the El Alamein position conform to what is often described as a soldiers' battle – which, in effect means that nobody is in control of events or has any idea of what is going on. The result at such times depends on the behaviour, under extreme conditions, of junior officers, NCOs and men. Little distinction can be made between combat or service arms since all are swept up in the collective urge

Vital as it was, fuel took second place to water. The containers were identical so these have all been clearly marked with 'W' to avoid mistakes.

to escape. Behaviour is unpredictable. On a bad day a hardened combat unit might fly unheeding while a bunch of lorry drivers turn and fight. Indeed, the history of the RASC at this point becomes a catalogue of courageous deeds that any regiment might be proud of and they were by no means alone in this.

To be evicted from established positions and pursued halfway across North Africa was something of a military disaster but it had this merit. At El Alamein British and Commonwealth troops were within easy reach of their main base and ports of entry on the Nile Delta.

British supply lines were shorter and more efficient as, in proportion, those of the enemy became longer and less reliable – this is a natural consequence of the fluctuating fortunes of war. In a region like the Libyan Desert, however, especially where it confronts a sea like the Mediterranean, the situation can be particularly bad. Short of evicting the enemy entirely from his base, the Germans had no obvious way to shorten their supply lines, even if they had control of the air and sea, because there were no adequate, intermediate ports that could handle supplies on a sufficient scale.

The build-up of supplies for General Montgomery's projected new offensive went on unabated. The provision of vehicles improved still further due to a change in the delivery arrangements. The recently created Corps of Royal Electrical and Mechanical Engineers (REME) took over some impressive Base Ordnance Workshops in the Middle East in 1942. Some were already manufacturing components, even including vehicle batteries, which only seem to have lasted about six months in desert conditions. Shortly before the Battle of El Alamein, REME also took over control of four large plants, which had been established since June 1941 for the assembly of vehicles delivered from Britain in a 'completely knocked down' state. This arrangement had been devised to assist in shipping by cutting down on volume and meant that more vehicles could be carried on a given vessel.

Although the 3-tonner was the standard by which all loads were measured the quantity of 10-tonners in the Middle East had also increased. All the same their carrying capacity was calculated in terms of 3-tonner loads and, during the preparations for the El Alamein battle this became more literal still. The area behind the line where dumps were being established was not as thoroughly reconnoitred as it might have been and large patches of very soft sand could be found. If a convoy of laden 10-tonners ventured into one of these it inevitably became stuck and the normal practice was for a succession of 3-tonners to go in and 'lighten ship', by unloading the stranded heavies until they could extricate themselves.

With someone as careful as Montgomery in command of the Eighth Army the pursuit of Axis forces after El Alamein was not the kind of bold thrust that Rommel had delighted in. Yet it still placed a great strain on

An assortment of wrecked lorries, mostly of North American origin, recovered from the desert and stored, awaiting repair.

American-built Dodge T215 panel van with various British modifications including the roof hatch and water can rack. The patch of gas detector paint can be seen on the bonnet and the RAF roundel on the roof serves as a general British recognition sign.

transport. The ports of Tobruk and Benghazi were recaptured and opened up in their turn but both were damaged and, even when fully restored, could not handle supplies on the scale required. The situation eased considerably after Tripoli was taken and the Army moved into Tunisia, but by then a high percentage of the transport had suffered considerable wear and tear, which could easily be measured by increased oil consumption. A repair programme was instigated and the change to a more temperate landscape eased the problem, but it brought new ones of its own. Road discipline had to be tightened. To drivers used to the wide-open desert spaces it took time to adjust. No longer could they just swan off into the blue to avoid a broken-down vehicle or get away from an air attack. Now it was a matter of keeping to the straight and narrow, on roads that had never been designed to take motor traffic, never mind the quantities now imposed upon them. During the build up for the Mareth Line battle, supply convoys from Tripoli were restricted to one narrow road and it is interesting to note that the old technique from the First World War, that of running a block system as if the convoys were railway trains, was adopted again.

The fact that American-built trucks were being supplied to the British Army from the first year of the war has already been established. Mention has also been made of large deliveries of Chevrolets direct to the Middle East. Under the terms of a rather selective neutrality act, trucks, and other military stores not considered aggressive in the conventional sense were not covered by any embargo. Thus, the modified act, signed by the President in November 1939, which lifted the embargo for all belligerents on condition that they paid for the goods and made their own shipping arrangements, did not affect trucks. This 'Cash and Carry' system, as the President called it, was

Inside one of the vast REME workshops in the Delta. Fitters are working on Canadian Chevrolet 3-tonners.

in any case slanted entirely in favour of Great Britain and France; Germany might be able to pay but her merchant shipping dared not risk the Atlantic. Even the Lend-Lease Act, the Master Agreement of which was signed in February 1942, did not entirely eliminate the need to purchase equipment from the United States, including trucks. Lend-Lease was not an open cheque book. Materials were supplied to an agreed scale but if an emergency arose, for example, the bombing of a large factory building lorries in Britain, then emergency deliveries from the United States to make up numbers had to be paid for.

Although the Americans, with their vast industrial resources, supplied huge numbers of vehicles to the British Army, Canada was not that far behind. Canada's achievement was that it graduated from the rank of small-scale producer in 1939 to a major supplier in a surprisingly short time. British dealings with the United States could cause irritation when priorities clashed but the Americans were in such a strong position that they inevitably got their way in the end. Canada could not compete and there is little doubt that the authorities in Britain sometimes treated the Dominion in a cavalier fashion when it came to getting what they wanted. And the Canadians were not entirely free of American influence either.

Canada's two main vehicle builders, Ford and General Motors, were in some respects subsidiaries of their American parents as any examination of their domestic products will show. Thus, when it came to building trucks for Britain the Canadians had to bend to British wishes while balancing these against their American-inspired production techniques and a more direct reliance on the United States for the supply of components. Hindsight suggests that in the long run this was not the best solution, yet it gave Canada the chance to establish an independent name for itself with the production of a series of very distinctive hybrids, which are still regarded by many with immense affection.

Canada's potential as a producer of military equipment had been investigated by Britain in 1935 and

BRITISH MILITARY TRANSPORT 1829-1956

A pair of Canadian Military Pattern 15cwts with early style cabs. Both have been extensively modified to cope with desert conditions. The nearer vehicle has a 7th Armoured Division badge on the mudguard, an A Squadron symbol on the door and, since the figure appears to be wearing an RTR beret and tank suit, they probably belong to the squadron transport.

two years later both Ford and General Motors produced prototype trucks. Both were 15cwt pick-ups with cabs, like their British contemporaries, that had the crew sitting virtually alongside the engine. The General Motors version, built at their Oshawa, Ontario plant, bore some resemblance to the British Bedford MW, as might be expected, but the Ford, built at their Windsor, Ontario, plant was very distinctive. The design is credited to a young engineer at Ford, Sid Swallow, and when the two companies agreed to harmonise production in 1940 it was the Ford-style cab that was selected for both versions. It was an example that some British companies might have followed.

When war was declared Canada was still gearing up for mass production but when France fell the need to replace lost transport demanded urgent action. As a first step the two major companies, joined by Chrysler with their Dodge range, turned out large numbers of militarised commercial models known officially as 'modified conventional' types to make up the deficit. Meanwhile, on instructions from Ottawa, Ford and General Motors expanded production of the new military types to match the existing British range from 8cwt to 3 tons, the latter mainly in 4 x 4 or 6 x 4 configuration. Indeed, Canadian production was directed far more to the adoption of four-wheel drive in all sizes than was normal in Britain. Known initially as Department of National Defence (DND) models, they soon became better known as Canadian Military Pattern (CMP) and the CMP lorry, with the distinctive Swallow cab that was applied to the entire range, soon became a familiar sight throughout the world.

Swallow himself was the first to admit that his design was only a start. Despite the fact that they were built to British requirements, even to the point of having right-hand drive, this did not extend to the engines, for British lorries were regarded as seriously underpowered by transatlantic standards. Canadian Fords used their regular V8 while the Chevrolet straight six, fitted in GM produced vehicles, was nearly as large. Designing a cab that could accommodate either of these engines without exceeding dimensions laid down by Britain was no mean achievement of itself, but it resulted in a cramped interior. Access to the engine was very restricted and the average driver, sporting a pair of Regular Army boots, experienced some difficulty just getting both feet onto the pedals. A long run could result in extreme discomfort. Swallow was posted to London quite early in the war but by 1942 a revised cab design was available. This was wider at the front, resulting in more leg room and better access to the engine and it also featured a reverse sloping windscreen. This small but effective innovation was intended to prevent the glass from reflecting sunlight, which would immediately draw attention to the vehicle at a considerable distance, no matter how well camouflaged or carefully driven.

The old Middle East battlefields from the First World War – Palestine, Arabia and Mesopotamia – did not assume the same importance in the Second World War. The centre of gravity had now shifted south and west because Italy was the main enemy, not Turkey. It did not prevent Axis forces from trying to create trouble, especially in Iraq and Persia, but the difficulty for them was that this time Britain had got there first. A special relationship, evolved from British mandates established at the end of the First World War, was one reason for the British – or more accurately British/Indian – presence, but vital supplies of aircraft fuel from the massive refinery at Abadan was a more pressing one.

The situation changed dramatically when the Soviet Union entered the war. Early German successes in the south created an uncomfortable scenario in which their forces, reaching the Caucasus, could push down between the Black Sea and the Caspian into Persia. The British responded forming the new Persia and Iraq Command (PAIC) and earmarking divisions to defend the Canal Zone. The defeat of the Germans at Stalingrad in February 1943 eased this threat but by that time the region had achieved a new significance. Under the terms of two Protocols, signed in October 1941 and June 1942, Britain and the United States agreed to maintain supplies of war materials and machine tools to the Soviet Union on a monthly basis. The first and most obvious route was the one used in the First World War, by sea around the top of Scandinavia. Nobody needs reminding what this involved, the saga of the Russian Convoys being one of the most harrowing of the war. A route from the Persian Gulf, overland and into southern Russia was a reasonable alternative and the trans-Iranian railway was improved and expanded to carry the stores. Both Britain and the United States supplied locomotives to work the line to its maximum capacity but, since most of the locomotives were steam and water in this region a scarce commodity,

A Canadian 'modified conventional' Ford 3-tonner with steel general service body.

BRITISH MILITARY TRANSPORT 1829-1956

it was decided to establish a parallel road route. In fact, a network of routes was created, road and rail linking Khorramshahr and Basra on the Shatt-al-Arab with Baghdad, Mosul, Teheran and the port of Bandar Shah on the Caspian. Another direct road route, duplicated by rail for part of the way, ran from Teheran via Tabriz to the frontier town of Dzhulfa and then into the Soviet Union on the western side of the Caspian.

It was this last route that probably carried most of the traffic and in time it was under intense pressure. The British had begun matters using mostly lorries hired in Persia with a mixture of civilian and military drivers but, as the Soviet demands increased, the Royal Indian Army Service Corps (RIASC) became heavily involved. The conditions were atrocious. The history of the RASC remarks that it was quite normal for a convoy to set off with crews wearing tropical gear, khaki drill shorts and shirts, but by the time they reached the other end a mixture of battledress, sheepskin overcoats and gumboots was dress of the day.* The same history contrasts British with American and Soviet convoy techniques. The RIASC employed the British block system of convoys organised as platoons, driven at a steady pace with fixed intervals and frequent halts. The Americans used their extended convoy system, which involved vehicles moving independently with roving maintenance crews on the road to pick up casualties. The Soviets simply gathered as many lorries as possible into huge convoys and then drove them flat out from one end to the other.

Both Allies criticised the British system for being too slow and methodical but, as the accident rate escalated and trucks started to wear out on an alarming scale, they came to see that slow but sure was not quite so foolish after all and started to conform. The American Red Ball Express system, which later on operated with such success in Europe evolved from US Army experience in this region.

At GHQ in Cairo, a plan to invade Sicily was already being drawn up while the fighting in Tunisia was still going on. It began on 10 July 1943 as a combined airborne/amphibious operation. From the supply and transportation point of view the greatest innovation has to be the DUKW. The RASC had one company available for the landings but it was a bit of an unknown quantity because the crews had very little experience of their new vehicles. A handful had been made available, about six weeks earlier, so some training could be done at Sousse on the Tunisian coast. About 230 DUKWs had been supplied to British forces in time for the landings and their value was appreciated at once.

The DUKW was effectively a GMC 2½-ton truck, fitted with a boat-shaped amphibious body designed by the New York yacht designers Sparkman and Stevens. Driven in the water by a single screw, and on land in the conventional manner, the DUKW proved surprisingly

Lines of new Canadian Military Pattern 3-tonners ready for distribution.

seaworthy for such a hybrid but it was the vehicle's ability to simplify ship to shore supply operations that made it so valuable.

Using Sicily as a springboard, the Allies then launched their forces into mainland Italy. The DUKWs began a supply ferry service across the Straits of Messina within two hours of the first landing but there was no opposition. Moving inland they proved difficult to manoeuvre through narrow village streets until a rough and ready road widening scheme was instituted.

A subsequent landing at Salerno on the west coast, timed to coincide with the Italian armistice on 9 September 1943, was not an immediate success since the Germans anticipated the move and resisted strongly. On the same day British forces captured Taranto, on Italy's instep, as part of a move to open up southern Italian ports, in particular on the east coast. Taranto was actually captured by airborne troops landing from the sea. They came complete with an RASC contingent but no transport at all – a conundrum that was solved by liberating whatever was required from local sources.

The masterplan for the Italian campaign was dictated by the geology of the country. The Apennine range, running like a spine down the centre, virtually split the country in two and lateral communications were poor. It was therefore agreed that the Americans would work their way up the west side while the British, with their Canadian, Indian, New Zealand, French and Polish allies tackled the east. Even with the Italians out of the picture the country itself conspired with the German defenders. Anything that even looked like a bridge was destroyed and every viable defensive position was held stubbornly.

As if these problems were not enough to contend with, forces in the Italian theatre were constantly losing experienced personnel, often whole divisions at a time, during the build-up

Typical of highway conditions on some of the long-haul supply routes in the Middle East, such as those in Persia, is this well engineered stretch on a cliff side. Here being used by British transport.

*(Various authors), *The Story of the Royal Army Service Corps 1939–1945* (Institution of the RASC and G. Bell & Sons, 1955)

A line of British manned DUKWs coming ashore over a Mediterranean beach.

in Britain for the forthcoming invasion of France. The Italian campaign became, in many minds, a second-class theatre and this applied to equipment as much as to men. The opposition the Allies faced was by no means second class and the fighting was hard throughout although, as the RASC history states 'the Italian campaign was administratively an engineer and transport battle'. When operations were taking place near the coast DUKWs continued to prove useful. In order to maintain an advance it was often quicker to move supplies a short distance by sea than wait until yet another bridge was repaired. Yet bridges would be required in the end and the Royal Engineers, using Bailey and Hamilton portable structures, were very much in demand. This requirement, in its turn, placed an extra load on the transport services who had to bring up the bridge components along with the plant, such as bulldozers, excavators and cranes, needed to prepare a site and handle material. An example, provided by the RASC history, is the 390ft-long Bailey bridge erected over the Trigno river. It required transport to the extent of six tipper trucks, two 10-ton lorries and 71 3-tonners. The same source also pointed out that, ingenious as they were, even Bailey bridges had their limitations. One created to bridge the River Sangro was 1,000ft long and, due to the length of the span, could only be constructed as a single lane. This inevitably created a serious bottleneck.

Another innovation for the Italian campaign, one it shared with the Pacific, was the use of Jeeps in the supply role. When the fighting led troops into mountainous terrain it proved virtually impossible to employ conventional transport. Pack mule companies undertook a lot of the work but the scale of resupply, especially of artillery ammunition, was beyond their capabilities unaided. Platoons of Jeeps, each towing a lightweight trailer, solved the problem most effectively. They could go almost anywhere and a platoon was capable of lifting up to 30 tons at a time.

The plan to be in Rome by Christmas 1943 proved to be unduly sanguine, German defensive positions on the Gustav Line and the Hitler Line proving hard to crack. The focal point of Monte Cassino, overlooking the Liri plain, conspired to put the entire campaign six months behind schedule. The Anzio landing of 22 January 1944 was intended to outflank the Cassino impasse and it, too, ran into stiff opposition. Indeed, once the initial beachhead had been established, Anzio turned into a situation not unlike the First World War except that the Allies had their backs very close to the shore. However, the supply problem was dealt with in a simple manner, considering the conditions. Early each morning 50 3-ton lorries, all fully laden, came ashore from LSTs (Landing Ship Tank) while 50 empty vehicles from the previous day were driven aboard. This went on for the best part of five months.

The final year of the campaign in Italy has little to offer by way of variety. It was a tedious struggle, often in atrocious conditions, which was eclipsed in the public mind by events in north-west Europe. However, in the final stages it did produce one transport innovation. Lake Comacchio, in the east of the country, on the Lombardy Plain, was regarded as a major obstacle in the advance to the River Po. The swampy area surrounding it limited the scope for using DUKWs so the RASC was introduced to another American amphibian, the LVT 4 or Buffalo, as it was known in Britain. In Italy they called it the Fantail on account of the hinged rear ramp.

Where the Buffalo was used by British troops in north-west Europe – for instance during the Walcheren landings in the Netherlands, and at the crossing of the Rhine – it was always operated by Royal Armoured Corps personnel, presumably because it served in the direct assault role, carrying infantry or guns. In Italy, with the RASC the assumption was that the Buffalo would be used in the supply role, after all it could handle a 4-ton payload. In the event they also served to move infantry and guns across Lake Comacchio and, in doing so, proved a great success.

British troops, Royal Tank Regiment by the look of the cap badge and beret, in unmarked Jeeps, probably newly delivered.

View from the bridge of an LST carrying transport, part of a convoy of the sort that was used to replenish the Anzio beachhead. The tall stacks on each side of the deck provide ventilation for the tank hold below.

7 SUPPLYING VICTORY

Vehicles with steel bodies or articulated semi-trailers were rarities in prewar Britain. During the war, thanks largely to the greater availability of steel, portable welding apparatus to effect quick repairs, and American influence, the benefits of metal-bodied vehicles and those with semi-trailers were finally accepted. By employing an articulated semi-trailer, the payload of a typical 3-ton chassis could be doubled.

7 SUPPLYING VICTORY

lorries, but another undoubtedly the lack of incentive to improve. Transport was a relatively low priority, compared with certain weapons, so resources had to be concentrated on production at the expense of technical development.

This is clearly reflected in monthly reports emanating from the Ministry of Supply, which was created by the Government in 1940. The first report appeared in October 1943, entitled *TT2 Transport Bulletin*. TT2 was a department of the Ministry responsible for the provision of wheeled vehicles and half-tracks to the services. Its bulletins were linked with a sister department created at the same time, the Wheeled Vehicles Experimental Establishment (WVEE). By 1940 the need to reconsider the controversial changes of 1928 was recognised. Tank and combat vehicle development was now catered for by the Experimental Wing of the Department of Tank Design (DTD) while supply vehicles, mostly unarmoured, became the province of WVEE. The former moved to Chobham while WVEE remained at Farnborough with a design department at Staines.

The bulletins were written in a frank, lightweight style but they did not always have much to report. New vehicles continued to emerge but in most cases they were imports, or modest improvements to British-built types, which the editorials sought to make the most of. Even then they were sometimes short on such information and in one issue spared some copy for the etymology of the name Jeep. In another they sought to explain 'Why not all 4 x 4s?' It was a question that was clearly bothering some people. In all but a few instances the four-wheel drive lorry had already replaced the 6 x 4 and, as anyone who worked with them could see, a 4 x 4 also had enormous advantages over the regular 4 x 2.

A transport convoy disembarks from an LST on a Mediterranean beach led by a Bedford OY 3-tonner.

One thing that should strike anyone who studies British military transport during the Second World War is how little it changed. Many of the types that were in production when the war began could still be found in service when it ended. There were improvements during that time, at least in detail, but the majority were recognisably the same and quite a few still in production. One reason was obviously the good, solid construction of most British

161

BRITISH MILITARY TRANSPORT 1829-1956

Typical of vehicles that saw service throughout the war, two essentially civilian types in military colours: a Triumph 3SW, 350cc solo machine followed by a Commer Q4. The markings indicate 4th Infantry Division, which later made such a name for itself in Burma.

According to the *Transport Bulletin* it was all a matter of balance. The 4 x 4 still being something of a novelty in Britain at the start of the war, British factories had all tooled up to produce a series of items for conventional lorries: one engine, one clutch, one gearbox and one driving axle per vehicle. Four-wheel drive production required extra machining facilities for the driven front axle on the production line, extra bevel gear cutting for the second differential and transfer box, plus the manufacture of Tracta joints, the universal couplings that enabled a driven front axle to steer. Since completion of vehicles was at the mercy of the slowest item on the production line this meant that the time required to build a 4 x 4 was effectively double that of a 4 x 2. Naturally the factories had steadily been increasing their machine tool equipment but even at best the construction of a 4 x 4 required about 30 per cent more man-hours than a 4 x 2, and this illustrated a second problem. Lorry production enjoyed no labour priorities, except in the case of some very large vehicles. As a consequence, skilled personnel were being siphoned off to higher priority industries or, if less skilled, called to the colours. By 1944 there were fewer people working in the British motor industry than there had been a year earlier, and the figure was expected to drop again in 1945.

A factory fresh Guy Quad Ant, still with the distinctive front end designed before the war.

Despite this rather depressing summary – which appears to add another variation to the old British complaint 'if God had meant us to have four-wheel drive lorries he would have provided suitable factories' – the *Transport Bulletin* was able to report some progress. In February 1944, it announced the return of a famous name. Guy Motors of Wolverhampton, for some time past concentrating mainly on building austerity lorries and buses for the civilian market, was now producing a four-wheel drive version of its Ant 15cwt truck. Not that it was anything outstanding, merely a truck bodied version of the obsolete Quad Ant field artillery tractor, but it initiated a trend to build all 15cwts as 4 x 4. A step which Morris-Commercial was due to take shortly. Other matters on which the *Transport Bulletin* pontificated at some length were the provision of steel, instead of wooden lorry bodies, and the growth of the semi-trailer type of load-carrying vehicle.

It was noted, even between the wars, that the traditional wooden load-carrying body was not ideal. Attempts had been made to 'metalise' wood by a patent process without much success but trials with steel or aluminium bodies seemed to show that they suffered more drastic damage and were not so easy to repair. By 1944 attitudes had changed. Steel was easier to clean than wood and it was not permanently contaminated by leaking oil or fuel. For service in the Far East it did not attract termites or generate fungi as wood did and, of course, it was less prone to catch fire. Naturally, steel was heavier, something over 1cwt when comparing steel or wooden bodies on a typical four-wheeled 3-tonner, but it was now much easier to repair. Most units were equipped with portable welding

Clearly a milestone event of a kind, a Fordson WOT6, 3-ton 4 x 4 on the assembly line at Dagenham. The '25,000' presumably refers to four-wheel drive vehicles built by all British manufacturers.

163

apparatus, unheard of in 1934, which meant that a damaged steel body could be patched up in situ. Carpenters, by contrast, were now rare and prized creatures. A lorry with a damaged wooden body could be out of service for days while it was repaired. If, said the *Transport Bulletin*, anyone was tempted to ask why, if steel was so good, it had not been used earlier the answer was that it had not been available.

Like steel bodies, vehicles with articulated semi-trailer attachments were something of a rarity in Britain before the war. The concept was tried but had not caught on except for heavy duty low-loaders used for moving plant, and a special lightweight type designed primarily to handle local deliveries from railway stations. In the United States, on the other hand, the semi-trailer had been recognised as an ideal combination and it was due largely to American influence that its virtues were finally accepted. Its lack of instant appeal in Britain is difficult to explain because it addressed a peculiarly British problem, although taxation conditions may have had something to do with it. The point was that, by employing a semi-trailer the payload of a typical 3-ton chassis could be doubled. This was because half of the load was carried by the tractor while the rest was borne by the trailer's own axle. Regular reports in the *Transport Bulletin* testify to the increasing demand for this type, mainly imported from Canada or the United States and it appeared with both 4 x 2 and 4 x 4 tractor units.

Another reason given for the new-found popularity of the semi-trailer was a worldwide shortage of alternative types of heavy haulage vehicles. This was said to be due to the priority given to artillery tractors and tank transporters, which absorbed most of the available production in this class. Another option, always more popular in Britain until the introduction of the semi-trailer from across the Atlantic, was the conventional drawbar trailer standing entirely on its own four wheels. Even a quick scan through representative issues of the *Transport Bulletin* will reveal that notices about trailers appear to exceed those on other types of transport to a surprising degree. This is further reflected in the remarkable number of British companies that specialised in the production of cargo trailers to the exclusion of anything else. Many of these firms made dozens of special purpose types for military use, all of which had to pass the same rigorous tests as the vehicles that hauled them.

Although the English Home Counties could not be described as one of nature's more rugged landscapes, it offered considerable variety to vehicle testers. Farnborough falls comfortably within this region but, by judicious use of what was available, complemented by a selection of artificial courses, WVEE was able to recreate a surprising variety of conditions. A road run to Hindhead along the North Downs included some short, steep climbs with sharp bends while the longer route to Salisbury offered straight, level sections ideal for high-speed runs. A disused brickyard at Bracknell provided a glutinous clay pit and the area around the nearby Fleet Pond was sandy enough to supply the odd dune. At Farnborough itself there was Hungry Hill, nicknamed the 'liver rattler', and a cross-country course in Long Valley known as the 'murder run', along with a deep wading-tank and a concrete slope designed to reproduce the angle between the ramp of a landing craft and the beach.

The establishment also used a mountain course in South Wales to provide a tougher challenge when long, winding hills and steep grades were required. A typical vehicle test involved a total of 10,000 miles: 7,500 on the road and 2,500 miles across country including 250 miles up and down Hungry Hill. This particular course had been designed originally to duplicate conditions on the North West Frontier of India by using blocks of granite embedded in concrete, which should have shaken most vehicles to pieces. Yet years of wear and weather had reduced these obstacles to what the *Transport Bulletin* called carbuncles so a new course, of concrete strips, laid out in an irregular fashion, had been constructed to keep livers rattling. If the vehicle survived the full programme of runs over this course it was then given a complete strip down in WVEE's own workshops where every component was examined before the final report was issued.

The amazing success of the DUKW during the Sicilian and Italian amphibious landings has already been mentioned, as has the tracked amphibian known to British troops as the Buffalo. These vehicles were but two manifestations of the ability of American industry to design and produce superb amphibious vehicles in a remarkably short time. For some strange reason this admirable ability was matched in Britain by a curious trait that resulted in some of the most bizarre and useless vehicles ever built. The tracked amphibian is, perhaps, too specialised to be covered in detail here but one has only to compare the American product with its British rivals, Argosy and Neptune, to appreciate the point. Britain's rival to the DUKW deserves closer scrutiny, however.

In its December 1943 edition, the *Transport Bulletin* went to some lengths to play down any suggestion of rivalry when it introduced Terrapin, the British alternative to the DUKW. British interest in amphibians can be dated to December 1942 when the British Truck Mission in Washington was instructed by the Ministry of Supply to consider the requirement for 300 DUKWs and 500 tracked amphibians of the Buffalo type. The American response was not encouraging. They had only placed a limited initial order for 2,000 DUKWs and these had already been allocated to the US Army. Britain eventually received nearly 300 for service in the Mediterranean, and would receive hundreds more in time when production expanded but – while the latter remained an unlikely possibility – steps were taken to produce a British equivalent.

A Bedford OXC semi-trailer combination with an enclosed, house-type body. Vehicles such as this formed part of the 'Golden Arrow' and 'Blue Train' command and signals convoys.

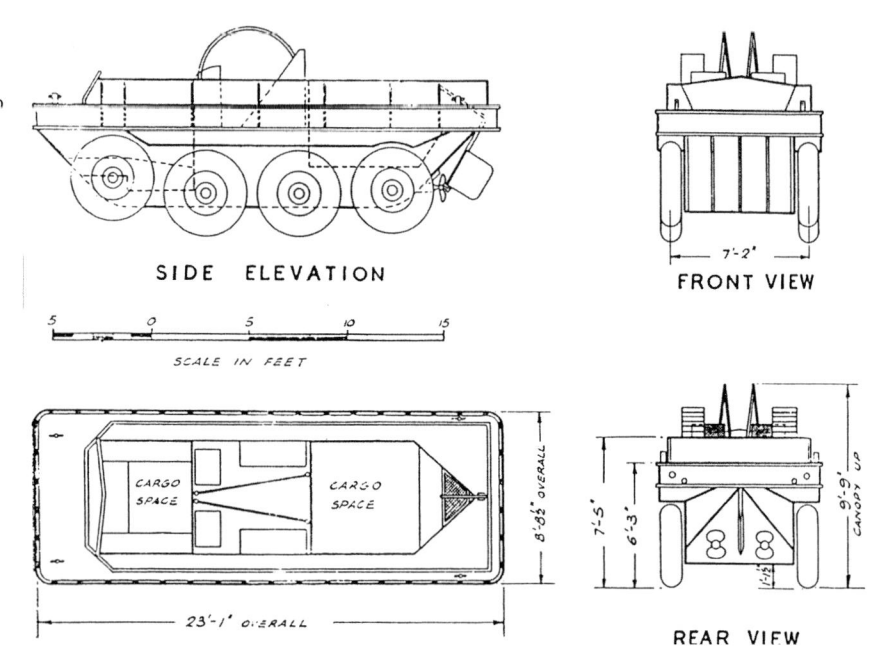

Outline drawings of the original Terrapin showing the two cargo holds and unusual wheel configuration.

SIDE ELEVATION

SCALE IN FEET

FRONT VIEW

REAR VIEW

A Terrapin in the water showing the central location of the helmsman/driver.

The logical course was to copy what the Americans had done. That is, to create an amphibious vehicle around the mechanical components of a standard 2½-ton Army truck. Unfortunately, it was claimed, there was no vehicle in production in Britain that lent itself to similar adaptation. The six-wheel drive version of the CMP 3-tonner comes to mind as a possible choice but there is no evidence to show that it was considered. Instead, the Ministry of Supply authorised the design and construction of something completely new, the Terrapin.

Terrapin's hull form was designed by the marine department of Thornycrofts but the production contract was handed to Morris-Commercial in Birmingham. It was an eight-wheel drive vehicle, powered by a pair of Ford V8 engines. It was driven in the water by twin marine propellers and steered with rudders or by varying the speed of each engine. The trouble was that this latter procedure was also adopted for steering on land. Although it was wheeled, Terrapin skid-steered like a tank by juggling the respective engine speeds to effect a change in direction. Since all eight wheels were fitted with large section, low-pressure tyres of the farm tractor type the strain of skid-steering all of them on a hard surface was appreciated. Consequently, it was designed in such a way that, on hard ground, only the four central wheels bore any weight. This simplified steering stresses to some extent but, to ensure it remained like this in its laden state, the Terrapin had no suspension in the conventional sense, just the cushioning

Canadian troops training with landing craft, the vehicle in this case being a Canadian Military Pattern 15cwt.

effect of the tyres. Advocates pointed to one great advantage: the Terrapin was designed to carry 4 tons as against the DUKW's 2½ tons. In fact, it was capable of handling 5 tons on land or in very calm water, but 4 tons was preferred to leave a safe margin. However, this required the load to be split, because the driver, or helmsman, occupied a central cab with separate cargo holds fore and aft. This was not a great problem except that, unlike the DUKW, a Terrapin could not handle a single, indivisible load like an anti-tank gun.

Early trials revealed a crop of faults and some naval experts cast doubt upon the Terrapin's seagoing qualities. They also disliked the fact that, when launching from a landing craft at sea, the Terrapin had to reverse into the water to avoid damaging the propellers. The Combined Operations Experimental Establishment (COXE) at Westward Ho! in North Devon used the DUKW as a yardstick during their trials and found the production Terrapin wanting. Ministry of Supply staff and members of the design team considered this unfair but one wonders what else COXE was supposed to use as a yardstick since the Terrapin was intended to fulfil a similar role. Whether it was fair or not the derogatory reports stuck and Terrapin was condemned. Ultimately 500 were ordered, the first 200 of which were rejected as unsuitable for active service but a few of the later ones were used operationally in Europe. Unfortunately, cooling problems rendered Terrapins unsuitable for service in warmer climes.

In an effort to overcome these problems, Thornycroft designed Terrapin II in 1943 and produced prototypes. This was a larger vehicle with a 10-ton load capacity and a much more sensible layout although it retained the twin-engine drive and rigid suspension. Earmarked for production with a view to operations in the Far East in 1945, it had not completed prototype trials when the war ended and the project was cancelled. When the study of history involves the consideration of motives or personality it is always suspect, but in reviewing this episode one wonders how much the events recorded were driven by jealousy or pride, encapsulated in the phrase 'Not Invented Here'. Ultimately, Britain obtained another 3,500 DUKWs, one or two of which were still in service with the British Army as late as 1996. Such clear evidence of a successful design makes it difficult to reach any other conclusion.

In Britain, most of 1943 and the early months of 1944 were dominated by preparations for the invasion of occupied France. From the transport point of view this raised the problem of landing. Lessons from Sicily and Salerno drove home the point that, in the initial stages at least before ports could be captured, all operations would have to take place across open beaches. This meant that vehicles of all types would have to wade through at least 3ft of water for a short distance between leaving landing craft and arriving on dry land, but no such requirement had been included in vehicle specifications.

As early as July 1940, Churchill had been badgering General Ismay, head of the military section on the War Cabinet secretariat, with memos demanding progress reports on the development of amphibious landing craft. One result was the formation of 110 Force at Inverary in Scotland, which later gave way to Combined Operations Headquarters. Early work on deep wading, as the ship-to-shore movement is called, was concentrated on the teeth arms. When it came to transport the manufacturers were asked to develop their own ideas. In the main it was a question of sealing the ignition system, maintaining an air supply and enabling the exhaust to escape.

The method finally adopted involved sealing all electrical components with a substance known as pressure plastic, mainly manufactured by the Bostick company. Air was supplied through extended pipes, normally attached to the roof of the cab, on the inside, but tests revealed that exhaust arrangements did not need modification. As long as the engine was running pressure was sufficient to keep water out. Thus prepared a vehicle would certainly run under water, even when the requirement was raised from 3ft to 6ft depth. However, there was also the ingress of water around the seams of gearboxes, axles and other moving parts to be dealt with and it was obvious that lubricants would either be washed off or destroyed by mixing with sea water so a far more extensive programme of preparation had to be developed. This involved a whole range of materials, a book of instruction for each type of vehicle and a series of processes, which had to be carried out in stages, up to the point where the vehicle was ready to board ship.

As a hedge against failure of the normal waterproofing system, Vauxhall Motors developed an alternative, which they christened the 'Giraffe'. It involved raising the engine and driver's cab of a lorry on a sub-frame, extending the gear change controls and interposing a chain drive into the system. The idea was that the chassis and load would proceed under water while the engine continued to run high and dry. It was applied to a normal Bedford QL 3-tonner and appeared to work well enough, but it was obviously a complicated solution that would have been even more difficult to apply to a normal control vehicle and extremely awkward to adapt for a smaller one. In the event it did not prove necessary.

Experience gained during the various Mediterranean landings contributed to the store of knowledge needed to effect a successful landing in Normandy, but the proposed assault was on a far greater scale. Looking at the larger picture first the planning staff of 21st Army Group worked out a scale of stores for British and Canadian forces for their sectors. The outline plan was to start landing stores over the open beaches and to maintain this until sufficient local ports, large and small, could be captured and restored to use. The artificial harbour, Mulberry B in the British sector, was included in

A typical vehicle park created in the days leading up to D-Day. Fordson 15cwts in the foreground, Bedfords in the middle rows and Canadian-built trucks beyond that.

the calculations, but always it seems with a good deal of caution as far as its capacity was concerned, and this caution was not misplaced.

For a few days after D-Day itself the army ashore would be supplied from Beach Maintenance Areas on the shore. As the beachhead expanded, roadheads would be set up further inland until a large Rear Maintenance Area could be set up to channel all supplies. Even at full capacity it was clear that the various ports around the Normandy shore would not be able to cope with the full scale of deliveries required, so the Mulberries, and the beaches around them, would remain active until the fighting moved east. As we shall see, even this was not as simple as it sounded then.

To give some idea of the scales involved the following figures were laid down as guidelines by 21st Army Group for the anticipated situation by midnight on D+3, that is three days on from D-Day. For ammunition of all kinds an estimated four days' full expenditure was to be in place by D+5. By the same date sufficient fuel would be needed to permit every vehicle in Normandy to move 50 miles. For other stores a system of packs was introduced, scaled to brigade level requirements up to D+10 and from then on to meet divisional demands. What this actually means in terms of getting material ashore, handling it, storing it, protecting it, issuing and distributing it can hardly be imagined. Yet all this work had to be done in the open, at the mercy of tides and weather to some extent, under the constant threat of air attack and on the fringe of an enormous battle. It is not to be wondered at that the scale of D-Day and what followed, along with the administration behind it, is still regarded with awe some 80 years later.

The exciting events that took place on mainland Europe tend to overshadow the tremendous amount of work done in Britain in the months leading up to D-Day. Many histories tell how the whole of southern England became, for the duration, one vast military camp. As thousands of men and vehicles congregated in the area with as much security as such a huge operation would allow, roads leading into the region were clogged with seemingly endless convoys, which tried the patience of local inhabitants waiting to cross the road on the way to work, getting children to school or simply shopping. In addition to normal loads such as fuel and ammunition, or the troops themselves, smaller types of landing craft, built at inland locations all over the country had to be moved, as did an equally vast fleet of dummy craft that were moved into the south-eastern counties as part of a massive deception scheme. The War Office retained its own pool of units to achieve this, working in conjunction with civilian lorries under the auspices of the Road Haulage Organisation.

As early as 1942, the Ministry of Supply actually hit upon the idea of waterproofing new vehicles and storing them in anticipation of an invasion. Unfortunately, this was a bit premature. Tests on sample vehicles early in 1943 showed that the materials used had deteriorated over time and that the preventative work would need to be done again. Responsibility for this was passed on to REME and two Wading Trials Centres were created, at Weymouth in Dorset, and Instow on the North Devon coast. The systems developed by manufacturers, and adopted by the Ministry, were modified as time went by and it was discovered that six weeks was about the longest period a prepared vehicle could be stored before use. REME worked out a programme in three stages. They would undertake the first stage while unit fitters and vehicle crews would complete the other two.

The first stage took place at the Concentration Area. It involved a full inspection of each vehicle, sealing of fixtures, test fitting of any special, additional hardware and application of anti-corrosion preparations; this all took about 50 man-hours and when it was completed subsequent driving was limited to about 200 miles. At the Marshalling Areas, closer to the embarkation ports, most of the remaining sealant was fitted, as was hardware such as breathing pipes and software in the form of waterproof aprons. This second stage took on average between four to five man-hours and restricted the vehicle to about 20 miles further driving. The final stage was carried out virtually alongside the landing craft at the point of loading. It involved covering the radiator and sealing all air inlets except the extended one. This only took half of one man-hour but, once done, the vehicle could not travel for more than about half a mile, that is on board ship in England and off again at the other end. And it is worth adding that the planning arrangements required that vehicles being sent over to France should be prepared for a wet landing all the way through to D+42, that is over halfway through July.

Naturally, all vehicles were fully laden when they left Britain. Their experiences on the French beaches varied due to the state of the tide and nature of the shore. In some cases they landed dry since, the beaches being so flat,

One of the two Wading Trials Centres was at Weymouth in Dorset. Here an Austin K5 with an apprehensive crew creates a bow wave as it manoeuvres in deep water.

it was often necessary for larger craft to dry out before discharging. In other instances, lorries could find themselves in 6ft of water, 300yds from the shore. Nonetheless, most vehicles got ashore safely and REME, who were responsible for the overall waterproofing programme, considered their part in D-Day a great success. Figures published in 1951 show that of some 14,000 B vehicles waterproofed for the landings 1.5 per cent were lost due to plunging into deeper water than they were prepared for; another 1.3 per cent were bogged down in soft clay or were wrecked by enemy action such as mines or air attack, while a mere 0.15 per cent were lost because their waterproofing had been badly done or because of incompetent driving.

It was in Normandy that the DUKW came into its own. For D-Day, 21st Army Group had 11 DUKW companies at the disposal of British and Canadian forces. The establishment of a DUKW company was based around 100 vehicles, of which 75 were divided between three platoons. This allowed a 25 per cent reserve for each company, which was essential on account of the extended maintenance procedures. Although inherently waterproof DUKWs were, as we have seen, built from normal truck components so that parts exposed to sea water, in particular axles and wheel bearings, needed constant attention and very regular lubrication.

On D-Day the first DUKWs were actually coming ashore as early as 9.00am, a mere 90 minutes after H-Hour. They were mainly loaded with ammunition, which they immediately dropped off at prearranged points called DUKW Cushions. Hazards encountered included German snipers lurking just behind the beaches, while at sea rolling smokescreens made navigation difficult. Having dropped off their loads the DUKWs were sent back again, to evacuate wounded personnel. The

Her Majesty Queen Elizabeth talking to men from the divisional transport echelon of the Guards Armoured Division before D-Day. The nearest vehicles are Dodge WK60 3-tonners.

nature of the anchorage, with its wide, gently sloping beaches, was such that fully laden vessels could often not approach closer than 5 miles, which meant longer round trips for the DUKWs. In addition, as the amount of shipping in the roadstead grew it became more difficult for DUKW drivers to identify the ship they were to unload and this was aggravated at night or when smoke drifted across the area. Damage to DUKWs was relatively light. By D+5, 36 had been damaged beyond repair, the majority by mines or shellfire, but three went down when an LST they were unloading was torpedoed.

Over the first few days there was a shortage of conventional transport so that the DUKWs, instead of trans-shipping their loads as planned, were obliged to take them a fair distance inland as the advance continued. This, according to one source, was the first

BRITISH MILITARY TRANSPORT 1829-1956

Fordson WOT6 3-tonners loading from a coaster at one of the Mulberry spud pierheads. The sea looks quite choppy.

time that it had occurred to anyone that DUKWs could be used as conventional transport. A revelation which, at this distance in time, seems rather surprising. Even so, continued road use caused a great rise in punctures. Despite the reserve of vehicles, the strain on DUKW companies was beginning to tell. By 10 June it was decided that the companies would rest during the dark hours so that arrears of maintenance could be done and drivers given the chance of some sleep. The history of 21st Army Group takes every opportunity of praising the DUKWs and their crews, at one point commenting that they were 'an outstanding success and contributed greatly to the maintenance of the forces over the beaches'.

Mercifully, air attacks never developed on a serious scale, due to the overwhelming superiority of the Allied air forces but also because the Luftwaffe was short of aircraft and was conserving what it did have just in case this operation turned out to be part of an enormous bluff. Nevertheless, the large fuel and ammunition dump of the British 3rd Infantry Division located near Sword Beach was bombed with the loss of over 100,000 gallons of fuel and 400 tons of ammunition, despite courageous attempts to save as much as possible.

Posterity has lavished attention on the artificial Mulberry harbours and, indeed, they were much praised at the time by the invading forces. Mulberry B, the British installation off Arromanches, was first used for unloading craft on 15 June (D+9) but it was severely damaged in a gale, which lasted from the 19th to 22nd. It was then reconstructed, using the remains of the American installation, Mulberry A, and put back into operational order. Even so it could only handle about 4,000 tons of stores every 24 hours and DUKWs alone could almost equal this. The greatest advantage of the whole port was the shelter it gave to small craft by its seaward defences, which enabled them to use the enclosed beaches in all weathers. The Allies were also fortunate to find that the small harbour of Port-en-Bessin, which lay more or less on the dividing line between the British and American sectors, was virtually intact and it became the major landing point for fuel for both armies from about D+5.

7 SUPPLYING VICTORY

The early success did not last, but for a while losses were less than anticipated and consideration was therefore given to slowing down the delivery of replacement vehicles. In the end it was agreed that to alter the build-up plans would only confuse matters and, as it turned out, the delay in taking Caen justified this decision. From D+8 to D+18, Corps Delivery Squadrons of the RASC mustered sufficient personnel to cope. Vehicles would come across the Channel in specially designated MT ships, which were equipped with adequate handling derricks. On arrival vehicles would be lifted out and placed aboard tank landing craft (LCT) or Rhino ferries for the run ashore. Rhino ferries were flat pontoons powered by a pair of large outboard motors, operated in British service by the Inland Water Transport service. Unfortunately, Rhinos did not function well in anything but flat calm conditions which, despite the fact that it was June, did not prevail at that time in Normandy.

After D+18 vehicles were delivered to the beach in bulk and staff at the receiving end were permanently troubled by a lack of drivers. In the RASC all personnel underwent a driving course, no matter what their duty, but this did not apply to the rest of the Army. In an emergency anyone found on the beach could be recruited for unloading, whether he could drive or not. Lack of previous experience notwithstanding, men were shoved into cabs, engines started, gears engaged and they plunged off landing craft ramps into the sea. How it affected these tyro drivers is not recorded, but it cannot have done the lorries much good at all. Once word of this practice got around units would often send a couple of drivers back to the beach with orders to hang around. Before long they would be pressed into an unloading party and, having found something suitable, promptly set off with it, back to their unit. This might be accepted as gamesmanship but the next stage, of lifting vehicles to satisfy the French black market, was nothing short of theft.

As American troops began their great encircling sweep around the German forces in Normandy, the British were engaged in some intensive fighting closer to the beachhead. The hinge to the German resistance was the city of Caen, which held out far longer than had been anticipated. The effect this had on transport was immediate. Lines of communication were short but broad, almost like the Western Front in 1916, and the result was the same.

DUKWs run a shuttle service during the Normandy landings alongside a beached Rhino ferry. Recovery vehicles at the water's edge are rescuing drowned vehicles while LSTs unload onto more Rhino ferries further out.

DISTRIBUTION OF TRANSPORT TO AN ARMOURED REGIMENT IN 1944

Details of the transport allocated to various military formations at different times during the war would fill many books but, as an example, the list below shows the distribution of transport to an armoured regiment in 1944.

A Echelon
Regimental Headquarters and Headquarters Squadron
Commanding Officer	Jeep (car, 5cwt 4 x 4)
Officer Commanding HQ Squadron	Jeep
Second-in-Command (Captain)	15cwt 4 x 4 truck
Squadron Sergeant-Major	15cwt 4 x 4 truck
Medical Officer	3 x 15cwt half-tracks
Mechanist Sergeant	15cwt half-track
Mechanist Quartermaster Sergeant	3-ton 6 x 4 lorry
Electrician	Loyd Slave Battery Carrier
Anti-aircraft	2 x twin Oerlikon 20mm trailers
Ammunition	4 x 3-ton lorries
Petrol	4 x 3-ton lorries
Water	2 x 15cwt tanker trucks
Office	3-ton lorry, house body

B Echelon
RHQ and HQ Squadron
Provost Sergeant	8 x solo motorcycles
Provost	5 x Jeeps
Medical staff	15cwt truck
Quartermaster	Jeep
Squadron Quartermaster Sergeant	15cwt truck
Technical Quartermaster Sergeant	15cwt truck
Armourer	15cwt truck
Tank spares	3-ton 6 x 4 lorry
Mobile Kitchen	3-ton
Officers' Mess and baggage	3-ton
Carpenter and 12 spare tank crews	3-ton
Anti-gas stores, baggage and blankets	3-ton

A Echelon
for each of three squadrons
Squadron Commander	Jeep
Fitter Sergeant REME	Armoured Recovery Vehicle
Mechanist Sergeant	15cwt half-track
Fitters	3-ton 6 x 4 lorry with compressor trailer or Loyd Slave Battery Carrier
Ammunition	7 x 3-ton lorries
Petrol	7 x 3-ton lorries

B Echelon
for each of three squadrons
Squadron Quartermaster Sergeant	15cwt truck
Officers' Mess	15cwt truck
Squadron stores and office	3-ton lorry
Mobile Kitchen	3-ton lorry and water trailer
Spare tank crews (7)	15cwt truck

Attached to regiment
Light Aid Detachment REME
Despatch riders	2 x solo motorcycles
Electrical & Mechanical Engineer Officer	Jeep
Personnel	15cwt truck
LAD Stores	3-ton lorry
No 1 Breakdown	3-ton lorry
No 2 Breakdown	6 x 4 recovery tractor

Armoured regiment Royal Corps of Signals troop
Electrician Sergeant	Jeep
Batteries and stores	15cwt truck
Instrument Mechanic	15cwt technical workshop
W/T Operator (Corporal)	15cwt wireless truck (No 22 Set)
Battery Charging	3-ton lorry

A proportion of lorries to be fitted with twin Bren anti-aircraft guns and carry a PIAT (Projector, Infantry Anti-Tank).

Traffic over these short routes became intense, one-way systems had to be introduced and roads deteriorated rapidly. Tipper truck companies of the RASC now found themselves working round the clock, supporting Royal Engineer and Pioneer Corps road repair groups who were permanently engaged in filling potholes, widening roads and creating temporary by-passes around narrow Norman towns. Indeed, tippers were very much in demand, even in forward areas where it was sometimes necessary to repair stretches of road under enemy fire even before tanks could be brought up; again, a situation that had been encountered in the First World War, but in those days only resolved by the use of manpower.

In the planning for D-Day and the weeks that followed, the high command had anticipated road transport operations once the troops were across the beaches and moving inland. Such operations had been codified in a military training pamphlet, *Mechanized Movement by Road*, published by the War Office in May 1944. The entire subject is examined in considerable detail and begins by explaining the terminology. Density, for instance, was described as the spacing of vehicles on a route and it was measured in 'vehicles to the mile' (vtm) while speed was expressed in relation to the distance covered in two hours, including short rest halts, as 'mi2h'.

As far as density is concerned, 30vtm was regarded as ideal for columns making strategical moves. It implied long convoys running with roughly a 60yd gap between vehicles. For moves by night, or in areas of greater risk, it advised that groups of between five and nine vehicles were the best arrangement; lorries within the group running closer together but maintaining the overall density. Drivers were given route cards stating the cruising speed to be observed and highly experienced

An interesting selection of vehicles engaged in road maintenance. In the foreground a Dennis Pig tipper, beyond that a steel-bodied CMP 3-tonner, then another Pig and, off to the left, a Karrier K6.

men were always selected to lead the convoy to avoid the problem of bunching. Even small changes of speed at the head of a column would convert into halts at the rear, leaving convoys vulnerable to air attack and generally slowing everything down.

Another interesting instruction, keeping in mind events in the First World War, was the subject of the driver's mate. The pamphlet emphasised that these men should not be referred to, or treated, as passengers. Instead they coined the term 'Vehicle Leaders' to make the point that these individuals had considerable responsibility for the safe progress of their vehicles, particularly at night. The man in the lorry at the head of every block of vehicles was the column commander and it was his duty to ensure that his block kept to its route and checked timings on the way. At night, the pamphlet insisted, if the commander could see the tail light of the last vehicle of the block in front he was too close.

The practice of classifying transport in

An Austin K2, four-stretcher ambulance, collecting a casualty.

echelons remained but the designations were altered. Top of the table now was F Echelon, which applied to vehicles that accompanied combat troops in action. Next came A Echelon, vehicles that were kept ready to provide immediate support for F Echelon. All other transport elements were designated as B Echelon.

The breakout from Normandy, following the long drawn out stalemate before Caen and the carnage at Falaise, came as a surprise. Some DUKW companies were hurried forward to provide ferry services over the River Seine but after that it was virtually a direct drive to Antwerp. In little more than one week, armoured units averaging 40 miles a day covered the 300 miles to Antwerp. They left a major problem in their wake as the original programme proposed the establishment of a vast Rear Maintenance Area at Rouen, but now this was simply overtaken by events. Antwerp was an ideal goal since it provided superb harbour facilities with just a short sea crossing from major British ports. However, it could not be used while German forces held the Scheldt Estuary and sealed off its outlet to the sea. The ports between, from Le Havre in the west through Boulogne, Calais, Dunkirk and Ostend were also unusable. German forces by-passed during the rush for Antwerp had retreated into them and, realising their value to the Allies, made every effort to stay there.

In order to capitalise on the precipitate German retreat through France, the British high command now decided to follow on their heels with a major force comprising 8, 12 and 30 Corps, but this would have stretched the lines of communication to breaking point. Instead, 8 Corps was pulled out of the line and all of its transport elements used to bolster the advance of the other two corps. Once again, behind the scenes, transport was manipulating the players. Those who pronounce upon the respective merits of Allied and German tanks in this period might arrive at more valid conclusions if they elected to study factors such as the reliability and availability of the lorries used by each side.

Naturally, as soon as the enemy had been driven out of the area, attempts were made to get the railways operating. Unfortunately, it had been a major task of the Allied air forces to wreck the French railway network in the months leading up to the invasion. Most important junctions had been ruined by concentrated bombing and any locomotive caught on the move was attacked by fighter-bombers. The first priority was to get a railway line running from Normandy into Belgium; to provide motive power, locomotives were brought over from Britain by landing craft. Meanwhile, the Inland Water Transport organisation was reactivating the canal system in Flanders and air delivery was being employed for small but vital shipments.

Even so, all these developments could not replace the huge Allied dependency on motor transport to fill the 400-mile gap between Antwerp and the Normandy shore. Smaller, intermediate ports were used as they were cleared of German garrisons but made little difference, while operations such as Market Garden added to the load. The Canadians showed considerable ingenuity when they adapted tank transporter trailers into load carriers and the idea was taken up by the British. It involved welding sides around the deck, formed from sections of perforated trackway, which created a

An incident during the advance, a convoy swings around a collection of abandoned and burning vehicles on the road.

The Austin K5 3-ton 4 x 4 GS lorry, which caused so much trouble in North West Europe.

Corps transport on the move through a damaged town. Fordson and Bedford 15cwts in front followed by a half-track ambulance.

trailer with a carrying capacity of 36 tons, if carrying ammunition, or around 500 jerricans of fuel. And it was fuel that everyone was desperate for. There is a record of one British unit, an RASC administrative section, which converted all of its vehicles, including a large office lorry, into petrol transport and, with office personnel driving, made a successful emergency delivery of their own.

It is at times like this that one hopes nothing else can go wrong, but it always does. Every vehicle was under pressure and the majority stood up to it well but the entire fleet of 1,400 Austin K5, four-wheel drive 3-tonners had to be withdrawn in early September on account of engine failure. This was diagnosed as piston trouble, but to make matters worse the same fault was discovered in all the replacement engines.

The closing months of 1944 saw increasingly bitter weather conditions hampering the movement of supplies. Most of this time was occupied with clearing the enemy from the Scheldt Estuary, preparing dock facilities at Antwerp and Ghent and fitting-out depots in Brussels for operational use. By this time the route from Normandy had established itself to the extent that rest stations, with all the basic hotel facilities, had been organised for drivers making these long runs. It is interesting to note that a vast number of horses and wagons, abandoned by the retreating Germans, were taken into service, particularly for local supply work around Antwerp, and this took some of the pressure off motor transport. In order to improve the manpower position, which was also getting difficult, some reorganisation took place in the establishment of RASC companies. The trend was towards increasing what was available at divisional level, at the expense of higher formations, the object being to release as many officers and men as possible for the infantry, to meet increasing demands from the Far East.

The Rhine was Germany's last major physical barrier and they defended it fiercely, destroying every bridge they could. Since it would take time to rebuild those needed for railways, it was essential to revert to road transport entirely and a large number of long Bailey bridges were thrown across at vital points. These naturally required extra transport to bring up their components but, with Belgian help, a lot of tasks hitherto undertaken by military transport were now being handled by local civilians, hired for the purpose.

East of the Rhine the weather continued to dominate, disrupting transport and the continuing road building programme. It is interesting to note that in freezing conditions a newly repaired road in the area might be able to handle up to 7,000 vehicles per day but if a thaw set in this was rapidly reduced to around 4,800. There was also extensive flooding and the DUKWs came into their own again. Huge tracts of land were covered in water about 3ft deep, which inhibited the use of all conventional transport unless full waterproofing practices were reinstated. This being impractical under the circumstances the RASC deployed their two surviving DUKW companies, which soon found

A NAAFI mobile canteen on a Fordson 7V chassis. Often getting a lot closer to the firing line than might be deemed wise, they kept the British Army running on its main staple – hot, sweet tea.

Victim of severe winter weather, a four-wheel drive 3-tonner the wrong way up.

themselves continually in demand.

As the Allies moved into Germany transport was required to deal with an increasing number of prisoners of war. These men included Germans who had to be taken out of the war zone and liberated Allied personnel for whom new clothing and food were required before they could be transported home. To add to their responsibilities, Allied troops were also having to deal with thousands of displaced persons and bring what succour they could to the survivors of each concentration camp that was discovered.

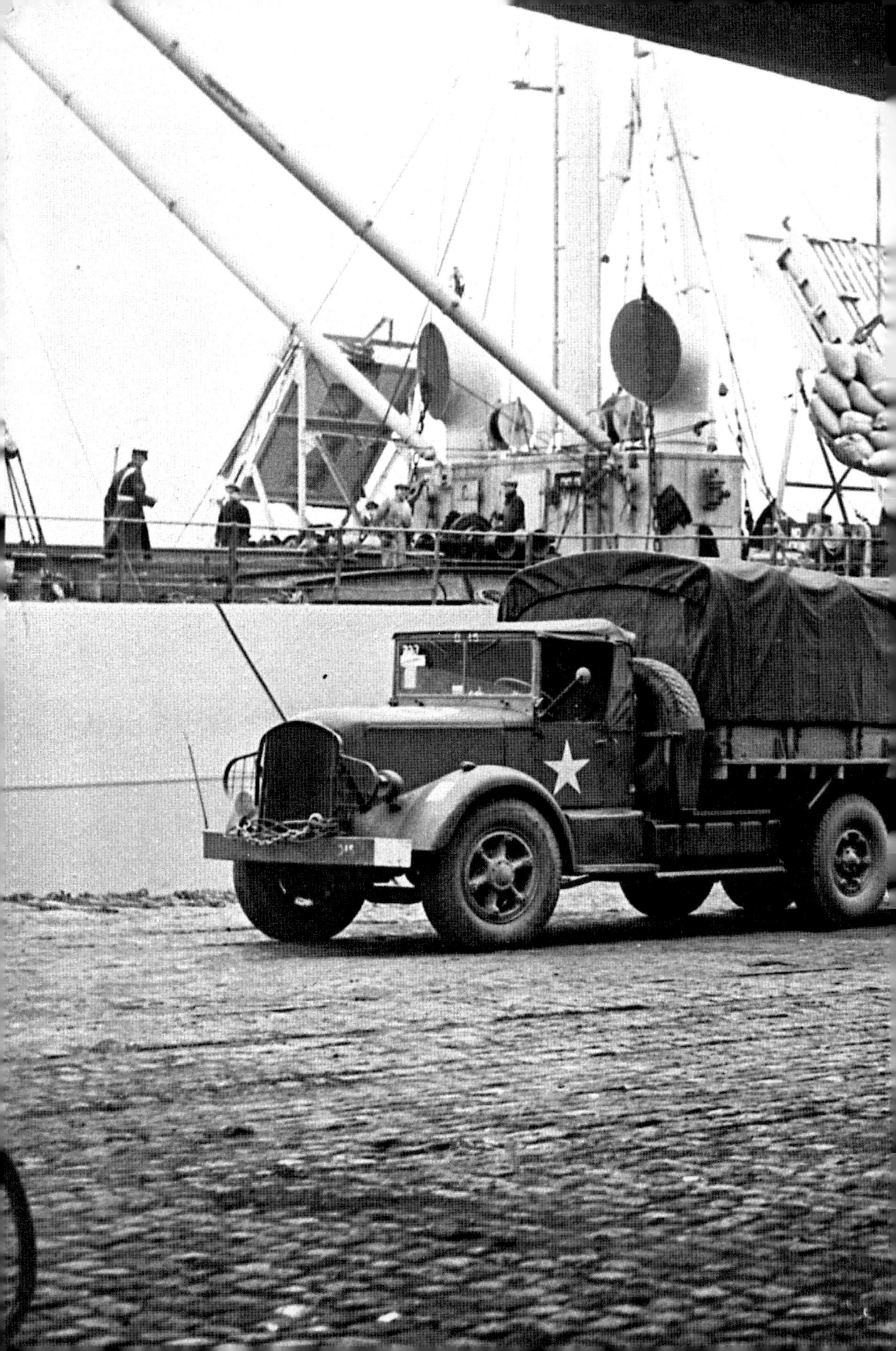

Mack type NR 10-ton lorries at Antwerp docks. Seen here in British service but with what appear to be Belgian civilian crews.

Gliders had been used to deliver not only troops but also light armoured vehicles and Jeeps direct to the battlefield during the Normandy landings and Rhine crossing. But the glider was essentially a short-range carrier. If vehicles were to be transported by air for greater distances then they would have to fit into conventional piston-engined aircraft and at that time the only suitable machine was the legendary C-47 Dakota, the military cargo variant of the civilian DC-3 airliner. In terms of vehicle carrying capacity the two vital factors were obviously weight and size. Maximum payload for the C-47 was 5,500lb of which 200lb would be absorbed by the weight of lashing down equipment.

This meant that one aircraft could carry a couple of Jeeps or one modified 15cwt truck. If a 3-ton lorry was taken to bits two Dakotas could be used to lift it, but tests revealed that about eight hours were needed to reassemble the vehicle after landing and then it could only be expected to last for about 5,000 miles. The main development of vehicles adapted to an air-portable state came very late in the war and is therefore associated, if only chronologically, with the campaign in the Far East to which we now turn. Much of the development work was done by TT2 and WVEE so the issue of *Transport Bulletin* for October 1944 is a useful source.

On the subject of 15cwts the new Morris 4 x 4 and similar Canadian types were ruled out on the grounds of weight. Austin Motors designed their K7 (which looked rather like an American Dodge) specifically for the airborne role, while Vauxhall Motors was developing something similar based on their type MW. However, the most unusual approach came from the Rootes Group in the form of the Humber Hexonaut, a tall, narrow, six-wheel drive vehicle powered by two Hillman car engines, which was also amphibious and skid-

A substantial Bailey bridge stretching across the river and flooded hinterland. Two Fordson 15cwts are on the bridge while a queue builds up along the narrow spit of land on the far side.

7 SUPPLYING VICTORY

DUKWs on the Rhine. Although they had no problems in the river this picture illustrates the difficulty of getting out. A suitable exit point has to be created, surfaced with trackway and well-marked before the DUKWs can start their ferry service.

steered like the Terrapin. It never developed beyond the prototype stage and was probably a bit too specialised. Of course, narrowness was not just a virtue in terms of air-portability, it was also an advantage in the jungle. The narrower the vehicle the less the trail had to be widened and it would certainly have helped around Kohima as explained below. However, the need for light patrol vehicles, perhaps towing a trailer load of stores, able to penetrate thick jungle country along manmade trails was seen as a useful asset; at least two British firms, SS Cars and Standard, produced a selection of what might well be called pygmy Jeeps for this role. Most could just manage to carry four men, who could equally carry the vehicle in an emergency and tow a small supply trailer, which was normally amphibious.

Since the 3-tonner was the backbone of the British Army the need to make it air-portable was paramount. In order to simplify the process, the manufacturers were requested to introduce modifications into their production procedures for a range of vehicles that would be identified, by the code APT as air-portable. The Bedford QL tipper, with winch, and the standard GS model were adapted as was the Karrier K6 winch lorry and both entered production.

Austin modified their K5 and Ford their WOT6 but neither entered production. The actual surgery required for each type differed in detail but all came with cabs that could be split at windscreen level and bodies that could be divided transversely. In the case of the Bedford QL a chunk of the chassis on the offside had to be removed along with the adjacent rear spring hanger.

An example of more specialised developments in Britain is this Jeep, equipped with infrared headlamps and binocular viewing device for the driver. Although the Germans are often credited with success in this field the Allies were also well advanced and used such equipment during the Rhine crossing.

183

BRITISH MILITARY TRANSPORT 1829-1956

Rear view of the chassis of the Bedford QL air-portable tipper. The top half of the cab is detachable to reduce height and the winch drum can be seen at the offside.

To embark vehicles onto the Dakota, the loading procedure involved partly dismantling the vehicle, mounting the chassis on four small castors and dividing the parts between two aircraft. One aircraft took the chassis, complete with engine and lower part of cab along with the axles, springs, fuel tank and exhaust system plus other details. The second aircraft contained the body in two pieces, the upper part of the cab and the doors, canvas tilt, wings and wheels. Whether it was worth the effort remains questionable. A larger aircraft might have been more practical and there are obvious risks in shipping one vehicle in two aircraft. What could be less useful than half of a Bedford QL?

From a transport point of view the war against Japan was a low-key affair in its early stages. The RASC had had a presence in both Hong Kong and Malaya prior to 1940 but it was small and, when hostilities began, many commercial vehicles and civilian drivers had to be hired to make up numbers. This was hardly a reliable source and locally recruited drivers were understandably reluctant to keep their jobs once the prospect of defeat became apparent. Forces in Burma were provided mainly from India and transport arrangements were in the hands of the Royal Indian Army Service Corps. This force was not mechanised on anything like the scale of the RASC and the majority of drivers were relatively inexperienced.

Even so there was no great difficulty over transport since fairly large stocks of American Ford and Chevrolet trucks were available. The problem in Burma was the roads, which had never been prepared for constant use by heavy motor vehicles.

The Japanese landed in Burma in January 1942. British reinforcements in the shape of 7th Armoured Brigade, withdrawn from the desert, landed at Rangoon towards the end of February. However, the Japanese soon sealed the coast and the only escape route was north. From Rangoon the tanks, with their own RASC company, began the drive northwards with the enemy in pursuit, surviving a series of ambush actions until they reached the Chindwin, where the tanks and transport vehicles had to be destroyed since no means of getting them across the river could be found.

Having chased the Allies out of Burma the Japanese halted to regroup while the monsoon season held sway. In India, meanwhile, efforts were made to establish positions close to the Burmese frontier from which a counter-offensive might be launched. Inevitably the supply situation was a key factor. The nearest railhead in India was at Dimapur and from here a single lane motor road wound its way into the mountains via Kohima and then down onto the Imphal plain where a track branched off to Tamu, on the border itself. Nowhere, not in the mountains nor on the plain, was it possible for motor transport to operate off the road. However, the road at least could be widened to permit two-way traffic. On the mountain stretches, where the road ran along ledges, this was done by the simple expedient of digging further into the mountainside, carrying the spoil across the road and using it to build up the outer edge. It was not a route for the faint hearted. The hills were steep, the corners sharp and the surface, particularly in the monsoon, dangerously slippery. A moment's distraction, a skid, and it was over the edge, often with fatal results. For new and inexperienced drivers it must have been a recurring nightmare, which was not made any easier by mud slides, rock falls and major avalanches, which occurred with monotonous regularity. At such times huge convoys built up, waiting for the road to be cleared and, on sections where the widening had not yet been done, this meant that the road was effectively blocked for miles.

The tiny Standard Jungle Jeep and trailer developed for service in Burma. The crew of four all sit on motorcycle saddles so it is difficult to imagine what they can be smiling about.

Although it has been shown that, to some extent at least, British military vehicles had been prepared for desert conditions in the Middle East it is clear that no consideration was given to operating in a tropical environment. In fact, many of the problems encountered in Burma and other jungle zones were the result of long-term storage rather

Chevrolet ambulances following a Lee tank on a jungle road in Burma.

than use. This applied in particular to communications equipment. Run a radio for an hour or two each day and its own heat keeps it free of humidity. But leave it in store for a few weeks without special protection and it could be ruined. As far as transport was concerned the main problem was with glass-faced instruments: in conditions of high humidity condensation before long caused an unpleasant fungus to build up inside, clogging the mechanism and obscuring the view.

A Tropic Proofing Experimental Establishment was set up in the unlikely surroundings of Mill Hill, a north-western suburb of London. The first move was to ensure that instruments were free from any moisture when they were sealed, which worked well enough during trials in Britain. However, Mill Hill lacks many of the more interesting tropical insects and, once in theatre, it was discovered that miniscule mites with tiny traces of fungus on their limbs could work their way into the instruments and set the process off. Work on tropic proofing was in progress, and making great strides, when the war ended and the programme was arbitrarily closed down with a predictable lack of foresight.

The campaign to drive the Japanese out of Burma depended mainly on two factors. The first was education, learning to get the measure of the enemy, match him at his own game and beat him. The second was, inevitably, supply. This depended so fundamentally on the availability of resources, and indeed men, that it was clear nothing dramatic would be achieved until the war in Europe was at least on the wane, if not won. Late in 1944, however, the historic actions at Imphal and Kohima proved that a moderate sized force, even when cut off by the enemy, could be supplied entirely by air. Not only did this enable them to resist, but ultimately to defeat their besiegers. In addition, a determination by the Allies not to relax through the monsoon period upset Japanese planning and in due course 14th Army began its advance on Rangoon. This was so entirely dependent on air supply that it has little to offer from the transport point of view.

In practice the advance of the 14th Army could be described as airfield hopping. Airfields were, in each succeeding bound, the primary objectives since the next stage depended entirely upon their capture. However, mechanised transport was needed for final distribution of supplies and four-wheel drive was deemed essential. Indeed, conditions were so bad that wheeled vehicles without four- or even six-wheel drive were quite useless. The ideal vehicle was believed to be the faithful old British 3-tonner, but in many cases it turned out to be the Jeep. Thus, the establishment of supply companies was reorganised to include platoons of 3-tonners, Jeeps and tracked carriers in order to provide the flexibility needed to deal with all conditions. Where even Jeeps and carriers could not go the mule could, with the added advantage that it could be eaten if air resupply failed. Four-wheel drive 15cwts were also considered suitable, but not being available in sufficient numbers were often replaced by six-wheel drive 30cwts, of American origin.

The ubiquitous DUKW also proved extremely useful in the Burma campaign, for amphibious landings, river crossings, floods and in some instances long-distance road runs if nothing else was available. One of the most amazing operations involving DUKWs occurred during the crossing of the Chindwin Valley. The road between Kalewa and Shwegyin being unusable it was decided to ferry everything down the river for 8 miles, with the DUKWs towing Royal Engineer pontoons. This was not just a supply operation. It involved combat troops, artillery and even tanks and was completely successful. The sight of DUKWs acting as tugs hauling tanks on pontoon rafts must have been one worth seeing. The same vehicles were later used to tow long sections of assembled Bailey bridge into position at Kalewa.

From the British point of view the campaign in the Far East has always been portrayed as a poor cousin, and there is no doubt that it was. However, such adversity often results in prodigies of improvisation and this was also evident. Now, with the war finally over it was time to take stock and, in the light of past experience, plan for the future.

A CMP 15cwt in Burma compared with a simpler form of transport. The quality of the road suggests somewhere in the immediate vicinity of Rangoon.

8 TOP GEAR

After the Second World War, the War Office came clean about its failures in the procurement of British-built military vehicles. For the postwar world it concluded that the Army had to specify precisely what it wanted; create a research and design establishment; and it needed to resolve the problems associated with building military vehicles for peace and wartime service.

In a confidential history published in 1951 (confidential, that is, in the security sense) the War Office admitted that they had got it wrong. Well, to be more accurate, they made it clear that the people running the War Office before the war had got it wrong. In fact, if anyone was responsible it has to be those who formed the Crosland Committee of 1935. What the authors of the confidential history, Majors Campagnac and Hayman said, was:

'The war made it very clear that shortcomings in the quality of military vehicles of British manufacture were due in a very large measure to reliance upon engines and chassis designed for commercial purposes with the object of avoiding penal taxation.' *

This realisation, the authors claimed, did not dawn upon the War Office nor the Ministry of Supply until 1944, but they doubted if the British motor industry had accepted it even then.

Campagnac and Hayman agreed that it was time for the divorce of military and commercial design. They acknowledged that military writers such as Hubbard and Kuhne had recognised it in 1920 and they could have said the same of Crompton in the aftermath of the Boer War. Now, they said, was the time for that divorce to become absolute; brave words.

In espousing this new policy, Campagnac and Hayman quote three paragraphs from a paper jointly prepared by the Assistant Chief of the Imperial General Staff (Weapons) and the Director of Special Weapons and Vehicles for the Organisation and Weapons Policy Committee at the War Office. Some of the points raised bear repeating again.

At the time the paper was prepared, September 1944, it claimed that there were some 55 different types of vehicles in service with infantry divisions and around 600 different types and makes in the Army as a whole. This, the authors of the paper suggested, placed an impossible strain upon maintenance and spares supply organisations. They went on to blame the position on pre-war policy, forced on the Army for reasons of economy, which meant that it had to rely on British manufacturers to supply its needs on a voluntary basis. As a result, according to the paper, when war did break out experience showed that commercial vehicles were quite

An Austin K9 fitted out as a Wireless Truck. The 4 x 4 K9 was Austin's first post-war design, introduced in 1952. It had a 1-ton capacity.

*Major R. Campagnac RASC and Major P.E.C. Hayman 15th/19th The King's Royal Hussars, *The Second World War 1939–1945: Army, Fighting, Support and Transport Vehicles and the War Office Organisation for their Provision* (The War Office, 1951)

unsuitable for the Army to use in the field and that the tendency was for the Army to require vehicles that departed more and more from commercial design. The conclusion was that the true Army vehicle had little commercial value, and vice versa. To quote the last two sentences directly:

'The commercial vehicle must be designed for economical use on good roads, clearance [meaning ground clearance] is of little importance and only sufficient power is required to enable it to operate on average roads. Military needs so differ from civil requirements that vehicles for Army use nowadays must be specially designed and built.'

Campagnac and Hayman concurred. The statement, they said, could not be more clearly put. But they went on to conclude that it was also impossible to rely on any foreign country for the production of equipment for service use so that any military vehicle must be capable of manufacture 'in the United Kingdom or the Dominions'.

Most of which, in an ideal world, was perfectly true; not just then, it always had been. After all the tank is specially designed and built for military use, as are any number of other curious vehicles that have no equivalent civilian purpose. Except in the most desperate circumstances armies do not convert civil engineering plant into tanks and, generally speaking, tanks are not a lot of use for much else. Why might not the same be true of lorries?

The answer, no doubt, is because they are lorries. Everyone knows what a lorry is, we see them every day, but how many of us are as familiar with tanks? They are a rare sight outside of military camps in times of peace and in that way they retain a degree of exclusiveness, a mystery most people cannot penetrate, so they are content to leave them to the experts. But if one sees a commercial lorry, especially on a farm or building site, it is difficult for the uninitiated to distinguish the qualities, or lack of them, which separate it from an Army lorry. It is there of course, we already have sufficient evidence for that, but would a parliamentary committee, anxious to protect a peacetime budget, grant much credence to the expert who pointed this out? Undoubtedly not, we have the evidence for that too. But you do not create Army lorries simply by painting civilian ones green.

However, in facing up to a brave new post-war world, Campagnac and Hayman were prepared to nail their colours to the mast in an official document – so the War Office must have concurred – when they said that three steps were now necessary before the ideal could be achieved. First, the Army had to specify precisely what it wanted; second, a research and design establishment must be created; and thirdly, the problems associated with manufacture of such specialised types for peace and wartime service had to be resolved.

If one goes back to the original subsidy scheme that evolved before the First World War it is quite clear that there was excellent cooperation between commercial manufacturers and the War Office. In 1925, a suggestion was put forward that a committee should be established, consisting of service representatives and members of the Institute of Automobile Engineers. This was rejected at the time although there were civilian members, drawn mainly from the road transport industry, on the Mechanisation Board. It surfaced again in 1943, when British methods of design and production were being compared (unfavourably, as far as the War Office was concerned) with those of Canada. Indeed, the British attitude was described as 'disturbingly complacent', a phrase that created considerable indignation at the Ministry of Supply. In theory the War Office view, that the Canadian approach was correct, prevailed but in practice it was too late to change until the war was over.

Late in 1944, the Controller General of Munitions Production engaged in preliminary discussion with the Society of Motor Manufacturers and Traders (SMM&T) and the result was very positive. To be fair the motives behind this approach, from the military point of view, were not entirely altruistic. The motor industry was not regarded as the best organisation to judge what the Army wanted but its support and goodwill was vital. The War Office believed that future vehicle requirements would only be met if the best brains in the country could be applied to their design. But the War Office also knew that it would never be able to pay these putative geniuses the kind of money they could command from industry. Thus, early in 1945, the SMM&T formed an Industrial Advisory Panel while, later in the year, the Ministry of Supply created its own 'B' Vehicle Committee.

The SMM&T, having a head start, got their report out first, on 24 January 1945. They had plenty to say but two points are worth noting here: first, that soldiers and civil servants could not design trucks; and, second, that industry was not geared up to meet War Office requirements. As to the first point, SMM&T did not believe that the War Office should create a design and development establishment. They could not see how soldiers and civil servants would be able to keep up with developments in the commercial field or changes in production techniques; nor did they believe that such people would be able to relate their concepts to existing, or future, mass-production techniques. However, if there had been any suggestion that the War Office was attempting to take advantage of the trade it soon became clear that this could work both ways. The SMM&T was equally aware that, under present arrangements, production facilities would never be able to meet War Office requirements in the event of war. In fact, they estimated that 75 per cent of existing plant would be unsuitable for such work and they felt that the War Office was being too idealistic. The simple answer was to persuade the authorities to water down their insistence on full implementation of the programme, in the event of war, and accept a proportion of modified commercial types. And the SMM&T had another suggestion.

If, they said, the War Office could bring itself to put pressure on the Government to adjust a few small matters, everything would be fine. They did not want much. Just a reduction in taxation rates for heavy commercial vehicles and large cars; a relaxation of those laws that restricted the weight, size and speed of lorries and a commitment to a comprehensive road improvement policy. Once these had been enacted the British motor industry would be encouraged to design and build a whole range of new vehicles, many of which would be ideal, or reasonably so, to meet many of the

The Austin K6, 3-ton 6 x 4, although a wartime development, saw a lot of post-war service. This one is shown transporting bridging equipment, a very unusual role.

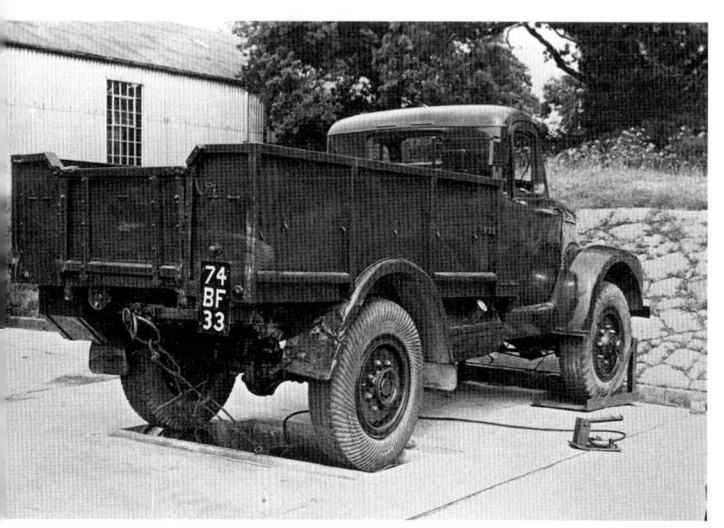

A typical example of a military vehicle built from commercial components, the Morris MRA1, a four-wheel drive 1-tonner, which never really proved suitable.

Army's requirements. The 'B' Vehicle Committee endorsed this view, proving that they, like the SMM&T, were heading for Cloud-Cuckoo-Land, but they could not agree to the trade taking over responsibility for design and development.

Once the war ended various branches of the Ministry of Supply were closed down. This included WVEE, which was now incorporated with the Fighting Vehicle Proving Establishment, formerly the Experimental Wing of the Department of Tank Design (DTD). The latter and its wheeled vehicle counterpart were merged to form the Fighting Vehicle Design Establishment in 1948. In 1952 these two branches were amalgamated to create the Fighting Vehicle Research and Development Establishment (FVRDE) with an address on Chobham Lane, Chertsey in Surrey. In fact, despite concern that the best brains in the business would follow the money, experience proved that these Government establishments were far more effective than industry when it came to applied research. In practice the establishments were also able to use other agencies, like the National Physical Laboratory, certain universities and industry itself to tackle specific problems.

Campagnac and Hayman's conclusion that the British could not afford to rely on foreign producers was surprising when viewed in the light of recent experience. Looking around the Commonwealth it was clear that, as things stood, only Canada was in a position to help on the grand scale, and even that would be difficult to achieve without American help. In any case, what Campagnac and Hayman failed to foresee was the extent to which the motor industry would develop its international status although there were signs, even then. Yet, when it came to meeting future requirements, summed up in the single word 'standardisation', they could only point to the United States as a guide.

Taking the American 2½-ton 6 x 6 as their model they explained how it had derived from a civilian product, created by the motor trade, and developed into a universal load carrier, towing vehicle and, of course, the DUKW. They probably could not have chosen a better example. What they wanted, they said, was the fewest possible types of engine and transmission for a range of vehicles which would not be 'Morris or Bedford or Austin, but British WD Pattern'. This, they announced, was in keeping with a General Staff policy document (the paper prepared for OWPC and mentioned above) of September 1944, which advocated standardisation, meaning 'the smallest possible number of types of vehicle'.

A great deal remained to be decided but the basic principles could be laid down. First, the selection of a range of engines and transmission would be geared to the various needs of divisional, corps, army and GHQ troops and the rule should be that any special designs of chassis or body should be built around these components. While it was accepted that the need for good cross-country performance would be higher at division and corps level, all-wheel drive, special tyres, good ground clearance, special braking systems and a good reserve of power were essential for all service purposes. The last factor was adequate power, in view of the need to go off the road or to tow trailers.

The endless military debate over the respective advantages of wheels or tracks was touched upon, although the fully tracked vehicle, as a supply carrier or tractor, was ruled out. Rather, Campagnac and Hayman were looking at the three-quarter track, based on the success of similar vehicles in the German Army as distinct from the half-tracks produced in the United States. Wheeled vehicles had the obvious advantages of being cheaper to produce and maintain, they were also faster and quieter on the road. Three-quarter tracks had the advantage of a lower silhouette – a lorry with adequate ground clearance being taller – and they could carry some armour if required. On a conventional lorry, weight of armour was bound to account for a significant amount of the payload. Then again, tracks would wear out more quickly than tyres but they gave a vastly improved cross-country capability.

On wheeled vehicles conventional, single-axle drive was ruled out entirely. Four-wheel drive should be a minimum requirement with six-wheel drive the ideal once a simpler, cheaper type had been designed. If light armour, sufficient to resist small-arms fire, covering the engine and crew cab for operations in forward areas, could be produced that was also welcome although its effect on carrying capacity was recognised. Further, special considerations were given regarding tank transporters and gun tractors but these fall outside our present study.

Ultimately, everything would be designed around a family of engines (petrol or diesel not being specified at this time) of the following types:

a 60bhp unit for a 4 x 4 Jeep type vehicle

a 90bhp unit for staff cars, all 4 x 4

a 180bhp unit which would suit a range of 4 x 4 vehicles in the 3-ton class, mainly for use behind the lines

a 180bhp unit for a 6 x 6, 3-ton chassis for frontline types such as load carrier, tractor and heavy ambulance

a 180bhp unit for half-tracks,

A Thornycroft Big Ben tractor with house-type semi-trailer. It is being tested on the ramp of a beached LST at Instow in North Devon.

improved versions of the American type, which would replace all 15cwt wheeled types, as well as small ambulances and tractors

a 350bhp unit for all heavy tractors, recovery vehicles and tank transporters; all 6 x 6, and the same engine in any future wheeled and tracked amphibians.

Further, with regard to the 4 x 4 type in the 3-ton class, Campagnac and Hayman hoped that this would interest commercial producers and might even result in a revival of the subsidy scheme. Everything else, they accepted, would not have any obvious civilian application. They went on to explain that they visualised the entire half-track range as being lightly armoured at the front and underneath to protect against small-arms fire and mine damage.

Considering body types – but limiting ourselves here to the immediate subject – they were looking for a general service load carrier, an armoured personnel carrier, house types for signals, office or workshops where a trailer would not do and semi-trailer tractors. Trailers, in general, they regarded as being of supreme importance since they avoided the penalty of building dozens of different types of bodies for powered chassis.

The above were all to be regarded as general recommendations. They were not intended to replace the kind of detailed General Staff specifications that were drawn up for each new design. Returning again to the general theme Campagnac and Hayman threw in a few more recommendations for good measure. These included rugged construction, a good turning circle, simplicity in manoeuvring and, it almost goes without saying, reliability and ease of maintenance. Then, just to make sure that nothing was overlooked they emphasised that the need for air-portability should be kept in mind, adding that the use of light alloys for construction should be investigated and that, during manufacture, as much attention as possible should be given to waterproofing.

These various recommendations were incorporated in a General Staff Policy Statement issued in November 1944, which preceded formal discussions between the Ministry of Supply and the British motor industry. Before these discussions had reached a conclusion, the War Office felt confident enough to announce that there was general agreement on the principle that military and civilian requirements were diametrically opposed. The War Office also stated that, in time of war, many smaller types of vehicle needed by the Army could be built that were 'in the capacity of existing tooling'. In other words, it seemed to be saying that there was a place for militarised commercial types after all!

At this point the War Office reverted to the ideal vehicle list and came to the conclusion that something was missing. The despised 15cwt truck, they were told, proved to be a very useful military type during the war. It was used in vast numbers by infantry units and was in demand as a general carrier and runabout by all branches of the service. The War Office countered by pointing out that 'it was generally accepted that the load was uneconomical', presumably forgetting that their original list specifically stated that a new type of half-track was required to replace all vehicles in the 15cwt class. In attempting to resolve this problem the various contributors proceeded to get themselves into a first-class muddle.

The first suggestion, for a continuation of the four-wheel drive 15cwt design, was rejected on the grounds that it would not be able to cope with frontline conditions. Improved performance could be achieved by employing six-wheel drive although this was considered uneconomical and difficult to design but the alternative, a 3-ton 4 x 4, was rejected as being too large. Inevitably, it was now time to compromise and the final suggestion was for a 30cwt 6 x 6 with the 90bhp engine which, the experts added, could also be produced as a passenger-carrying vehicle. In effect what we have here is a reinvention of the 1927 Morris-Commercial D Type with a driven front axle.

A revised list was drawn up to incorporate this new type whereupon, believe it or not, the entire programme was reconsidered! This was due to a sudden realisation that existing production resources in Britain and the Empire, while capable of meeting peacetime requirements, would not be able to satisfy demand in the event of war. This seems so blindingly obvious that one wonders why it did not feature as the starting point of the whole discussion. A cynical civilian might be tempted to say that this was typical of the military approach, but perish the thought.

To pursue what followed could be tedious, but it is difficult to resist quoting the final sentence. 'Army troops not required to operate in forward areas might be provided with 4 x 2 chassis'! A draft copy of the revised proposals, as they stood at this stage, was then shown to the Deputy Director General of Mechanisation at the Ministry of Supply. He promptly shot a few cherished ideas down in flames and two of these must be mentioned. He could, for instance, see no great difficulty in creating a 15cwt 6 x 6 in the 90bhp class because it would be developed from the proposed 4 x 4. He saw no advantage in producing a 30cwt 6 x 6 and, most strangely of all, recommended that they drop the 3-ton 4 x 4.

The result of all this mental effort was a list, in the form of a table, which appeared in February 1945 (see Table 8.1 on page 196). The table was published as General Staff Policy Statement No 35 in November 1945 and it remained as official doctrine until 1947.

Having considered ideals at such unforgivable length it is now time to examine what really did happen.

In 1942 the experimental department at Rolls-Royce, then managed by W.A. (Roy) Robotham, was engaged in testing a long-bonneted Bentley car known, on account of its performance, as the 'Scalded Cat'. On trial one day the car first achieved a top speed of 101.5mph and then managed to climb the tortuous Porlock Hill, on the edge of Exmoor, entirely in top gear. This was done without making any changes to the car, the rear axle ratio remained the same, and it argues much for the quality of the engine that it was able to respond to both demands without any change.

The engine of the Scalded Cat was a 170bhp straight eight, 3½in stroke by 4½in bore of F-head configuration; that is, with overhead inlet valves and side valves controlling the exhaust. This was nothing new. Most early cars had used the F-head arrangement including the original Royce models of 1904. However, it had fallen from favour and Rolls-Royce only reintroduced it in 1938 for technical reasons. The engine was first fitted into an experimental Rolls-Royce known as Big Bertha before the war and a six-cylinder version, rated at 120bhp, was fitted into a prototype Bentley, known as the Corniche.

Robotham was, in fact, testing both Big Bertha and the Corniche in Germany and France a few days before war broke out and, in the hurry to get back the Bentley had to be left on the quayside at Dieppe where it was later destroyed by a German bomb.

TABLE 8.1

Published in 1951, this lists a range of proposed military vehicles for the post-war British Army.

Serial No	Chassis (a)	BHP	Types of Body (a)	Priority
1	4 x 4	60	British light car	1
2(b)	4 x 4	90	Staff car; scout car; 3-ton including some technical bodies; light artillery tractor (d)	2
3	6 x 6	90	Light load-carrier GS (c); light artillery tractor; light ambulance	7
4	6 x 6	135	3-ton, including some technical bodies; heavy ambulance	5
5	6 x 6	180	3-ton, including some technical bodies; 10-ton GS; field and anti-tank artillery tractor	4
6	6 x 6	350	Tank transporters; medium artillery tractors; intermediate and heavy AA tractors; heavy breakdowns; heavy tractors	6
7	¾-tracked	80	Field and anti-tank artillery tractors; load and passenger carrying vehicles; some technical bodies	3
8	¾-tracked	350	Medium artillery tractors; heavy breakdown, intermediate and heavy AA tractors	8
9	Fully tracked	180	Field and anti-tank artillery tractors; load and passenger carrying vehicles; some technical bodies	1 (e)
10	Fully tracked	350	Medium artillery tractors; heavy breakdown, intermediate and heavy AA tractors.	2 (e)

(a) Wheeled and ¾-tracked chassis and associated bodies to be considered for transport by air.
(b) A chassis was already being designed for carriage in the Dakota.
(c) 30cwt payload most desirable, but the vehicle must not be greater in silhouette than the obsolete 30cwt 4 x 2.
(d) Only required in Serial 2 if the 6 x 6 vehicle in Serial 3, plus the new light artillery gun could not be made air-portable in one Class I load (2,000lb).
(e) Serials 1-8 and 9-10 inclusive were at that time the responsibility of two separate Ministry of Supply departments – hence the duplication of priorities.

The fact that cars like the Scalded Cat were still being tested as late as 1942 is something of a surprise but the experimental department at Rolls-Royce was rather an exclusive set. The main factory at Derby had been turned over to production of the Merlin engine for the RAF and Robotham took over the ruined Clan Foundry at Belper for his small team. Since work on their post-war car programme was seen as somewhat incongruous at the time, and petrol rationing ended the practice of testing experimental cars, Robotham was seconded to the Ministry of Supply and, with his team at Belper undertook other work, as recounted elsewhere in this series.*

If the 120bhp, six-cylinder engine of the Bentley Corniche is taken as the standard unit then the straight eight of the Scalded Cat was created by adding a cylinder to each end. Likewise, a cylinder could be trimmed off each end to create a four-cylinder version, which was fitted into another experimental car called the 'Ripplette'. As things turned out this range of engines was never used for car production – excluding the 16 Rolls-Royce Phantom IV limousines produced for the Royal Family and other heads of state, which employed the straight eight. Instead this family of power packs, with its standardised range of components, turned out to be just what the War Office needed for its proposed range of post-war military vehicles.

According to his autobiography, Robotham found his period with the Ministry of Supply very trying and he left in August 1943. On his return to Belper his main concern was the future of car production but he seems to have got wind of the various discussions, outlined above, for future military vehicles. He was convinced that the range of standard engines, known as the B series, would be ideal and sought out ways of convincing the War Office. His first step was a trial run in the Scalded Cat. Robotham took with him a senior officer, Major-General Charles Dunphie who was then serving on the General Staff. On the basis of this trial, he appeared to have obtained a contract for Rolls-Royce to build a version of the Universal Carrier with the straight eight in it. In fact, events did not progress in quite this personal way since the War Office was already negotiating for a new carrier and Rolls-Royce was but one of a number of firms involved. Their machine, the CT24, did not prove successful but the same engine was used in two other prototypes and it was clearly regarded as an improvement on its nearest rival, the Ford V8.

The three basic engines in the B series were the four-cylinder B40 at 80bhp, the six-cylinder B60 at 130bhp and the big eight-cylinder B80 at 165bhp, all with the same size cylinders. There were various marques and variants for specific applications but the only one that should be noted here is the B81, which was essentially the B80 enlarged to 3¾in bore. The B81 delivered a maximum 220bhp. It is worth noting that in each case, when compared with the ideal engines originally specified by the Ministry of Supply, the Rolls-Royce range did not meet the horsepower requirements and there was nothing approaching the big 350 unit intended for the largest vehicles. However, when the Rolls-Royce engines were all tested in the latter days of the war and after in a variety of vehicles ranging from a Morris-Commercial 15cwt to a Scammell recovery tractor, the performance in all cases was extremely good.

Adapting the engines for military use drew on all the recent wartime experience. The entire ignition system had to be fully suppressed in order that it should not interfere with the operation of radio equipment; likewise, the electrical system had to be sealed against the effect of tropical conditions and made as thoroughly waterproof as

*D. Fletcher, *The Universal Tank* (The Tank Museum, 2021)

BRITISH MILITARY TRANSPORT 1829-1956

An Austin Champ in front of a wartime half-track serving in the communications role during an exercise in Occupied Germany.

possible. Naturally, these requirements applied to all vehicles and, although it clearly worked, the degree of thoroughness caused a maintenance nightmare. Even a relatively simple task such as checking the gap on the points became a major operation, even more so on the larger engines, which had twin contact breakers. All engines in the military range also had the Ki-gass cold start equipment fitted, which injected ether into the manifold.

The wartime habit of austerity did not evaporate at the end of the war; indeed, the impression remains that the Government of the day did everything it could to foster it. Many essential, everyday items continued to be rationed and any overt display of flamboyance was severely frowned upon. The British armed forces still had worldwide responsibilities just as they had in 1919 and a lot of this was due, once again, to the potential Soviet threat, which was now far better organised. From the military transport point of view there were no serious shortages. Vehicle production had been sustained in order to support an expanded commitment to the Far East war and, when this was cut short by the dropping of the atom bomb, it meant that adequate stocks were available. Although the Army was not exactly enjoined to live off its fat, as it had been in 1919, it was obliged to in any case, yet the ambitious wartime programme survived. Indeed, it had already begun.

In 1944, specifications had been drawn up for a British replacement for the Jeep, based on the General Staff requirement. Design work was shared between FVRDE and the Nuffield organisation, which resulted in an ugly field car, the 'Gutty', appearing in 1945. Three prototypes were built and duly

198

abandoned. Then, in 1949, as part of the Nuffield Group, Wolseley Motors built three prototypes of a similar vehicle called 'Mudlark' and followed this with a small pre-production batch. The engine used in both cases was the Rolls-Royce B40.

In 1952, while trials of the Mudlark were still proceeding, Nuffields amalgamated with Austin to form the British Motor Corporation and the new organisation came up with the 'Champ', in conjunction with FVRDE. Bearing in mind the uncertain deliberations on the advantages of independent suspension it is interesting to observe that in the Champ, and other military prototypes built under the post-war scheme, it was a major feature. The Austin Champ employed short, longitudinal torsion bars for each wheel station. It also had a five-speed gearbox with independent reverse and, to assist in deep wading, a permanent schnorkel-type arrangement mounted on the front, offside mudguard. Upon entering service the Champ attracted a lot of attention. Opinion was divided over whether such a sophisticated machine was indeed more useful to the Army than something simple, like the Jeep, or the slightly less basic Land Rover, but there was no doubt at all that in terms of cost the Champ was way ahead of its competitors. By 1954, one Champ cost approximately three times as much as a Land Rover.

The discussions already recorded on the respective advantages of 15cwt or 30cwt vehicles, whether 4 x 4 or 6 x 6, which had confounded the original Ministry of Supply deliberations, took another twist in 1947. Working in conjunction with the Rootes Group, FVRDE came up with a design for a

A Humber FV1600 series 1-ton truck in the wading tank at Chertsey. The device on the right side of the cab is the engine breather and all appears to be going well although a tow rope is still kept handy.

The Vauxhall FV1300 6 x 6 prototype undergoing tests in a swamp. The shallow tray body has simply been fitted to hold ballast weights and a loose spare wheel.

Third prototype of the impressive Bedford BT three-quarter tracked vehicle based on wartime German designs.

4 x 4 light truck for a payload of 1 ton. It was probably the only capacity that had never been discussed. Rootes produced a prototype in 1950, under the Humber marque, and production followed in 1952. Early models had a soft-top canvas cab but the main batch came with a stylish, coach-built hard-top cab with covered manholes in the roof for both driver and assistant. Indeed, the cab was so well styled the question arises as to what possible advantage it could offer to a military vehicle. It must have been vastly more expensive to manufacture than a utilitarian type and even more difficult to repair in the event of damage. Perhaps it was an inevitable result of the 'no-expense-spared' mentality that lay behind the entire programme; virtually all the specialised military vehicles built at this time were the same in this respect.

The Humber, built to FV1600 specification, used the B60 engine, and again had independent, torsion bar suspension. It had a superb performance and was extremely popular for its comfort and handling but again the price placed it in the luxury category. Even so, in this case the War Office seems to have got its money's worth because the chassis was used as the basis for the armoured utility vehicle, known as the Humber Pig, which gave the British Amy nearly 30 years of valuable service.

In 1949, the General Staff addressed the problem of the 3-ton class. Working in conjunction with Vauxhall Motors, FVRDE produced a 6 x 6 design (FV1301), which appeared in prototype form in 1952. Why Vauxhall chose to use their own name instead of the Bedford marque is not clear but the resulting vehicle, which again was of striking appearance, never entered production and the project was cancelled in 1953. The Vauxhall would have employed the B80 engine and both Albion and Thornycroft used the same power unit in military designs of their own that were offered in the mid-1950s. Only Thornycroft's Nubian entered limited production.

In 1951, Leyland Motors built the prototype of a B80-powered cargo truck in the 10-ton class. This, however, is better known for its dual role as an artillery tractor and recovery vehicle, both of which are outside the scope of this work. Indeed, the entire story of the development and use of the B-series engines goes far beyond the limited subject of military transport and, since it is covered in considerable detail elsewhere, need not concern us any further.*

Returning again to the original Ministry of Supply programme of 1944 there were references to a half-track in the 15cwt class, which never saw the light of day, and a three-quarter track for which a whole range of tasks was envisaged, including a cross-country load carrier. Although nothing was ever done to develop anything within the standard programme the concept had been anticipated to some extent by Vauxhall Motors. Like many other British manufacturers, Vauxhall had undertaken evaluation of captured enemy vehicles during the war, one of which was a German three-quarter tracked personnel

*P. Ware, *In National Service* (Warehouse Publications, 1995)

carrier. In 1945 they built six prototypes of their own which, for want of anything better, employed a pair of Bedford six-cylinder engines rated at 136bhp; a long way short of the 180/350bhp specified by the Ministry. Again, however, this project was closed down at the prototype stage.

Between 1951 and 1953, British forces were involved in the Korean War, as part of the United Nations forces under American command. The transport of British and Commonwealth forces involved was almost exclusively of Second World War vintage with the Bedford QL continuing to give an excellent account of itself. Indeed, at one point it was compared very favourably with the vaunted GMC 2½-ton 6 x 6. Early in 1951, an RASC company was boosted by a Royal Canadian Army Service Corps (RCASC) platoon equipped with the latter American vehicles. In the frightful winter conditions British crews discovered that the cab-over-engine layout of the Bedford provided a lot more warmth than the GMC cab and it is reported that the American vehicle suffered far more from broken springs than did its British counterpart. The official view that the four-wheel drive 3-tonner had no place in the post-war Army was probably unrealistic anyway, but if not events such as Korea should have proved them wrong. Many of those men who served in Korea have drawn parallels with the First World War. The Allied retreat to the Han River, following the Chinese invasion, has so much in common with events following the German offensive of 1918 that it is positively eerie. In grim

Bedford MW 15cwts and a Universal Carrier destroyed by enemy shelling during the Korean War.

Bedford QL 3-tonners and an AEC Matador gun tractor at a base camp in Korea.

BRITISH MILITARY TRANSPORT 1829-1956

An excellent example of a CT-type vehicle. A Humber 1-ton 4 x 4 crossing a tank bridge.

weather, sometimes approaching 60 degrees of frost, convoys ran a shuttle service alternating parties of infantry and stores from one staging post to the next ahead of the advancing Chinese. Exhausted drivers fought to stay awake, driving around the clock, just as their fathers had done in the First World War.

Sometime, certainly before the Korean War, somebody realised that the ambitious programme devised by the General Staff and Ministry of Supply was not only prohibitively expensive but entirely beyond the scope of the British motor industry, especially in peacetime. Coming back down to earth is never easy and it is always liable to be taken too far in the other direction once the descent has built up momentum. The normal British response, under such circumstances, is compromise but in this case it seems to have resulted in an even bigger muddle.

According to a document issued in 1950, new military vehicles would be divided into groups, selected by purpose and identified by letter groups. At the forefront came CT chosen, it is said, from the end letters of the word CombaT. Then there would be GS (for General Service) and finally CL on CommerciaL. It is not difficult to foresee what the Army was getting at; it is back to the business of horses for courses again.

CT, or combat vehicles, would be those types built to the most stringent General Staff specifications. Combat was an odd choice of word to describe them since they were not fighting vehicles in their own right but, in theory at least, they could operate where fighting vehicles could go and to that extent would, presumably, be found in those combat areas that armoured fighting vehicles operate in.

The General Service types, on the other hand, were not as general as all that. They were essentially commercial models adapted, under FVRDE guidance, into military vehicles with an adequate cross-country performance. The most significant military modifications would be four- or six-wheel drive as appropriate, the use of WD Pattern split-rim wheels and heavy-duty tyres. Ground clearance would be improved, engines screened for electrical interference and many detailed changes made to suit their military roles but they would retain their commercial engines, axles, springs and so on. Commercial types are exactly what the name implies; that ever popular standby, the ordinary lorry painted green.

All of this must have been disappointing enough for those who had worked so hard to create an exclusive military programme, to provide the British Army

The Ford Thames E4 would fit well into the GS category. The cab is based on a current Commer design for commercial vehicles, the engine a Ford V8, but the chassis has been modified to four-wheel drive and is seen here fitted with an ambulance body for military purposes.

Although not precisely an example of a vehicle in the commercial category this 1947 2.1-litre Standard Vanguard saloon photographed in the Middle East does represent an unmodified civilian vehicle in military service.

A Leyland Martian undergoing stability tests on the tilt bed at FVRDE.

203

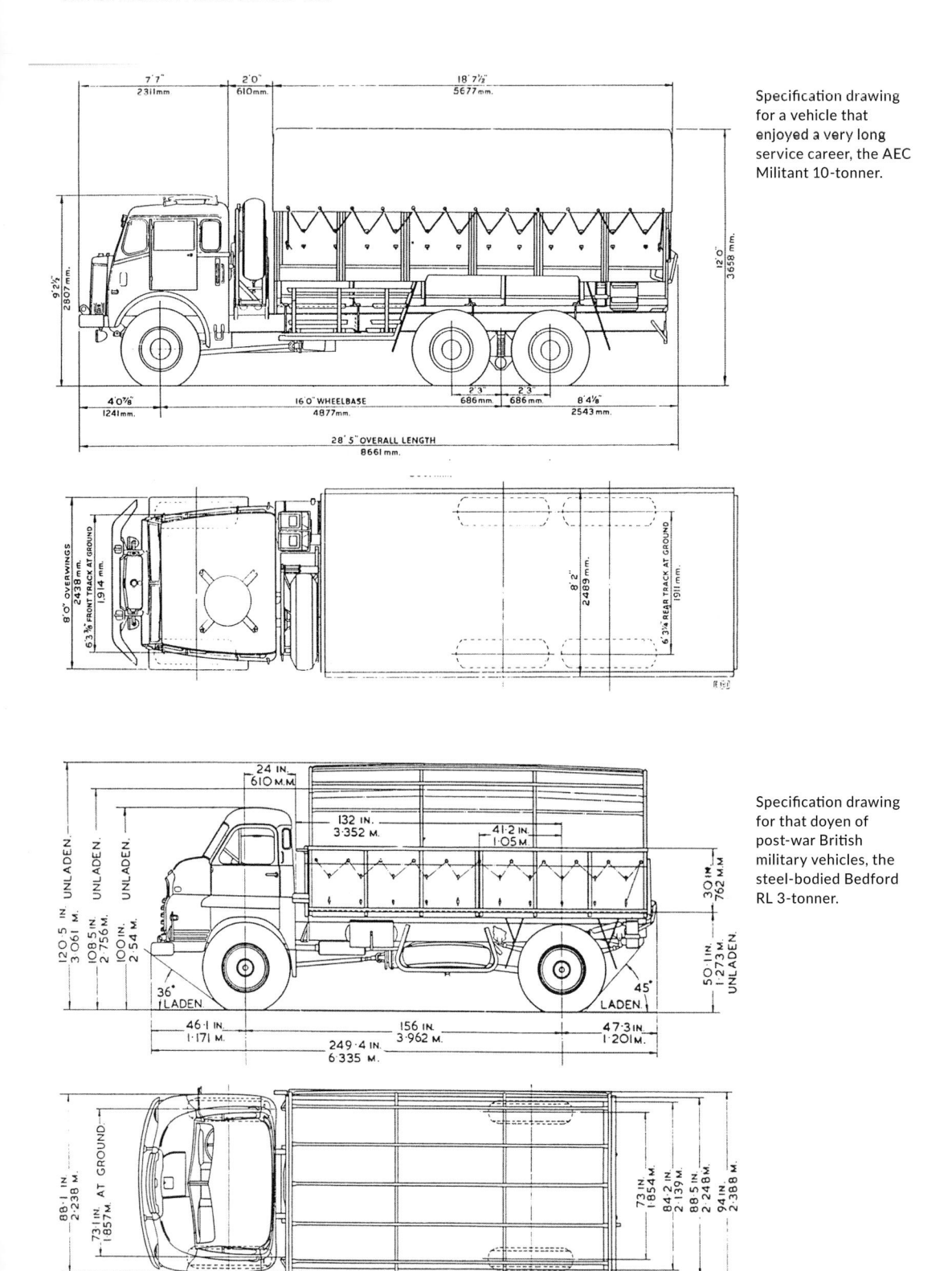

Specification drawing for a vehicle that enjoyed a very long service career, the AEC Militant 10-tonner.

Specification drawing for that doyen of post-war British military vehicles, the steel-bodied Bedford RL 3-tonner.

with an almost ideal range of support vehicles regardless of cost. What made it worse was the proposed scale of production for the three classes. According to the 1950 paper, 45 per cent of all production would be of Commercial types; 39 per cent General Service and a mere 16 per cent Combat. And these figures were calculated at a time when most of the exotic vehicles described above were still being developed for production. When it is realised that out of the entire CT range only three vehicles – the Austin Champ, Humber FV1600 and Leyland Martian – of the main types ever went into production, it is clear that CT vehicles were hardly worth worrying about in the full scheme of things. If they had any claim at all to statistical significance it would have to be in terms of cost, but that will probably never be calculated. Of course, it was not all bad news. Other extremely good things came out of the original programme, at least as far as the engines were concerned. Although they do not fall within the scope of this work it is worth remarking that the B-series engines were used extensively for other military projects, notably light armoured vehicles such as the Ferret, Saladin and Saracen or later supply types such as the amazing Stalwart.

In 1954, FVRDE held the first of a regular series of displays which, it was hoped, would serve as a showcase for British military vehicles, not only for sale to other armies but with an eye to commercial business too. The FVRDE site at Chertsey was chosen as the venue and visitors were invited to inspect a static display of vehicles and also watch them perform over a road circuit, cross-country course and, where appropriate, through the wading tank. FVRDE also used the occasion to show off their own expertise and facilities because the equipment on offer included fighting vehicles and therefore, by definition, the organisation's own input.

A design which did not enjoy much interest from the military is this four-wheel drive version of the Leyland Comet 3-tonner. It was just one of many such designs that were examined at FVRDE.

One company that must have benefited from the FVRDE shows was Land Rover. This early Series I is equipped with sand channels and semaphore indicators. Before long it had entirely eclipsed the Champ and become a major export success story.

A comprehensive little booklet was published for the occasion. Each exhibit, of which there were over seventy, had its own double page entry. They included production vehicles and prototypes of everything from lightweight trailers to tank transporters and combat vehicles, including tanks. In the booklet's introduction, the Minister of Supply, Mr Duncan Sandys MP, made a particular point of welcoming overseas visitors and ensured that they would be aware that many of the vehicles on display had civilian

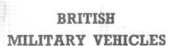

The cover of the FVRDE's booklet for the first of its vehicle displays held in 1954.

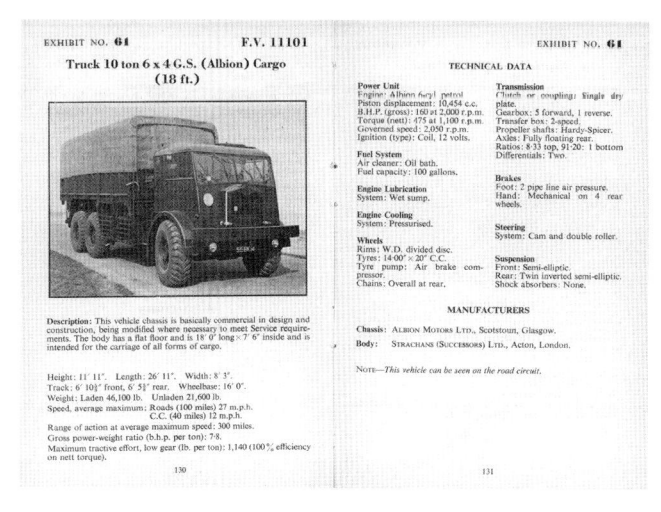

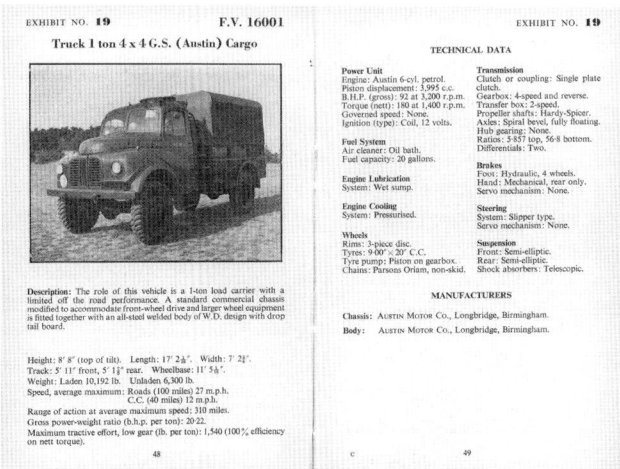

Each display vehicle had its own double-page spread inside the booklet, with a specification and photograph.

applications. The event was presented in conjunction with the Society of Motor Manufacturers and Traders whose president, Mr A.B. Waring, made the same points but went out of his way to praise the facilities at FVRDE.

The booklet did not identify CT, GS and CL-types as such but there were coded references that give the game away. When describing a CT type, for instance, details such as tropicalisation and waterproofing are emphasised. When a GS vehicle is shown the key phrase is usually something to the effect that it is a commercial type, modified with four-wheel drive and secondary gearbox for service use. And the CL-type description invariably includes the phrase 'a commercial design modified to meet service requirements' without in any way specifying what the modifications might be. Load carriers appear in the 1-ton, 3-ton, 5-ton and 10-ton classes but, in terms of variety the ranges are dominated by 10-tonners in both 6 x 6 and 6 x 4 configuration, these last representing most of the genuine CL-types. However, bearing in mind earlier forecasts that there was no future requirement for a 3-tonner in four-wheel drive configuration it is interesting to note three makes, Bedford, Commer and Ford, all of which entered production and service.

Indeed, if one vehicle may be singled out as proof that the original insistence upon perfection was entirely misguided it has to be the classic Bedford RL 3-tonner. In essence this was Bedford's commercial S-Type 7-tonner of 1950, reworked to four-wheel drive, with a WD approved steel GS body by Park Royal of London. Admittedly, Bedford had the advantage over its competitors of experience gained with the equally admirable wartime QL but that cannot detract from the fact that, in the RL, the British Army had one of the best all-round road and cross-country vehicles of the age at a tiny fraction of the cost that it would surely have taken to develop a custom-built type. Production exceeded 73,000 units for a variety of roles and the type was still in service 30 years later.

By 1956, the year in which our study closes, the number of exhibits shown at Chertsey exceeded 80. The companies producing vehicles remained about the same but the range of types had expanded considerably. To give but two examples: AEC Ltd displayed a rigid 8 x 4 chassis as the basis of a bulk refuelling vehicle while Bedford showed a 31-seater coach, with Mulliners body, which could be adapted as an ambulance to take 16 stretchers. This would almost certainly qualify as the first purpose-built military bus.

In November 1956, British and French troops landed in Egypt to contest President Nasser's right to nationalise the Suez Canal. A small RASC party landed with the first wave of paratroops and, backed up by a larger force landed from the sea, appropriated whatever local vehicles they could find and created an improvised bus column. Following in their wake was the RASC divisional transport column of 3rd Infantry Division, which had exchanged all its old QL 3-tonners for the newer Bedford RL model. In the event a ceasefire was already agreed by the time they arrived and the entire Allied force would leave Egypt before Christmas. Brief as it was, this sharp little war provided a new lesson in logistics for the British since it was the first time that helicopters had been employed extensively in the re-supply role. Some American helicopters had helped to supply Commonwealth units during the Korean War but this was the first time that the British had used them in this way on any scale.

It is, therefore, a good time to leave the subject for now. The helicopter is never likely to replace the earth-bound vehicle entirely, but it has altered things dramatically since 1956. If anything is clear from this superficial study it must be that lessons, even those learnt the hard way, do not appear to stay learnt.

Centurion tank of 6th Royal Tank Regiment in Egypt during the Suez Crisis supported by a Bedford RL and Austin K9, the former displaying the white 'H' allied recognition symbol.

Although this cab design was never adopted, the AEC Mammoth Major eight-wheeler shown at FVRDE was in every other respect a standard commercial type.

INDEX

A
Abadan, oil refinery 155
Abbott, Colonel Sir Frederick 11
AEC Ltd 57, 59, 105, 111
   3-ton 6 x 4 lorries 59, 111, 136
   eight-wheel all-wheel drive lorries 209
   Mammoth Major 8 x 4 truck 208
   Matador four-wheel drive tractor 136
   Matador six-wheel drive tractor 136
   Militant 10-ton truck 204
Afghan War 1919 88
El Agheila 144, 149
air-portable vehicles 182-3
Akroyd-type (paraffin) engine 28
El Alamein 142, 150-1, 152
Albion Motors 99, 115, 136
   30cwt lorries 95
   3-ton 32hp lorries 74, 85, 86, 137
Allen and Simmonds, steam engines 35
Allenby, General Edmund, 1st Viscount 75
ambulances
   Austin K2/Y 137, 176
   Bedford coach 208
   Chevrolet 186
   Ford Thames E4 4 x 4 203
   ATS/FANY drivers 135
   Car conversions 59
   El Hakkim rescue 72
   half-track 178
   Mesopotamia 76, 86, 155
   trailers 83
Amiens, Battle of 69
ammunition parks 120, 51, 113
amphibians
   Argosy 165
   DUKWs 156-9, 165, 167, 171, 172, 179, 192
   Hexonaut 182
   landing craft 78, 164, 167, 168, 170, 173, 177
   LVT 4 Buffalo 159, 165
   Neptune 165
   Terrapin 165-6
Antwerp 51, 176, 177-9
Armstrong-Whitworth, Armstrong-Saurer 5-ton trucks 114
Army
   8th Army 149, 152
   14th Army 186, 187
   III Corps 61
   8 Corps 176
   12 Corps 176
   30 Corps 176
   Guards Armoured Division 171
   1st Armoured Division 125, 135
   7th Armoured Division 154, 185
   3rd Infantry Division 172, 208
   4th Infantry Division 162
   22nd Guards Brigade Group 148
   7th Armoured Brigade 185
   Army Balloon Factory 15
   Army Group, 21st (British and Canadian) 168, 169, 171, 172
   Army Motor Reserve (AMR) 33
   Army Service Corps (ASC) 23, 26, 45, 89
   606 Company 56
   ambulance companies 84
   MT companies 77, 92
   see also Royal Army Service Corps (RASC)
aromatics, petrol additives 123
Arquata 79
Arrol-Johnston, 16hp four-seat motor car 34
Ashanti War 1874 14
Associated Equipment Company (AEC) see AEC Ltd
Austin
   15cwt platoon truck 105, 114, 133, 139
   20hp ambulance 45
   30cwt lorries 137
   2-ton workshop vehicle 78
   Champ 198, 205
   K2/Y heavy ambulance 137, 176
   K5 3-ton four-wheel drive 137, 170, 177, 178, 183
   K6 3-ton 6 x 4 191
   K7 15cwt 182
   K9 1-ton truck 207
Australians, Light Car Patrols 72
Austro-Daimler 6 x 4 116
Autocarrier tri-car 37
Automobile Association (AA) 63
Auxiliary Omnibus Park (AOP) 63
Auxiliary Territorial Service (ATS) 135
Aveling & Porter Ltd, steam rollers and traction engines 9, 14-5, 17
Aveling, Thomas 14

B
Badcock, Colonel, on Model-T Fords 73-4
Baghdad 76-7, 156
Bagnall-Wild, Captain R.K. RE 24, 30, 34
Bagnold, Major Ralph RASC 103, 105, 143
Bain, trucks 62
Balaclava, steam railway 10
Balloon, Steam Sapper 15
Bandar Shah 156
Barrie, Isaac, haulage 141
Basra 71, 75, 76, 157
Beadon, Colonel R.H. RASC 77, 78
Beatson, A.M. 54
Beda Fomm 144, 146, 149
Bedford
   15cwt truck 122, 133, 178
   30cwt lorry 137
   3-ton lorry 120, 144
   5-ton tipper 137
   BT three-quarter track prototype 200
   coach thirty-one-seater 208
   Giraffe wader 168
   MW 15cwt 201
   OXC articulated semi-trailer 165
   OY 3-ton bread carrier 137
   QL 3-ton four-wheel drive 137, 183
   QL tipper 183
   RL 3-ton truck 207-8, 209
   WH 2-ton lorry 106; *see also* Vauxhall Motors
Belsize 2-ton lorry 49

INDEX

Benghazi 149, 152
Berkshire Manoeuvres 1893 15
Berna trucks 62
'Blue Train', command and signals convoy 165
Bluebell, steam-powered cart 12
Boer War 4, 17-18, 25, 29, 81, 189
boilers
   Field-type 13
   pot-boiler 13
   vertical 13, 21
Botha, General Louis 82
Bovington Camp 104
Boydell, James 10, 11
Brabazon of Tara, 1st Baron 141
Brennan, Louis 36
bridges
   Bailey bridges 158, 161, 179, 182, 187
   Hamilton bridges 158
   pontoon bridges 14
   tank bridges 202
bridging train 136
British Expeditionary Force (BEF)
   World War 1 44, 50, 51, 54, 68
   World War 2 119, 120, 124-5
British Motor Corporation 199
British-Berna, 3.5-ton trucks 62
Broad, Lieutenant-General Sir Charles 88, 107-11
Brooke motor car 28
Brooklands, vehicle testing 34, 41, 42
Broom & Wade, internal combustion vehicles 35
Buffalo, amphibian 159, 165
Buick
   27hp six-cylinder tractors 60, 65
SS *Bulawayo* 17
bulldozers 158
Buller, General Sir Redvers 18
bullock carts 12
Burford-Kégresse, half-tracks 93, 94
Burma Campaign 162, 185-7
Burrell
   steam tractors 34
   steam-crane tractor 34
Burrell-Boydell engine 11
buses
   B-type double-decker 41, 51, 53, 54, 59, 63
bus columns 33, 108-9
Daimler 3-tonner 34, 61
charabancs 42, 63, 108
double-deck trailer 13
double-decker 51, 54, 129
Milnes-Daimler 21, 22, 32, 33, 34, 37
RASC Omnibus Companies 107-8
single-decker 107, 108, 129
Bussing designs 33, 44

C

Caen, German resistance 173, 176
Calais, British transport vehicles 69, 121, 176
Cambrai, Battle of 66
Campagnac, Major R. RASC 189, 94
Canada, vehicle production 126, 153
Canadian Army, mechanisation of 132
Canadian Military Pattern (CMP) models 154, 156, 167
cars *see* motor cars
Caterlorry 90-1
caterpillar tracks 10
caterpillar tractors and train 73, 77, 79
   see also Holt caterpillar tractors
Cautley, Colonel Sir Proby 11
Central Bus Company 41
Centurion tank 209
chain-drive vehicles 3, 39, 41, 43, 44, 65, 168
Chanak, Turkey 92
Charlotte Dundas, steam-powered boat 9
Chenab, Ransomes steam engine 13
Chevrolet
   30cwt trucks 116
   3-ton Canadian trucks 153
   ambulance 186
   see also General Motors
Chief Inspector of Subsidised Transport (CIST) 49
Chindwin river 185, 187
Chitral, armoured car 101-2

Churchill, Sir Winston S. 51, 65, 121, 134, 168
Churchill tank 141
Citroën, André 93, 96
Citroën-Kégresse, staff cars 93
Clarkson, Thomas 32-4
Clayton & Co, and MTC subsidy scheme 42
Clayton & Shuttleworth, steam lorries 55
Clement-Talbot, 30cwt lorries 92
coaches *see* buses, single-decker
Colvin, Colonel R.B. 32
Combined Operations Experimental Establishment (COXE) 167
Combined Operations Headquarters 168
Commer
   15cwt trucks 106
   30cwt four-wheel drive tractor 111
   3-ton chain-drive lorry 3
   Beetle 137
   Q2 truck 137
   Q4 truck 162
   Q15 truck 137
   Queen Mary aircraft transporters 137
   Raider 30cwt lorry 104
   short-wheelbase tractor units 137
   War Office subsidy trials 41, 42
Commercial Motor Transport Exhibition 1933 98
compound steam engines 17, 19, 24, 25, 27, 35, 82
convoys 50, 57, 61, 64, 72, 74, 95, 101, 103, 110, 120, 124, 147, 152, 156, 165,170, 175, 185, 202
   air attack 147, 175
County of London, 25th Cyclist Battalion 36
cranes 9, 14, 34, 97, 140, 158
Crawford, Colonel 115
Crimean War 9, 10
Crompton, Colonel R.E.B. 12-14, 20, 23, 26-7, 29, 35, 43, 47, 90, 189
Crosby, F. Gordon 90
Crosland Committee 1935 98,

209

106, 120, 189
Crossley
  30cwt lorry 97
  3-ton 6 x 4 lorries 97, 104, 115
  3-ton searchlight lorry 147
  ambulance 20/25hp 45
  armoured cars 101
  charabancs 108
  four-wheel drive independent suspension 114
  tenders 74
Ctesiphon, Battle of 76
cyclist battalions 36, 37

D
D-Day 141, 169-171, 175
Daimler
  3-ton lorries 34, 61
  double-deck buses 51
Dakota C-47, military transport 182
Dauntless trucks, four-wheel 116
Davidson, General A.E. RE 34, 100, 103, 115
De Dion omnibuses 33
demobilisation 1919 89
  ex-service vehicle auctions 89
  see also mobilisation of subsidy vehicles
Dennis
  3-ton Pig tipper 137, 175, 200
  subsidy trials 41
Dennis-Stevens 3-ton petrol-electric lorry 117
SS *Denton Grange* 18
Department of Tank Design and Experiment 90, 93
desert conditions 144, 151, 154, 185
diesel engines 98, 116
Dimapur railhead 185
Diplock, Bramah J. 29-30, 90
divisional transport 18, 37, 44, 121, 146, 171, 208
Dodge
  modified conventional types 154
  T215 panel van 152
  WK60 3-ton trucks 171
  Dominant trucks 6 x 4 116
donkeys, assistance to mechanised transport 82

Drag, steam-powered cart 9-10
drivers
  ATS 136, 155
  civilians 102, 140, 184
  Special Reserve 42, 50
  training in World War 1 59
  driving school, Rawalpindi 86
Du Cross Cab Co 36
DUKWs 156-8, 159, 165, 167, 171-2, 173, 176, 179, 183, 187, 192
Dunkirk, loss of vehicles 122-4, 176
Dunphie, Major-General Charles 197
Dzhulfa 156

E
Egypt
  Canal Zone 155
  Suez Crisis 209
  vehicle specification 103
  in World War 2 168
eight-wheel drive 166
Endless Railway 10-2
engines
  Bedford 6-cylinder 136bhp 201
  breathers/schnorkels 199
  Chevrolet straight six 154
  compression checks 123
  Dorman four-cylinder 48
  Ford V8 166, 197, 203
  ignition systems suppression 197
  Knight sleeve-valve 74
  Rolls-Royce 170bhp straight eight 197
  Rolls-Royce B series 197
  Tylor JB4 37, 61; *see also* internal-combustion engine
Enrolment Scheme, for steam tractor owners 35
Ensign lorry 82
ERF, 6-ton 2C14 truck 139
Europe, Western Plan 106
excavators 158
Experimental Military Hauling Engine 27
Experimental and Motor Sub-Committee (of MTC) 23, 26-7

F
Falaise 176
Feltham, RASC MT Depot 132
Ferret, light armoured vehicles 206
Fiat 15 ter 78, 91
Fighting Vehicle Design Establishment 192
Fighting Vehicle Research and Development Establishment (FVRDE) 192, 198-200, 203, 206, 209
  Chertsey vehicle displays 206-8
fire engines 13, 45, 139
fire tenders 137
First Aid Nursing Yeomanry (FANY) 58, 135
flexible trackway 145
Foden
  6-ton truck 139
  6 x 4 10-ton diesel lorries 139
  steam lorry 20-1, 22, 31, 56
food, transportation of 44, 50, 83, 112, 113
Ford
  15cwt truck 154
  2-ton truck 114
  3-ton lorry 147, 155
  anti-aircraft decoy 148
  box bodies 65
  Canadian Ford 148, 155
  Model-A, pick-up 102
  Model-T *see* Model-T Ford
  Thames E4 4 x 4 ambulance 203
Fordson
  15cwt trucks 169, 189
  30cwt 4 x 4 trucks 138
  3-ton 4 x 4 trucks 138
  7V NAAFI canteen 179
  WOT2 15cwt anti-aircraft truck 135
  WOT6 3-ton 4 x 4 truck 5, 183
  WOT8 30-cwt office truck 143
Fosters of Lincoln 26
four-wheel drive 15, 29, 78, 80, 106, 111, 114, 115, 132, 133, 136, 137, 139, 140, 154, 161, 163, 178, 179, 187, 192, 193, 194, 201, 203, 207, 208
  15cwt trucks 154

210

INDEX

30cwt lorry 53
1-ton truck 199
3-ton lorries 113, 159, 174
1951 recommendations 121, 125, 171
Bedford, QL 3-ton 132, 134, 137, 168, 183, 184, 201, 208
independent suspension 114-115, 199
Karrier K6 175, 183
tractor units 137, 164
Fowler
B5 & B6 Lion class 10nhp compound 24, 25
compound engines 19, 25, 82
compound road locomotives 82
steam tractor 26, 28, 34, 35, 37
tracked trailers 77, 111
French, General Sir John 54
Frog, traction engine 16
fuel
coal 13, 16, 18, 20-5, 27
coke 22
paraffin 21, 28, 32, 34, 35, 38, 41
rationing 140-1
wood 13
see also diesel engines; petrol
Fuller, Colonel J.F.C. 90
FWD Motors 93, 111

G
Gallipoli Campaign 77-8, 92
Gardiner, Captain 18
Garner
30cwt four-wheel drive tractor 97, 111
Gazala Line, retreat 150
General Motors 102, 116, 153-4
6 x 6 truck 192, 201
see also Chevrolet; DUKWs
General Strike 1926 106, 108
German East Africa 81
German South West Africa 82
German Spring Offensive 1918 68
'Giraffe', wading vehicle 168
Girba Oasis, Senussi campaign 1914-15 72
Girouard, Percy 18
gliders, delivery of light vehicles 182
'Golden Arrow', command and signals convoy 165
Greece, war with Turkey 1921-22 92
Greek Government, fuel supply at Salonika 78
Greenwood's Corner, Waziristan 100
ground clearance 4, 48, 120, 132, 190, 203
GS wagons 64, 68
gunboats 75
Gurney, Sir Goldsworthy 9-10
Gustav Line 159
'Gutty' field car 198
Guy Motors 93, 97, 117, 125, 138, 163
15cwt truck 125
15cwt Ant trucks 136, 163
15cwt Ant 4 x 4 trucks 162, 163
30cwt lorry 93, 94
3-ton trucks 97, 145
3-ton four-wheel drive tractor 106
3-ton 6 x 4 lorries 95
double-deck bus 138
Otter 3-ton petrol-electric searchlight lorry 117
El Hakkim, Senussi campaign 1914—15 72
armour 94, 193
Wool trials 104
see also tracked vehicles

H
Halfaya Pass 148
Hall of Dartford, and MTC subsidy scheme 42
Halley
30cwt lorry 93, 95
Chain-drive lorry 65
Haliford
Petrol-electric lorries 39
Hamilton, Ronald 134
Hardy Motors, 3-ton four-wheel drive tractor 111
Hathi tractor 111
haulage industry 38, 140
Hayman, Major P.E.C. 15th/19th KRH 189-90, 192-4
Hele-Shaw, Professor 30
helicopters, supply role 209
Herepath, John 9, 10
Hindenburg Line 63
hire of civilian vehicles 101; see also mobilisation of subsidy vehicles
History of the Ministry of Munitions 58, 66
Hitler Line 159
Hobart, Major-General Percy 143
Holden, Colonel RE 34
Holden, James 27
Holt 75hp caterpillar tractor 73, 77, 79; see also tracked vehicles
Home Guard, transport needs 132
Hornsby, internal combustion tractors 28, 31, 35
Horses 9, 11, 15, 16, 47, 64, 179
Hounslow Barracks 9
Howard, traction engines 16
Humber
8cwt pick-up 119
1-ton 4 x 4 FV1600 truck 199, 200, 202, 205
Hexonaut six-wheel drive amphibian 182
Pig 200

I
Imphal 185, 186
impressment of civilian vehicles 40, 50, 54, 68, 106, 117, 119, 120, 125, 135
India
Eastern Plan 106
internal security operations 84
lorry fleet 85-6
pacification of Waziristan 100-1
roads 85, 100-1, 104
Indian Army
4th Indian Division 148
4/16 Punjabi Regiment 101
6th Infantry Brigade 75
Royal Indian Army Servic Corps (RIASC) 156, 185
Supply and Transport Corps 84
Indian Standard Lorries 85, 86
infantry, BEF transport needs 50-1
infrared headlamps 183
Inland Water Transport service 173
Institute of Automobile Engineers 190
Internal-combustion engine 8, 21,

211

31, 32, 34, 35, 117
Ireland, armoured lorries 88
Islington Agricultural Hall, vehicle auction 89
Ismay, General Lionel, 1st Baron 168
Italian Campaign 157-8
Italy
 allied assistance to 62, 79, 80

J
Jeeps 158, 159, 161, 174, 182, 183, 187, 193
 pygmy Jeeps 183, 185
 search for a replacement 198-9
Jeffery, quad vehicles 111
Johnson, Lieutenant-Colonel Philip 90-1, 93, 111
jungle conditions 183, 185

K
Kalewa 187
Karrier
 30cwt lorries 111
 K3 3-ton four-wheel drive tractor 111
 K6 four-wheel drive 139, 175, 183
Kégresse, Adolphe 90, 93, 94, 96, 111, 116
Keller tractor 29
Kerr, Stuart, steam engine 30
Khorramshahr 156
Khyber Pass 88, 101
Ki-gass cold start equipment 198
Kitchener, Field Marshal Earl 18, 78
knocking 123
Kohima 183, 185, 186
Korean War 201-2, 209
Kroonstad 18, 23
Kurds, breakdown recovery not tried 77
Kurna 75
Kut-al-Amara 76

L
Lake Comacchio 159
Lakeman anti-aircraft mounts 134
Lakeman, Major Tom RTR 134
Lamerton, W. 11

Lancashire Steam Motor Carriage Company 21; see also Leyland Motors
Lanchester motor car 28
Land Rover 199, 205
landing craft 78, 164, 167, 168, 170, 173, 177,
Landing Ship Tank (LST) 159, 171, 173, 193
Lancia IZ lorry 91
Laycock Engineering Company, 3-ton lorry 61
Le Mans, BEF transport depot 120
lead, in petrol 123
Lee tank 186
Leland, Lt-Col F.W. ASC 76-7
Lettow-Vorbeck, General von 81
Leyland Motors 21, 39, 42, 89, 98, 139, 200
 30cwt ambulance 45
 30cwt lorries 41, 45
 30cwt Lynx 138
 3-ton lorries 41, 46, 77
 3-ton 6 x 4 Retriever 139
 3-ton X-type lorry 44
 3-ton Comet 4 x 4 205
 5-ton Bull Terrier 6 x 4 lorry 96, 97
 10-ton cargo truck prototype 200
 10-ton Hippo 139
charabanc 42
double-deck bus 41
eight-wheel all-wheel drive lorries 105
fire engines 45
Indian Standard Lorries 86
Martian 203
MTC subsidy lorries 38-41
tanks 139
and war surplus vehicles 89
see also Lancashire Steam Motor Carriage Company
Light Armoured Motor Battery (LAMB) 74
Light Car Patrols, Libyan Desert 72
light patrol vehicles 183
Lloyd, Major F. Lindsay RE 23
Lloyd George, David 57
Locomotives 9, 54, 55, 82, 155,

177
London General Omnibus Company 51, 59
Long, Major-General S.S. 99
Long Range Desert Group 103
lorries
 articulated semi-trailer 160, 164
 breakdown lorries 140
 cabs 6, 36, 37, 41, 97, 103, 132, 154, 183
 chain-drive 3, 41, 43
 conversions
  from buses 54
  to run on rails 81, 86
 crane lorries 140
 CT vehicles 205
 in East Africa 81
 experimental 8 x 6 89
 in Gallipoli and Salonika 78-9
 CL Type 206, 207
 CT Type 206
 GS bodies 119, 208
 GS vehicles 206
 off-the-shelf 61
 paraffin lorries 34
 petrol-electric 35, 117
 rigid six-wheelers 89
 searchlight 116, 147
 six-wheel drive 136, 166, 182, 187, 193, 195
 tippers 41, 175
 trials 41, 42, 43, 97, 104, 105, 111, 114, 163, 167, 170, 186, 199
 troop-carrying 63, 124, 131, 133
 WD Pattern 192;
 see also subsidy schemes *for lorries by load weights see under individual manufacturers*
Lowca Engineering Company, steam tractor 35
lubrication 74
'lurries' 23

M
Mack 118, 127, 181
 EH 3-ton 4 x 2 truck 127
 NR 10-ton truck 181
Mackworth, Colonel A.W. 17
McLaren Steam Sapper 17
Maintenance 24, 30, 35, 37, 57,

INDEX

59, 87, 146, 194, 198
   Mesopotamia 76
   India 156
   Normandy landings 169, 171, 172, 176
   North Africa 149
Mareth Line, battle 152
Marne, river 51
Marshalls of Gainsborough, internal combustion vehicles 35
mass production techniques 120, 191
Maude, General F.S. 76-7
Maudslay 139
   3-ton lorries 47
   6-ton 4 x 2 Militant 139
   RAC Trial 1907 30
   subsidy trials 41
Maxwell, General Sir John 78
meat, transportation of 37, 44
Mechanical Traction Committee (MTC) 22-39 passim, 41, 43, 47, 49; see also subsidy schemes
Mechanical Warfare Board 98-100
Mechanical Warfare Experimental Establishment (MWEE) 89, 99, 108, 112, 116
Mechanisation Board 99, 114, 190
Mechanisation Experimental Establishment (MEE) 108, 114
Mechanized Movement by Road, pamphlet 175
Mechanized and Armoured Formations, the 'Purple Primer' 88, 107
Mercedes-Benz, rigid 6 x 4 112, 116
Mercedes-Daimler 21
Mersah Matruh
   Senussi campaign 1914–15 71-2
Military Tractor Type A 65-6
Milne, Field Marshal Sir George 109, 110
Milnes-Daimler
   3-ton paraffin lorries 21, 34
   motor omnibus 32
   petrol lorry 37

Mimi, motorboat 81
Ministry of Munitions 57, 58, 62, 66
Ministry of Supply 127, 161, 165-7, 170, 191, 192, 194-5, 197, 199, 200, 202
   'B' Vehicle Committee 191
   Deputy Director General of Mechanisation 195
   discussions with the motor industry 194
Ministry of War Transport 129, 141
Misheifa, railhead 149
Mitumba mountains, Royal Navy and 81-2
mobile canteen 179
Mobile Division (Egypt) 143
mobile divisions 112, 133
mobile kitchens 97, 174
mobile office 55, 88, 116
mobile workshops 55, 97
mobilisation of subsidy vehicles 35; see also demobilisation 1919
Modern Formations, the 'Purple Primer' (revised) 88, 107-10
monorail 36
Mons, retreat from 51, 54
Montagu of Beaulieu, 2nd Baron 84-6, 88
Monte Cassino 159
Montgomery, of Alamein, Field Marshal Viscount 90, 151
Moore-Brabazon, J.T.C., Lord Brabazon of Tara 141
Morris, William R., Viscount Nuffield 116
Morris-Commercial
   8cwt truck 105, 107
   12cwt van 103
   15cwt 107, 139, 143, 197
   15cwt 4 x 4 182
   6 x 4 lorries 139
   CDF 30cwt lorry 103, 121
   CS8 anti-aircraft truck 134
   D Type 8 x 6 lorry 89, 195
   four-wheel drive independent suspension 114
   MRA1 1-ton four-wheel drive 192
   Terrapin 139, 166-7, 183
   Viceroy single-deck bus 108

Mosul 77, 156
Motley anti-aircraft mounts 134
motor battalions 133
Motor Car Exhibition at Olympia 1906 28
motor cars 28, 33, 93
   ambulance conversions 59
   Army Motor Reserve (AMR) 33, 51
   World War 1 volunteers 54
motor industry, discussions with the Ministry of Supply 189, 191, 194
Motor Track Train 111
Motor Transports in War (Wyatt) 47
Motor Volunteer Corps 33
motorcycles 54, 110, 135
   Douglas 54
   tracked 90
   Triumph 3SW 350cc 162
Msus, Field Maintenance Centre 149
MT companies 24, 51, 132, 135, 143
MT ships 173
Muirhead, Richard 12, 13
Mulberry Harbours 141, 168, 172
mules 18, 83, 84
Munich Crisis 1938 116-7, 143
'Municipal' bodies 41
Munitions Production, Controller General 191
Murmansk 87

N
NAAFI, mobile canteen 179
Napier
   ambulance 58
   lorries 33, 81, 82
   motor car 28
   taxi 36
National Bus Company (of Chelmsford) 32
National Physical Laboratory 192
navigation, desert driving 143, 171
Neptune, amphibian 165
Newton, Colonel Henry 65
Newton tractors 65
Niblett, Herbert 20, 95-6, 105, 111

213

Normandy landings 161, 168, 171, 173, 176-7, 182
Norperforce 75
North African theatre 142-52
Norway Campaign 121-2
Nuffield Group, 'Gutty' field car 198
Nuffield, Viscount 116
Nugent, Capt RE 23, 24
Nugent, Col RE 84

O
omnibuses see buses
Operation Battleaxe 148
Operation Brevity 148
Operation Crusader 148
Operation Market Garden 177
Operation Overlord; see Normandy landings
Organisation and Weapons Policy Committee (OWPC) 189, 192
Overland, tractors 65
Ox-drawn transport, in East Africa 81
oxen, traction engines and 19

P
SS *Pacific Coast*, ignited petrol vapour 122
Packard, trucks 62, 77
Pagefield, Subsidy A-Type lorry 42, 48, 61
Pakenham, Thomas 18
Panhard four-cylinder (16hp) taxi 36-7
paraffin tractors 38
Paris
 Automobile Exhibition 1906 28
 defence of 51
Passchendaele 64
Paul, Brigadier-General G.R.C. 43
Pedrail wheels 29, 30, 90
Peerless trucks 56, 62, 74, 76, 77, 90
 armoured cars 108
 tracked conversion 91
Persia 75, 77, 155, 156, 157,
SS *Persia* 86
Persia and Iraq Command (PAIC) 155
petrol 22, 38, 174
 cans 49, 67, 68

consumption 61, 149
distribution of 120, 144, 178
lead additives 123
MT72 123
MT80 123
octane grades 123
rationing 197
tax 98
unleaded 123
see also fuel
petrol-electric lorries 35, 117
Petrol Executive 68
petrol tankers 68
Pierce-Arrow, trucks 62
Pioneer Corps, road-making 175
Po river 159
pooling system 68
Port-en-Bessin, Normandy 172
prisoners of war 69, 179
public service vehicles 98, 129

Q
Qantara railway 73
Queen Mary aircraft transporters 137
Queen, Steam Sapper 16

R
Raglan, General Lord 10
Rainhill trials 9
Ransomes engines 13
Ransomes, Simms & Head 12
Ransomes, Simms & Jeffries 27
Ravee, Ransomes steam engine 13
Rawalpindi, driving school 86
Rawlinson, Toby 54
Razmak camp 100, 101
rearmament, vehicle production intentions 114
Red Ball Express convoy system 156
Red Cross Society 60, 68, 135
refuelling, of MT columns 27, 35, 68
refugees see displaced persons
registration numbers 68
Renard road train 31, 32
Renault 60, 96
 6 x 4 10CV 94, 96, 116
Renault, Louis 96
Renolds, chain-drives 43
Reo lorries 81

repair programmes see maintenance
Rhine, crossing of 159, 179, 182
Rhino ferries 173
Ricardo, Harry 98
Richborough Military Port 69
Riley 9hp car 103
Road Haulage Organisation, and D-Day 141
Road and Rail Traffic Act 1933, road haulage restrictions 106
road trains 105
Roadless Traction Ltd 90, 93, 111
Roberts, David 30
Roberts, Field Marshal Lord 18
Robotham, W.A. (Roy) 195, 197
Rocket, steam locomotive 9
Rolls-Royce
 Bentley Corniche 197
 CT24 Universal Carrier 197
 Phantom IV 197
 Ripplette 197
 Scalded Cat 197
Rommel, General Erwin 145, 150, 152
Rootes Group 139, 182, 199
Rouen Advanced Mechanical Transport Depot 54
Rear Maintenance Area 176
Royal Air Force 77
 AEC Matador 136
 Commer Q2 and Q15 137
 Crossley four-wheel-drive 3-tonner 137
 Dodge T215 152
 high octane fuel use 123
 in Russia 87
 Merlin engine 197
Royal Army Ordnance Corps (RAOC) 99, 104
Royal Army Service Corps (RASC) 78, 99, 103, 117
 advance to Antwerp 178-9
 Corps Delivery Squadrons 173
 Divisional RASC units 128
 DUKW companies 173-8, 183
 in the Far East 184-5
 Italian campaign 157-9
 in Korea 201
 Motor Coach Companies 132
 MT Companies 92, 132, 143
 Normandy landings 173-8

INDEX

Omnibus Companies 107
retreat to El Alamein 150
Rhine crossing 183
Sicily landings 156
at Suez 1956 208
Tank Brigade companies 113
tipper truck companies 158, 175
Training College 95, 96
troop carrying lorries 63, 124
see also Army Service Corps (ASC)
Royal Artillery 23, 44, 78, 80, 93, 104
Royal Automobile Club (RAC) 30, 31, 51, 54
Royal Canadian Army Service Corps (RCASC) 201
Royal Electrical and Mechanical Engineers (REME) 151, 153, 170-1, 174,
Royal Engineers 6, 11, 14, 15, 23, 24, 56, 63, 79, 87, 104, 140
 45 Steam Road Transport Company 17
 bridging train 136
 Electrical Engineers (RE) Volunteers 20
 road making 55, 63
Royal Flying Corps 41, 45, 58, 68
Royal Gun and Carriage Factory 39
Royal Lancers, 12th Battalion 124
Royal Naval Air Service 51, 57, 78
Royal Naval Division 51
Royal Navy 51, 58, 75, 81, 147
Royal Tank Corps 101, 104, 105, 109, 112, 115
 1st Brigade 112
 5th Battalion 60, 109, 115
 8th Light Tank Company 101
 see also Tank Corps
Royal Tank Regiment 134, 135, 159, 208
 6th Royal Tank Regiment 209
rubber, loss of Malaya and 123
Russia
 British military intervention post 1917 86-7
 overland supply route 155

S

Saladin, light armoured vehicles 206
Salerno landings 157, 168
Salisbury manoeuvres 1898 17
Salonika 78-9
Sandys, Duncan 206
Sangro river 158
Sappers and Miners 101
Saracen, light armoured vehicles 206
Saurer trucks 62, 114, 116
Scammell 140
 mechanical horse 3-wheel trucks 140
 recovery tractor 197
Scholfield, Major G.P. 17-20, 23
School of Military Engineering, Chatham 14
scout cars 68; *see also* motor cars
searchlight vehicles 97, 116, 147
Sebastopol 10
Senussi campaign 1914-15 71-2
Shadow Factories 139
Shahur Tangi ambush 1937 101
Shatt-al-Arab 75, 156
Shave, Mr, Mechanical Warfare Board member 98
Shell, primary fuel distributor 68
Sicily, invasion 156
Sidi Barrani 149
signposts, desert 144
Sinai Desert campaign 1916 73
Siwa Oasis, Senussi campaign 1914-15 71
six-wheel drive 136, 166, 182, 187, 193, 195
Smuts, General Jan Christian 81
Society of Motor Manufacturers and Traders 41, 191, 206,
Sollum, Senussi campaign 1914-15 71-2
Somaliland campaign 1903 38
Somme, Battles 61, 66
South African Army Service Corps 82
 anti-aircraft decoy lorry 148
spare parts 35, 38, 40, 66, 102, 113, 120
 interchangeability of 33, 38
 'knocked down' vehicles 151
 seeds of disaster 83, 120

Sparkman and Stevens, DUKW design 156
SS Cars 183
 pygmy Jeeps 183
 staff cars 54, 90, 93, 135
Stalingrad 155
Stalwart, light armoured vehicles 206
Standard
 2.1-litre Vanguard 203
 Jungle Jeep 185
Standard Oil Company, Salonika 78
standardisation 126, 192
 of controls 39
Star ambulance 76
steam rollers 15, 54, 79
Steam Sappers 14-5
steam tractors 26, 28, 34, 37
Steam Transport on Roads (Templer) 15
steam vehicles
 compound 17, 19, 24, 25, 27, 35, 82
 legal restrictions 26
 military interest 12, 15, 35
 overtype 20-1, 53
 range 15, 26, 32
 undertype 21, 27, 28, 30, 36
Stephenson, George 9
Stephenson, Robert 9
Stewart & Co, steam tractor 35
Stirling lorries 38
Straker Steam Vehicle Company 21
Straker-Squire 22, 33, 34
 ambulance 34, 44, 45
 lorry 44
 omnibus 44
 steam lorry 10, 11
Streeter, G. 94-5
Struma river, front 79
Studebaker
 tractors 65
 trucks 62
Sturrock, Archibald 12
subsidy schemes
 Class A 3-ton lorries 40, 42, 46, 47, 49,
 Class B 30cwt lorries 40, 42, 49
 hoped for revival 194
 mobilisation 59

215

see also lorries; Mechanical Traction Committee (MTC)
Suez Canal, Turkish attacks 73
Suez Crisis 1956 208
Sunbeam
  12/16hp ambulance 47, 60
  staff car 54
Supplementary Transport, Chief Inspector 117, 119
supply columns
  Tank Brigade manoeuvres 112-3
  Western Front 50-1, 66
  see also convoys
supply lines
  airborne 187
  Anzio 159
  problems in France 121
  Western Desert 151
  supply trains 18, 30
suspension 22, 45, 48, 90, 93, 95, 114-5, 166, 167, 199
Sutlej, Ransomes steam engine 13
Suvla Bay landings 78
Swallow, Sid, Ford designer 154
Swift, 10-12hp two-seater motor car 34
Swinton, Sir Ernest 93
Switzerland, vehicle supplies to Britain 62
Sword Beach 172

T
Tabriz 156
Talbot
  charabancs 108
  tenders 3, 57, 76
Tank Corps 40, 53, 66, 90, 111
  5th Battalion 60
  F[6th] Battalion 64-5
  see also Royal Tank Corps
Tank and Tracked Transport Experimental Establishment 99
tanker lorries *see* petrol tankers
tanks
  Centurion 209
  Churchill 141
  Lee 186
  Mark IV 60
  Department of Tank Design and Experiment 90, 93
Tanzania 81

Taranto 157
Taskers of Andover, steam tractors 26, 35
Tatra heavy lorry 116
taxation
  commercial vehicles 98, 100, 116, 164, 189, 191
  on petrol 98
taxicabs
  Home Guard requisition scheme 132
  machine-gun transport 36
  mobilisation exercise 1940 129
  requisition of 37, 54
'Taxis du Marne' 1914 129
Teheran 156
Templer, Lieutenant Colonel J.L.B. 9, 15-8
Terrapin, amphibian 139, 166-7, 183
Territorial Army 32, 34, 36
Thomson, R.W. 12-3
Thomson road steamer 12
Thornycroft 20-3, 49
  30cwt paraffin lorries 34
  30cwt petrol lorry 31
  3-ton four-wheel drive Nubian 140, 200
  3-ton six-wheeler 101, 104
  6 x 4 lorries 57, 59, 63
  6 x 4 Tartar 140
  Amazon crane lorry 140
  Big Ben tractor 192
  chain-drive 2½-ton lorry 41
  colonial steam lorry 22
  internal combustion tractors 34, 35
  J Type lorry 67, 92
  MTC subsidy lorries 41, 42-3
  Terrapin design 167
Tilling, petrol-electric lorries 35
Tobruk 148-9, 152
Toutou, motorboat 81
Townshend, Major-General Sir Charles 75-6
tracked vehicles 65, 90, 93, 105
  armour 89-90
  Colonel Johnson's designs 90
  Colonel Newton's design 65
  three-quarter track 193, 200
  tracklayers 30, 35, 90

see also half-tracks; Holt caterpillar tractor
Tracta joints 162
traction engines 10, 12, 14, 15, 17-20, 23, 24, 26
traction trains 24
  Army Service Corps 23, 26, 45, 56, 89
  India 9
  South Africa 17
tractors
  artillery 111, 136-7, 139, 163, 164, 196, 200
  Buick 65
  Military Type A 65-6
  short wheel-base 136
  steam tractors 26, 28, 30, 34, 35, 37
  tracked 65, 73, 105
  see also tracked vehicles; transporters
traffic patterns, World War 1 61
trailers
  ambulance 83
  articulated semi-conversions 137, 140, 164
  double-deck 13
  drawbar 164
  light 206
  supply 73
  tanker 24
  tracked 77, 111
transport echelons 112
  Normandy 175-6
  Western Desert 146
Transportation on the Western Front 60
transporters
  aircraft 137
  tank 137, 140, 164, 177, 193, 194, 196, 206
  see also tractors
Trapmann, Captain A.H. 47
trench warfare 51, 56, 60, 65
tri-cars 37
Trials
  North Wales 1930s 104, 114
  steam-powered vehicles 9, 10, 12, 28, 32
  Studland Bay 104
  War Office Experimental Convoy 1932 103

INDEX

Wool (Dorset) **1925** 104
see also vehicle tests
Trigno river 158
Tripoli 145, 149, 152
troop-carrying vehicles 63, 124, 131, 133
see also buses
Tropic Proofing Experimental Establishment 186
tropical conditions 82, 87, 185, 197
TT2 Transport Bulletin 161, 182
Tunisia Campaign 156
Turkey
   Gallipoli Campaign 77-8
   war with Greece **1921-22** 92
tyres 14
   cross-country 15, 29
   Dunlop oversize 106
   Dunlop Runflat 123
   Goodyear tyres 62
   heavy duty 203
   oversize 73
   pneumatic 45, 76, 77, 85, 91, 93
   sand tyres 103, 126
   solid 44, 48, 86
   studded 34
   see also wheels

U

United States
   'Cash and Carry' system 152
   Lend Lease 153
United States Army, mechanisation of 132
Universal Carriers 197, 201

V

Vauxhall Motors
   3-ton 6 x 6 (FV1300 prototype) 199
   3-ton 6 x 6 (FV1301 prototype) 200
   three-quarter track prototypes 200
   see also Bedford
vehicle design
   amphibians 165, 194
   Canadian 153
   half-tracks 89, 90, 93, 94, 104

need for standardisation 39, 126, 192
   RASC Training College 94-6, 99
   subsidy scheme pre-**1914** 38
vehicle displays, Chertsey 206, 208
vehicle list, post-World War 2 194
vehicle parks 169
vehicle production and development, World War 2 198
vehicle specification 103, 168
vehicle tests 164; *see also* trials
Verdun, supply columns 57
Vickers-Armstrong, tracked lorry 105
Vickers-Carden-Loyd light tractor 104
Vulcan, 30cwt lorry 93

W

Wading Trials Centres 170
wading vehicles 168, 199, 206
Walcheren landings 159
Walker Bros, and MTC subsidy lorries 42, 48
War Office Experimental Convoy **1932** 103
Waring, A.B. 206
water
   supply for steam-power 24, 82
   tankers 119
Waterloo, Battle of 10
waterproofing of vehicles 168, 170-1, 179, 194, 206
Wavell of Cyrenaica, General Archibald, 1st Earl 144-6, 148
WD Pattern Bogie 96, 97, 99
Wellington, Duke of 6, 9-11
Wellington steam tractor 26
Westminster, Duke of, in World War 1 54, 72
Wheeled Vehicles Experimental Establishment (WVEE) 161, 164-5, 182, 192
wheels
   traction engines 11, 12, 13, 15
   twin at rear 12
   WD Pattern 203
   see also tyres

White 118
   760 10-ton truck 126-7
Wolseley 60
   3-ton lorry 58
   ambulance 45
   motor car 28, 29
   MTC subsidy lorries 42
   'Mudlark' 199
Wolseley, Sir Garnet 14
women
   drivers 135, 136
   vehicle production 125
Wood, Major-General Sir Elliott 19
Wool, vehicle trials 104
Woolwich Arsenal 11
workshop facilities see maintenance
World War 1 46-69
World War 2 118-187
Wrigley, motor parts 61
Wyatt, Horace 47

Y

Ypres Salient 63-5

BRITISH MILITARY TRANSPORT 1829-1956

THANKS TO

The Tank Museum wishes to thank and acknowledge the following, whose kind support enabled *British Military Transport 1829-1956* to be republished in late 2022.

Alan Atkinson
Benjamin Hutchins
Matthew Tyler
Ben Leah
Rob Shipman
Deborah Parkes
Iain Reid
Steven Harker
Jerzy Hevelke
Andy Dinh
Cameron Moeller
Duncan Stevens
Victoria Taylor
David Gorton
Robert Rewcastle
Samantha Field
Ildefonso Gómez Yáñez
Paul Lowther
Mick Graham
Jeff Freeman
John Walker
Robert Bull
David Pyle
Chih-Yung Chang
Donald James
Thor Greve
Peter Bailey
Ross Hillman
Mike McGurgan
Nigel Wilton
Colin Avern
Andy Rhoades
Derek Maunder
John Bagley
John Elgie
Todd Schavee
Peter Noble
Jordan Graham
Matthew Hudson
Adrian Hampton
Michael Mills

Steve Foster
Stephen Stuck
Kye Woods
Greg Jewell
William T. Wright
Ken Macdonald
Chris MacKay
Michael Rhodes
Robert David Parkin
Michael Williams
Stephen Bettany
James Grover
Tom Morris
Nicholas Slater
Ian Stanworth
Julie Cox
Anthony Hillier
Peter Faulkner
Oscar Levy
Nigel Fairhurst
Stephen Harvey
Richard Stephen Purvis
Skyler Wake
John Shill
Ian Merriman
Stuart Carter
Janis Sorenson
Edward Adkins
Ian McKinnon
Neil Boston
Patrick Woodford
Geoff Titterton
Neil Atkinson
Gerald Pierson
Julian Davies
Michael Catt
Meredith Russell
Andrew Witherspoon
Andrew Bird
Dave Hickman
Kevin Hann

Ian Clarke
Alan Smith
Glynn Beresford
Warren Mason
Harry Johnson
Robert Hector
Richard Evans
Tom Williams
Ethan Beal
Gavin Kratz
James Mcinnes
P.D. Jarman
Geoffrey Boby
Douglas Nicholson
Jack Rimmer
Hugh O'Donnell
Chris Naden
Robert Mundell
Mike Whitcombe
Graeme Thomas
Wayne Birks
Michael Orris
Mike Warren
David Powell
Tim Yow
David Garoz Esteban
George Exon
Alan Atkinson
Graeme Carruthers
Stephen Belton
Paul Trevett
Ryan Brewis
Robert Peach
Peter Savill
David Hulme
Andrew Grayman
Anita Jennison
Samantha Green
Philip Livingstone
Wirton Philippe
Terence Young

THANKS TO

John Blackmore
Kevin Hudson
Graham Hough
Nigel Savage
Luke Webb
Steven Browning
Glenn Harrison
Robin Braysher
John Edwards
Michael John Bishop
Anna Bartoszewicz
Colin Webb
Matthew Kaye
Thomas Platt
Nicola Lillywhite
Martin Roberts
David O'Farrell
David Magee
Ian John Whitear
Colin Needham
James Hall
Lynn Norcliffe
Clare Wilkinson
Susan Anchor
Mark Ansell
Owen Adamson
Anthony Brown
David Rowland
Tom Badger
Maximilian Broden-Barbareau
Ian Roberts
Matthew Hynett
Kevin McAlinden
Graham Crymble
Alberto Corradine
Malcolm Ivison
Euan Smith
Martha Wells
David Morris
Bryan Donald Surridge
James Scrivener
David Allen
Melvin Avery
Wayne Weddle
Lindsey Haycock
Piers Wilson
Robert Mountford

Derek Gard
Charles Stevens
Edward Sealey
John Zahra
Thomas Breitenbacher
Neil Holden
John King
Axel Macdonald
Joshua Garston
Charles Canova
Tomasz Blaut
Darren Rolfe
Tim Lowe
Graham Hurst
Chris Ryan
David Farrell
Peter Morrison
John Doran
Roger Houston
Nigel Sait
John Gibbons
Simon Quinn
Austin Hindley
Simon Cannon
Peter Smith
John Hill
Peter Martin
Björn Unell
Tom van der Vlist
Ian Costar
Radu Dumitrean
Scott Parkinson
Rodney S. Arneil
Kathleen Moots
Paul Thomson
William Gunter
Bryn Stevenson-Davies
David Wade
Philip Dale
Roberts Daniel
Chris Simpson
Nicholas Noppinger
Alan Neocleous
Paul V. Scourfield
Nick Godwin
Alexander Burnett
Simon Burrough

Christopher Worsley
Marion Bahnerth
Alyssa Ryder
Mark Demmen
Mark Campbell
George McLean
Ron Owen
Robert Ingham
Rachel Bowen
Mike Burgess
David Richardson
Stuart Gumm
Alex Phillipson
Rick Williams
Brenton White
Hamish Davidson
Joseph Blackett
Ceri Thomas
David Johnston
Keith Bispham Miller
Paul Colebrooke
Joseph Checkley
Martin Gregory
Len Newman
Alan Northcote
Gordon Matthews
Neil Burt
Robert Scott
John Fearn
Gary Matfin
Graham Wilby
Tancred Cassar
Michael Rhodes
Jason Spicer
Tim Cook
Paul Tamony
Geoff Ayres
Robert Bond
Douglas McMillan
Keith Terry
Markku Hyttinen
Ross Kennedy
Trevor Corrin
Michael Monroe
Alan Ross
Tyler Steele
Gene Smith

BRITISH MILITARY TRANSPORT 1829-1956

Justin Grootenboer
Martin Jones
Terry Rowsell
Steve Bastable
Simon King
M.J. Roche
James Christopher Cutts
Peter Sutton
Mark McCuller
John King
Richard Payne
Richard Dallimore
John Robertsom
Terry Cotter
Stephen Lord
Steve Smith
Stephen Cairns
Alan Long
David Gray
Jan-Cees Grinwis
Robert Metcalfe
Teresa Smith
Norm Day
Rebecca Addicoat
Samuel Greenhill
Neil Inglis
George Corrie
Daniel Boggild
Trevor Rawlinson
Richard Davies
Neil Mason
Jason Ward
Chris Bill
Andrew Perkins
John Melrose
Guenter Kortebein
Robert Swaine
Jason Field
Christopher Tubb
Johnny Doyle
Peter Vernon-Lawes
Andrew Wilkinson
Chris Binnie
Thomas Rye
Martin Mickleburgh
Paul Malmassari
Jedd Connolly

James Webb
Craig Cowie
Gavin Taylor
Sue Jenkins
John Zrimc
David Hewson
John Green
Ben Hughes
Anthony Cairns
Alexander Losert
Ryan Cook
Mark Yearsley
Maria Vazquez Lopez
Adrian Ferguson
Paul Lipscombe
Martin Clouder
Amanda Butler
P. Hennessy
Derryck Madden
Gary Norris
Jean Lewis
Malcolm McEwan
M.J. Hill
Ian Mcnally
Paul Hutchings
Dot Tracy
Amber Stahl
Michael Freeman
John Twigge
Stuart Bestford
Richard Bradley
Gary Hewings
David Mason
Jan Meyer-Kamping
Chris Stevens
Uwe Springhorn
Anthony Bird
Alan Johnson
Edward Shoop
Simon House
John Ingleby
Johan Van der Bruggen
Marc Lecuit
Phil Bargery
Kathleen Gulson
Philip Kaye
David Pepper

Keith Stafford
Peter Dicks
Gareth Sewell
Henry Boulton
Anbe Hironobu
Liam Cooney
William Walter Hill
William Gunning
Jeremy Bond
Annie and Michael Bradley
Mark Paines
Bennett Horner
Charles Taylor
Neil Cowell
Christopher Dunmill
Ian Price
Ian Hambelton
Nigel Barrett
Karolina Phelps
Richard Gibbon
Lee Smith
Colin MacNee
Peter Tipping
Philip Jobson
Brian Sanders
Alex Blair
Antony Vickers
David Foster
Richard Cooper
John Hutchinson
Mike Matthews
Steve Percy
David Fraser
James Andrew
William Pointing
Steven Bannister
Nick Vaughan
Gabriel Necsuleu
Richard Bishop
David Bottomley
Eugene Lefeuvre
Rob Carson
Brian McGinley
Robert Dickinson
Eero Juhola
William A. Siddons
Stephen Wall

THANKS TO

John Cavanagh
Nicholas Piper
Adam Burton
Sam Anderson
David Mansfield
Graham Rhodes
Martyn Keen
Philip McCarty
Paul Perry
Gwynne Fright
Matthew Lambert
Hamish Davidson
Piers Jackson
Cobweb Williams-Manton
Paul Bussard
Andrew Downs
Dwight Luetscher
Matthew Finck
Wayne Mills
Anthony Witham
Justin Rollinson
Thomas Paine
James Carty
Tony Price
Jared Lee
Scott Harwood
Brian Douglas
Javier Tapia
Campbell Harris
Edward Paul Anderson
Eddie M. Redfearn
Charles Hoagland
Lowell Wong
John Rauscher
Larry Geno
Glen Cooper
David Krigbaum
William Neilus
Adrian Symonds
William Mckibben
Chris Bridgman
Ka Ki Leung
Rejean Paquette
David Batho
Øystein Mork
Benjamin L. Apt
Larry Deornellas Jr

Geoffrey Mawson
Andy White
Kieran Hall
Merle Steeves
Steven Dyer
Rob Lee
Paul Demato
Nicholas Brodar
Tim Prestia-Cook
Oliver Pearcey
Patrick Bailey
Joseph Jolley
Andrew Noble
Franz Biedermann
Stuart Purvis
Robert Frisch
Alan Batten
John MacFarlane
Phil Eyden
John Simpson
Callum White
Alexander Estermann
Richard Cammack
Tim Wrate
Dave Howling
Josh W. Salazar
Jeffrey Ware
Eric Maple
Graeme Campsie
Mark Niblett
Murray Kennedy
Mark Mills
John Beck
George G. Hill
Mark Ploszay
Friedrich Klett
David Woodside
Terry Hall
Richard Briscoe
Patrick Crelly
Keith Walker
J. Tweddle
Alan Mincher
Sidney Road
Lachlan Harris
Colin Bracher
Sean Smart

Andrew Hunter
Barry Canning
Daniel Moore
Paul Nuttall
Simon King
James Cridland
Matthew Zembo
Bob Baal
Aiden Terris
Craig Abrahams
Anthony Sampson
Fiona Jakielaszek
Simon Snodin
Charlotte Dillon
Philip Moor
Alan Titcombe
Martin Littlecott
Staley Snook
Oliver Austin
Filip Björklund
John Tapsell
Thomas Lucas
Robert Obermeier-Hartmann
Connor Coolbaugh
Alan Knuth
Ryan Maclam
John Buckle
Michael Guerin
Jack Shearer
Stuart Woods
Iain Mellors
Adrian Johnson
Michael Hall
Zebulon Swinney
Stuart Hanley
Duncan Curd
Nigel Chappell
John Parr
Jan Andersson
Bradley Mitchell
Trevor Povey
Alexei McDonald
Mark Bentley
Alvin Chan
Nicholas Sadler
Steve Merrett
Paul Button

BRITISH MILITARY TRANSPORT 1829-1956

THANKS TO

Doug Parry
Christian Bastow
Stephen Turner
Matt Davies
Neil Kindlysides
Gareth Williams
Ben Dummer
Gary Dhillon
Mark Fowler
Paul M. Wilde
Scott Gill
Julie Bettinelli
Frederick Brown
David Bullen
Geoffrey Giles
Andrew Pritchatt
Jacob Tierney
Nick Jones
Stuart Hudson
Matthew Smith
Michael Rorer
Richard Box
John Convery
Ray Peterson
Roman Smith
Colin Baddeley
Chris Pilags
Russell Barnes
Andrew David
Sean Smart
Pierre Pellerin
Nicholas Biddle
Paul Grainger
Robbie Macauley
Joshua Hiscock
Ian Rainford
Roger Peachey
David Paul Williams
Antony Kirmond
Eric Hollis
Justin de Lavison
Richard J. Tugwell
Stephen Gregory
Rodney Anderson
Hugh Dennis
Isaac Dennis

Martin Killick
Matt Klotz
Steven Barnes
Mark Hollowell
Ian Collins
Bryan Perrington
Alan Anstruther Black
K. Simpson
David Chapman
Tizian Dähler
Kirsty Meredith
Alexander Gibson
Steven Parkes
John Meadows
Lawrence Rhyce
Chris Burberry
Paul Cocks
Donald Holmes
Jason Hofer
Robert Coach
Alex Malcom
Philippa Bowden
Alexander Ridler
Gordon Chrisp
Paul Condren
Nigel Rumble
Chris Saulpaugh
David Mapley
Jim Evans
Ray Young
Grant Kenny
Mark Ambridge
Charles Jones
Ian Duffin
James Knight
Edward Hervey
Anthony Grindle
Kenneth Lilley
Colin Poulter
Marici Reid
Jacob Wright
Jordan Taylor-Jeal
Robert Feast
Nigel Colverson
Deborah Schouten
Jonathan Barnes

Mike Woolnough
Heather Brown
Larry Stone
Alfie Green
Phil Loder
Michael Woong
James Nicholls
Michael Brothwell
Nick Wynn
Neil Illingworth
Chris Wright
Michael Pytel
Nigel Titchen
Noah Bly
Phil Burrows
Tony Gaynor
Robin Elliott
Eric Dellaquila
Keith Matthews
Albert Lecuyer
Sarah Burt
Jaroslaw Chojnacki
Jean Grieten
Tim Ellerby
Thomas Hignell
Jonathan Frere
Rocco Plath
Nicholas Davis
Pat Coughlin
Gayle Bailey
Pierre Hedström
Steven Grace
Scott Kerr
Jonny Nilsson
Leonard Thomson
Sean Cuddy
Stuart Harrison
Brian Smith
W. Lindsay
Vivian Symonds
Ian Willy
Alan Lodge
Thomas Stromberg
Susan Logan
Kevin Dyke
Andrew Wood

THANKS TO

Gary Burns
Bradley Kirk
Sean Holder
Simon Barnes
Fraser Durie
Helen Rogers
Colin Little
Erik Miller
Neville Mullings
Dennis Krag
Paul Jones
Keith Allan Langton
Geert Arends
Keith Major
Bill Allan
Mark Bevis
Michael Patey
Ian Bullion
Stewart Garnett
Andrew Woodward
Jamie Todd
Ben Hughes
Nicholas M. Maris
Naomi Ecob
Arran Hartley
Oliver Beddoe
Mattias Sjösvärd
Colin Gibson
Samuel Tuck
Thomas Brooks
Paul Walsh
Tony Hearn
Alex Wrotek
Simon Norburn
John Andrews
Jason Singleton
Mark Barnett
Matthew Faiers
George Gillett
David Sedano
Sarah Gray
Daren England
Paul Liddiard
Terry Light
Brian Nelson
Charles Knapp

Ian Bryer
Kenneth Zichal
Chris Brook
Phil Puddefoot
Matthew Hurley
Jeremy Lawson
Cammie Lamont
Simon Smith
Thomas Sitch
John Hill
Aidan Lloyd
Kjartan Bergsson
M. Reynolds
Danny Hin
Paul James
Hongrui Zhang
Marcel Tromp
Tim Barr
Paul Nuttall
David Chapman
Carson Thomas
Allan Sinclair
Trevor Hayman
Kevin Page
James Carter
Andrew Osborne
Aaron Supinger
Glenn Bainbridge
Andrew Temple
Steven Blackburn
Tina Rydberg
Matthew Spreadbury
Lukas Milancius
Ben Couldwell
Thomas Williams
Børge Arild
Eisa Alkalbani
Alastair Powers-Jones
Liam Riordan
Stephen McGuire
Peter Feeney
Taylor Jay
Patrick J. McNamara
Kristine Janusas
Kjell Arne Randen
Anthony Stewart

Wes Lunney
Louis Devirgilio
Paul Taylor
Clive Thomas
Willem Marinus Stoutjesdijk
Leslie Stephenson
Kelvin Bampfield
Ethan Candy
Salvador Cadengo
Steven Adams
Cameran McKie-Jones
Daisy Ticehurst
Nikolas Eibich
Mario Saliba
Daniel Nye
Karen Lee Zachry
Panzerwrecks Ltd
Paul Hutchinson
John Wright
Mr Michael Townsend
Ian Featherstone
Andrew A.
Matt Magee
Bryan Davis
Andy Kirk
Tom Williams
Scott Mccrindle
David Butterfield
David Hindmarsh
Simon Ashcroft
Liam Adams
Katie Jones
Jonathan Bordell
Graham Cooper
Martin Jones
Mark Hiles
Mark Gregory
Robin McEwen
Ewan Spence
Douglas Swanson
Alan Hall and Shade Kelly.